FORD ANGLIA, PREFECT 100E 1953-62 AUTOBOOK

A Workshop Manual for the
Ford Anglia, Prefect and Popular 100E
including Escort, Squire and Thames
5 and 7 cwt Vans, 1953–1962

by

Kenneth Ball
G I Mech E

and the
Autopress Team of Technical Writers

AUTOPRESS LTD
BENNETT ROAD BRIGHTON BN2 5JG ENGLAND

SBN 85147 038 6

Books by the same author

1100, 1300 AUTOBOOK
1800 AUTOBOOK
AUSTIN A30, A35, A40 AUTOBOOK
AUSTIN HEALEY 100/6, 3000 AUTOBOOK
BMC AUTOBOOK THREE
BMC AUTOBOOK FOUR
FIAT 850 1964-69 AUTOBOOK
FORD ANGLIA, PREFECT 100E 1953-62 AUTOBOOK
FORD CONSUL, ZEPHYR, ZODIAC 1, 2 1950-62 AUTOBOOK
FORD ESCORT 1967-69 AUTOBOOK
FORD ZEPHYR, ZODIAC AUTOBOOK TWO
HILLMAN MINX SERIES 1-5 1956-65 AUTOBOOK
JAGUAR 2.4, 3.4, 3.8, MARK 1, 2 1955-67 AUTOBOOK
JAGUAR XK 120, 140, 160, MARK 7, 8, 9 1948-61 AUTOBOOK
MGA, MGB AUTOBOOK
MG MIDGET TA-TF AUTOBOOK
MINI AUTOBOOK
MORRIS MINOR AUTOBOOK
ROOTES 1965-67 AUTOBOOK
ROVER 60-110 AUTOBOOK
ROVER 2000 1963-69 AUTOBOOK
SPRITE, MIDGET AUTOBOOK
SUNBEAM RAPIER, ALPINE 1959-65 AUTOBOOK
VAUXHALL VIVA HA AUTOBOOK
VAUXHALL VIVA HB AUTOBOOK
VAUXHALL VICTOR 1, 2, FB 1957-64 AUTOBOOK
VAUXHALL VICTOR 101 1964-67 AUTOBOOK
VAUXHALL VELOX, CRESTA 1957-68 AUTOBOOK
VOLKSWAGEN AUTOBOOK ONE

The AUTOBOOK series of Workshop Manuals covers the majority of British and Continental motor cars. For a full list see the back of this manual.

CONTENTS

First Edition   August 1969

Printed in England by
G. Beard & Son
Brighton

ACKNOWLEDGEMENT

My thanks are due to the Ford Motor Company Ltd for their unstinted co-operation and also for supplying data and illustrations.

I am also grateful to a considerable number of owners who have discussed their cars at length and many of whose suggestions have been included in this manual.

Ditchling

Kenneth Ball G I Mech E
Associate Member Guild of Motoring Writers

INTRODUCTION

This do-it-yourself Workshop Manual has been specially written for the owner who wishes to maintain his car in first class condition and to carry out his own servicing and repairs. Considerable savings on garage charges can be made, and one can drive in safety and confidence knowing the work has been done properly.

Comprehensive step-by-step instructions and illustrations are given on all dismantling, overhauling and assembling operations. Certain assemblies require the use of expensive special tools, the purchase of which would be unjustified. In these cases information is included but the reader is recommended to hand the unit to the agent for attention.

Throughout the Manual hints and tips are included which will be found invaluable, and there is an easy to follow fault diagnosis at the end of each chapter.

Whilst every care has been taken to ensure correctness of information it is obviously not possible to guarantee complete freedom from errors or to accept liability arising from such errors or omissions.

Instructions may refer to the righthand or lefthand sides of the vehicle or the components. These are the same as the righthand or lefthand of an observer standing behind the car and looking forward.

CHAPTER 1

THE ENGINE

1:1 Description

The engine described in this Chapter is fitted to Anglia and Prefect (1953 onwards), Escort and Squire Estate cars, Thames 5 and 7 cwt vans (1954 onwards). It is of four cylinder type, the cylinders being cast integrally with the upper half of the crankcase. The crankshaft which is statically and dynamically balanced, runs in three main bearings of the steel-backed replaceable type.

With a capacity of 1172 cc this side-valve engine features inlet valve heads and ports which are larger than those of the exhaust. This gives improved volumetric efficiency. An exhaust heat control valve is fitted to models produced prior to June 1957 and this is fully described in **Chapter 2, Section 2:9**.

The cooling system incorporates a water pump and thermostat. The lubrication system is by pressure feed from a submerged gear pump to the camshaft and crankshaft bearings and to the big-end bearings and valve tappets. The timing chain is lubricated by controlled flow from the front camshaft bearing.

Full technical information including torque tightening figures is given at the end of this manual in **Technical Data** and detailed drawings are given in **FIGS 1:1** and **1:2**. All nuts and bolts are AF sizes with the exception of one or two odd ones on carburetter and electrical components.

1:2 Operations with engine in place

Work on the cylinder head, manifolds, valve assemblies and water pump may be carried out with the engine in position but attention to other engine components should be given after removal of the unit. Before starting any operations we emphasize the importance of preparation and the following will give guidance to the reader.

Remember that the parts of a modern car are made to extremely fine limits and any ideas of filing to enable a fit to be made, or bending to take up wear are not to be entertained. During all dismantling operations, any part which is obviously worn should be replaced as reassembling it will only mean carrying out the same work

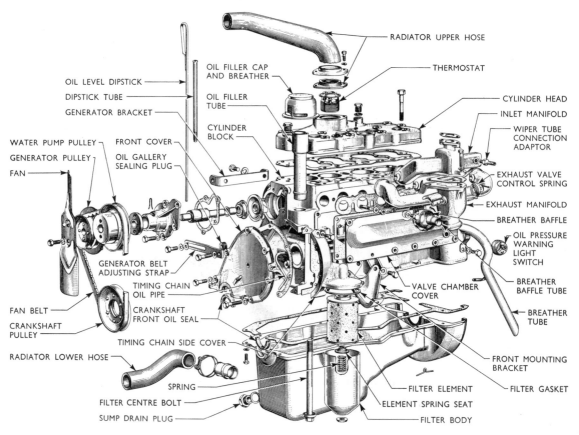

FIG 1:1 Engine exterior components

again at a later date apart from disappointing the operator with poor performance on completion of his labours.

Sound preparation:

Any vehicle which has covered a reasonable mileage will present the operator with the following problems:
1 External dirt.
2 Tight, rusted or seized nuts and screws.
3 Dismantling unfamiliar assemblies.
4 Diagnosis of defective items in complex assemblies.
5 Inability to remember order of reassembly.
6 Tuning and adjustment.

1 The need for scrupulous cleanliness in all operations connected with automobile repair and overhaul cannot be overstressed. A wire brush (not on aluminium parts) or stiff bristle brush is recommended for initial cleaning using two containers of paraffin. Final drying off may be done with non-fluffy rag or by rinsing in petrol.

The use of water soluble degreasers is not recommended for the home mechanic due to the resulting wet and danger of water penetration to vital parts. Great care must be exercised to blank off ports and holes wherever dirt or grit could enter during operations. Any rag used for blocking such holes must be large enough to prevent any chance of a piece being pushed in and subsequent

removal overlooked. Coloured vinyl tape is a useful material to stick over holes if the metal is cleaned well prior to fixing.

2 Many obstinate screws can be made to move by liberal use of penetrating oil or anti-crorrosive fluid. Tapping the spanner with a hammer sometimes proves effective on seized nuts as does hammering on the end of a metal screwdriver to start tight screws. Great care must be exercised with any screw thread and any hammer blows must be given with the nut in place and flush with the end of the thread. Never use Stilson or toothed jaw pliers on nuts unless the flats have worn and the nut is to be replaced. Screwed studs can usually be removed by using a locknut together with the existing one and unscrewing normally with an open-ended spanner.

Heat is often useful as a last resort to free seized parts but make sure there is no danger from adjacent petrol tanks or fuel lines and that gaskets or seals are not going to be spoilt. Keep any heat localized, using asbestos shields (cooking mats are useful) where necessary.

Always support parts where possible before hammering and make sure the car itself is adequately jacked-up—it is very easy to become so engrossed that you fail to notice that a block or axle stand has slipped!

3 Dismantling an assembly is something which very

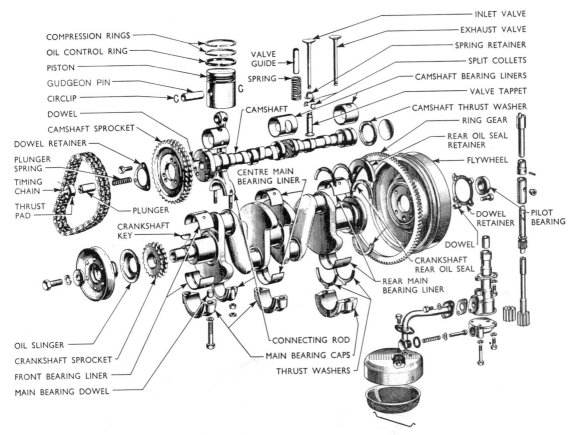

Labels on diagram:
COMPRESSION RINGS
OIL CONTROL RING
PISTON
GUDGEON PIN
CIRCLIP
DOWEL
CAMSHAFT SPROCKET
DOWEL RETAINER
PLUNGER SPRING
TIMING CHAIN
THRUST PAD
CRANKSHAFT KEY
OIL SLINGER
CRANKSHAFT SPROCKET
FRONT BEARING LINER
MAIN BEARING DOWEL
VALVE GUIDE
SPRING
CAMSHAFT
CENTRE MAIN BEARING LINER
PLUNGER
CONNECTING ROD
MAIN BEARING CAPS
THRUST WASHERS
REAR MAIN BEARING LINER
CRANKSHAFT REAR OIL SEAL
INLET VALVE
EXHAUST VALVE
SPRING RETAINER
SPLIT COLLETS
CAMSHAFT BEARING LINERS
VALVE TAPPET
CAMSHAFT THRUST WASHER
RING GEAR
REAR OIL SEAL RETAINER
FLYWHEEL
DOWEL
DOWEL RETAINER
PILOT BEARING

FIG 1:2 Engine interior components

often causes the home mechanic most trouble. Clean and inspect the part very carefully, note countersunk screws, flush-seating spring retaining plungers and fine joint lines as clues to the method of assembly. Decide whether that obstinate threaded collar or flange might have an opposite thread!

Always work over a sheet of paper on a bench. Make drawings and notes on how the various pieces were positioned when you started taking the item apart. Mark mating surfaces and edges with scratches or dots (never on spring metal or anti-roll bars etc, as this may lead to a fracture). Electrical wires and terminals should always be marked for subsequent identification.

4   There are many indications for finding worn, defective or malaligned parts.

The telltale traces of oil leakage and rusty water stains are immediately able to lead the operator to worn oil seals, gaskets etc. Mating surfaces very often have burrs which prevent perfect seating, this is often the case around stud holes and can cause persistent leakage from cylinder head gaskets and rear axle flanges.

Worn bearings and bushes need expensive equipment for accurate measurement but the operator can usually make a reasonably close check by isolating any movement to the part concerned and ensuring that any wear is not being transmitted or magnified from adjacent components.

A watchful eye for unusual rubbing marks on parts not usually expected to bear them may indicate something bent, worn or distorted (e.g. bright marks on one side near the top of a piston might indicate a bent connecting rod or tight gudgeon pin. Tyre rub marks against the chassis frame under a wing might indicate lock adjustment, worn steering joints or hub bearings).

When fitting a new part, always compare it with the original to ensure no modifications have been made since the production was first introduced.

5   Reassembly can present problems where parts are not marked or there are alternative courses open to the fitter. Very often surrounding paint or rust marks will indicate the position, or internal examination of passages and ports will show at once the way round an item must go to connect or fit correctly.

The pressure side of nuts and screws will usually show whether a plain or spring washer is to be used on replacement.

The bedding-in characteristics of all moving mating parts are such that they will show corresponding rubbing marks (e.g. pistons and cylinder walls, shafts and bushes) and enable correct assembly to be carried out.

6   When checking clearances and tolerances make sure that the feeler gauge is giving a true indication. In the case of tappets, the bearing surfaces may be worn

unevenly and this will give a false reading. Similarly, torque readings for nut tightening can be misleading if the thread is tight or damaged in any way. Bearing end float measurement may be difficult to ascertain if thrust washers or retaining nuts have bearing surfaces which are not perfectly true. Castellated nuts whose holes do not line-up with splitpin holes may be rubbed down to provide the additional part turn.

Assemblies which are smooth in operation outside the vehicle sometimes bind or become stiff when fitted. This **may be** due to the pull of the mounting bolts and can be overcome by fractional adjustment of the unit concerned. Starter motors and steering boxes are prone to this and loosening the fixing bolts and giving a slight movement one way or the other will often ease the operation of the part concerned.

Engine tuning should always be carried out with the unit at normal running temperature. **Remember always carry out one adjustment at a time and observe its effect upon performance.**

Whenever an overhaul or repair has been carried out it is always a good plan to check the tightness of nuts and screws after a few hundred miles of running as both heat and vibration cause them to settle down.

1:3 Removing the engine

On vehicles built prior to August 1954 the engine and gearbox must be removed as one unit. On later vehicles the larger floor inspection cover gives access to the top two clutch and flywheel housing bolts and enables the engine to be removed separately from the gearbox.

1 **All vehicles.** Drain the cooling system by means of the radiator tap and retain antifreeze if used. Remove the engine splash shield by removing six retaining screws. Release the air cleaner clamp and supporting stay from the cylinder head (dry gauze type only). Drain the oil from the sump and replace plug. Disconnect the battery and starter lead.

2 Disconnect all leads, wires, choke and accelerator controls. Unscrew the exhaust pipe clamp bolts and remove the two halves of clamp.

3 Detach the fuel pump feed pipe and **plug the end of the pipe to prevent loss of fuel from tank.** Disconnect top and bottom radiator hoses at the radiator, unscrew the temperature gauge unit from the cylinder head and disconnect heater hoses. Remove the radiator from front bulkhead after removal of four bolts.

4 Disconnect rubber wiper tube from manifold. Disconnect HT and LT leads from the coil. Note distributor index setting, remove locking washer and screw holding the distributor to the cylinder head and lift away after detaching HT leads from plugs.

5 Unscrew No. 3 sparking plug and replace with an engine eye bolt (part A/CEY.6004). Alternatively, a conventional lifting sling may be used. (Although not essential, at this stage, for convenience, the starter motor, generator and fan blades may be removed.) Release the engine mountings by removal of single nut on the engine mounting foot.

Early vehicles (prior to August 1954):

6 Drain the gearbox and retain the oil. Remove gear-

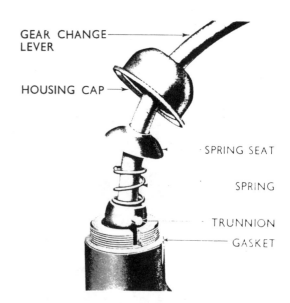

FIG 1:3 Gearchange lever

FIG 1:4 Upper clutch housing to flywheel housing bolts

change lever by unscrewing the plastic knob and withdrawing the rubber housing cover. Ensure gearlever is in the neutral position and unscrew the housing cap (see **FIG 1:3**). Withdraw the lever carefully and cover the gearbox aperture to prevent the entry of dirt.

7 Remove **eight** self-tapping screws and the floor inspection cover.

8 Mark the rear axle pinion flange edge with the corresponding rear universal joint flange edge, remove the four retaining bolts, lower and pull the propeller shaft

to the rear, thus withdrawing front universal joint sleeve from the gearbox extension housing.

9 Slacken the pinch bolt on the clutch hydraulic operating cylinder mounted on the clutch housing. Withdraw cylinder forward. Disconnect earthing strap from the right rear gearchange housing bolt.

10 Unscrew the speedometer drive cable from the gearbox extension housing and withdraw. Cut the locking wire from the gearbox extension mounting bolts, remove bolts and flat washers.

11 Lift out the engine complete with gearbox by raising it slightly by means of the lifting gear and pulling whole assembly forward and to the left to clear the battery.

Later vehicles:

12 Remove **ten** self-tapping screws from the floor inspection cover and remove the cover. Remove the top two flywheel housing bolts (see **FIG 1 : 4**). Place a jack or suitable support under the gearbox housing and remove the remaining clutch to flywheel housing bolts.

13 Lift the engine slightly and move it forward to clear gearbox main drive gear.

1 : 4 Removing and replacing cylinder head

1 Drain the cooling system (the water will flow more freely through the radiator drain tap if the pressure filler cap is first removed). If antifreeze is used, retain coolant for further use. Remove the air cleaner. Slacken the upper radiator hose clamp and on later models the lower hose clamp as well. Unscrew the water temperature gauge connection from the cylinder head.

2 Detach HT leads from the sparking plugs and LT lead from the coil terminal. Note distributor index setting and remove the retaining screw and washer and lift out the distributor from the cylinder head.

3 Disconnect the heater hoses (if fitted) at the cylinder head end and then remove the oil filler cap.

4 Unscrew the fourteen cylinder head bolts a little at a time in the same sequence as for tightening (see **FIG 1 : 5**). The head may now be lifted away. Withdraw the dowel pin fitted between the head and block of later engines. If the cylinder head does not come free at once, turn the engine over (handle on commercial models. **On passenger cars** place in gear, jack-up one rear wheel and turn the road wheel) with sparking plugs in place and utilize compression to loosen the head. **Never use a screwdriver or wedge in an attempt to prise the head off.** Gentle tapping with a wooden mallet is permissible.

When refitting the cylinder head ensure absolute cleanliness of both head and block surfaces and remove any burrs round bolt holes etc. Always fit a new gasket (early models **without** dowel pin Part No. 100E.6051.A later models **with** dowel pin 100E.6051.B) placing the smooth face downwards. Gasket cement is not recommended.

Replace the cylinder head bolts and screw them only finger tight. At this stage refit the distributor which has offset driving dog (match large and small segments with coupling in cylinder head hole). The refitting of the distributor **now** will ensure alignment of shank

FIG 1 : 5   Order for slackening or tightening cylinder head nuts

FIG 1 : 6   Manifolds (prior to June 1957)

holes in both block and cylinder head before tightening of head.

5 Tighten cylinder head bolts a little at a time in the sequence given in **FIG 1 : 5** until correct torque setting is obtained (see torque settings, **Appendix 2**—65 to 70 lb ft).

6 Reset distributor to its original position on timing index and replace all the other parts in reverse order to that given for dismantling. Refill the cooling system, run the engine and test for leaks. When normal running temperature is reached, check torque setting of cylinder head bolts.

1:5 Servicing the head and valves

1 Remove the head as given in the preceding section. Scrape all carbon deposits from the combustion surfaces with a blunt tool and give a final finish with a wire brush. Particular attention should be given to the mating surfaces of both head and block. Prevent carbon from entering the water passages, bolt holes etc.

2 Disconnect the choke and accelerator connections from the carburetter. Detach wiper tube from the manifold. Remove the fuel pipe from the carburetter. Release the exhaust pipe from the manifold by unscrewing two nuts on the securing clamp.

3 Unscrew the four securing nuts and washers from the studs securing the inlet and exhaust manifolds and remove manifolds together with gasket.

4 Providing the carburetter flange gasket and the inlet to exhaust manifold gaskets are in good order, further dismantling of this assembly is unnecessary. Clean all surfaces thoroughly and make sure that the slots on the inlet port faces are clear.

Should the inlet and exhaust manifolds require to be separated, always use a new gasket (see **FIG 1 : 6**) and replace connecting bolts only finger tight until complete manifold has been fully tightened against its port face gasket to cylinder block. Finally tighten the inlet to exhaust manifold bolts fully.

5 Replacement of the manifolds is a reversal of the preceding instructions. Always use a new gasket on the cylinder block face studs. Details of the exhaust heat control valve are given in **Chapter 2, Section 2 :9**.

6 Disconnect the wire to the oil pressure warning light switch at the rear end of the valve chamber cover. Remove the breather pipe after removal of two securing bolts. Disconnect the fuel feed pipe from the fuel pump and plug the pipe to prevent petrol loss. Remove the two retaining nuts and spring washers and withdraw the fuel pump. Unscrew the nine valve chamber cover securing bolts and remove the cover and gasket.

Replacement is a reversal of dismantling procedure but before doing so make sure all oil galleries are clear and mating faces are clean. Use a new cover gasket.

Two of the nine valve cover retaining bolts are shorter than the others, these must be fitted one in the upper centre bolt hole and the other in the bolt hole which is **third from the front of the engine in the bottom row.**

7 Cover the crankcase openings in the valve chamber with clean rag to prevent dirt or small parts entering the sump. Obtain a suitable clamp-type valve spring compressor and turn the engine until the first valve is fully seated. Using the compressor to compress spring, withdraw the split collets. Remove the compressor tool, lift valve head and remove the spring retainer and the spring. Withdraw the valve.

Repeat operation with the remaining seven valves. **Keep each valve and its associated parts in numerical order for exact replacement.**

Before giving attention to the valves it is now the time to remove carbon from the piston crowns and the valve ports. Each piston should be brought to the top of its stroke and the carbon removed with a blunt tool. The application of grease round the edge of the piston will prevent carbon particles falling down the cylinder walls which may cause scoring or ring sticking. It is an

FIG 1 :7   Grinding-in a valve

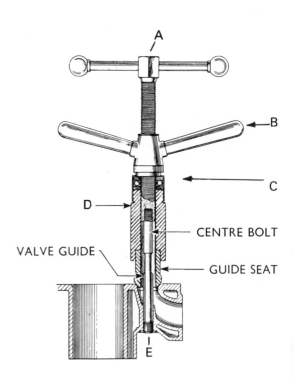

FIG 1 :8   Valve guide removal tool

advantage to leave a ring of carbon round the edge of each piston crown for oil control purposes. Do not damage the valve seats when removing carbon deposits. Once everything is clean, the work of valve grinding may commence.

8 Check the valves for distortion of stem. If they are bent or worn, discard and fit new ones. If the seats show light pitting then the valves should be hand ground. Place each valve in turn into the guide from which it was removed and rotate the engine until the valve is fully seated. First using coarse greased-mixed grinding paste and finishing with fine grade, rotate a rubber suction-cup tool between the palms of the hands (see **FIG 1 : 7**), lifting and dropping the valve every few seconds. When both seats have a smooth matt grey band (not more than $\frac{3}{16}$ inch wide) devoid of all black spots, then wash away all trace of grinding paste with petrol. Repeat the process on each valve.

Where the seats are too burnt for hand grinding, they should be recut after first removing the glaze with abrasive cloth. A suitable 45 deg. cutter may be hired from most hire shops or garages. The removal and insertion of valve seats is best left to a service station.

The valve guides should be examined and if they show severe wear when checked against a new valve stem and the Wear Limit Tables in **Technical Data** they should be replaced. A simplified tool can be made up for their removal based on **FIG 1 : 8**, in which 'A' is a threaded rod to be a sliding fit in the valve guide, 'B' the adjusting nut, 'C' thrust washer, 'D' a piece of steel tube of similar outside diameter to a valve seat insert and slightly longer in length than a valve guide. 'E' is an internally threaded ring of slightly smaller diameter than the external diameter of the valve guide. To use, insert 'A' and screw 'E' on to the threads as they protrude from the bottom of valve guide. Position tube 'D', washer 'C' and nut 'B', **then** tighten 'B' thus withdrawing the guide.

To fit new guides, use a drift, preferably stepped, to give a clearance between top of valve guide and cylinder head machined surface of $\frac{15}{16}$ inch final position.

Valve springs should be checked for **free** length (1.98 inch) and replaced if they vary from this.

9 Lightly oil and replace the valves and springs using the compressor tool. Then fit the valve spring retainers. The split collets should be engaged in the recess in the valve stem whilst the compressor is released and a dab of thick grease may be found useful to keep them in position. The replacement of each valve, spring, retainer and collets should of course be carried out with the tappet on the heel of its cam (lowest point).

10 The valve clearances should now be adjusted. Inlet and exhaust valves have the same clearance when the engine is cold should be between .0115 to .0135 inch.

Counting from the front of the engine the valve sequence is:

1–4–5–8 — *Exhaust*
2–3–6–7 — *Inlet*

then rotate engine and with

Valves fully open	Valves to adjust
1 and 6	3 and 8
3 and 8	1 and 6
2 and 4	5 and 7
5 and 7	2 and 4

FIG 1 : 9 Checking valve clearances

FIG 1 : 10 Timing marks (internal)

Using a feeler gauge whilst maintaining pressure on valve head (see **FIG 1 : 9**), adjust clearance by holding the tappet with one spanner and turning the adjuster with another. No locknut is used as the adjuster screw is self-locking.

The following operations should be carried out with engine removed

1:6 Removing timing gear and camshaft

1 The camshaft is driven from the crankshaft by a non-adjustable double roller chain. For access to the timing gear carry out the following operations.

Remove the fourteen sump bolts and lockwashers, lift off the sump and cork gasket. The sump front flange contains the bottom half of the split crankshaft front oil seal (see **FIG 1:1**). Unscrew the crankshaft pulley bolt (a sharp blow on the spanner is the most effective way to do this) and remove the plain and spring washers. With a suitable puller, withdraw the pulley wheel and remove the oil slinger disc.

2 Unscrew the six bolts and lockwashers from the engine front cover, remove together with gasket. Detach the spring and plunger located in the front of the camshaft which is designed to control camshaft end float.

3 Turn the engine until the marks on both the crankshaft and camshaft sprockets are in-line (see **FIG 1:10**). Bend back the camshaft sprocket locking tabs and remove the retaining screws and locking plate. (On early models a locking wire is used and passes through the heads of the three retaining screws.)

The camshaft sprocket can now be eased off and the timing chain slipped off the crankshaft sprocket. If the timing chain has badly stretched it should be replaced. The two sprockets should be checked for wear and if replacement is necessary, the crankshaft sprocket may be removed by the use of a suitable puller.

4 To remove the camshaft, dismantle the valves as described in **Section 1:5** and remove the fuel pump. Withdraw the small dowel which is exposed when the valve chamber cover is removed (use a $\frac{3}{4}$ inch long screw for this) and remove the distributor and oil pump drive gear and bearing.

Now turn the engine upside down when the tappet blocks will move away from the camshaft. Remove the camshaft, taking great care not to damage the bearing or cam surfaces. The tappets may now be withdrawn if required. A tappet which is not worn should drop slowly into its guide when lubricated. Ensure the tappets are returned to the same guides from which they were removed.

It is not recommended that the camshaft bearing bushes should be removed or replaced by the reader. However, the brass thrust washer behind the camshaft flange may be replaced if the original is worn. This washer should be fitted with chamfered face **away** from the camshaft flange.

1:7 Replacing the camshaft and timing gear

1 Lightly oil the camshaft bearings and guide the camshaft into position, taking care not to damage the bearing surfaces.

2 If the crankshaft sprocket has been removed it may be replaced, making sure that the timing mark is showing to the front. Place the chain over the crankshaft sprocket and engage the camshaft sprocket in loop of chain so that both timing marks are in-line with each other and the sprocket centres.

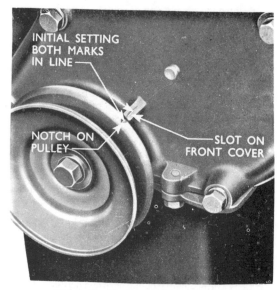

FIG 1:11   Timing marks (external)

FIG 1:12   Distributor drive coupling

3 Locate the camshaft sprocket on the camshaft flange, engaging the dowel (two dowels on engines produced prior to October, 1957). Position the locking plate and enter the three retaining screws. Check the alignment of timing marks and sprocket centres once again and fully tighten the retaining screws. Secure with tabs or wire according to type.

4 Check that the timing marks are in alignment before replacing distributor drive. Should the engine cover be in position the external pointers should be in-line

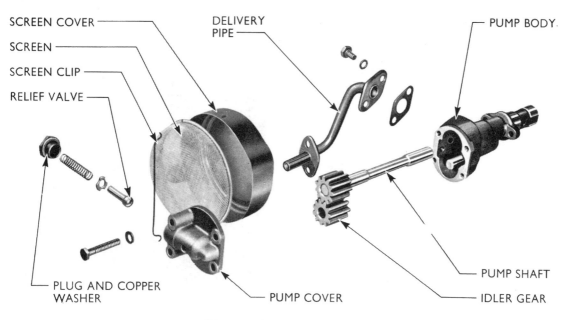

SCREEN COVER

SCREEN

SCREEN CLIP

RELIEF VALVE

DELIVERY PIPE

PUMP BODY

PLUG AND COPPER WASHER

PUMP COVER

PUMP SHAFT

IDLER GEAR

FIG 1:13 Oil pump components

(see **FIG 1:12**) with No. 1 piston on compression stroke with both valves closed.

Install the distributor drive gear so that when it is fully engaged, the coupling shaft is in the position shown in **FIG 1:12**. Ensure that the holes for the retainer dowel are aligned and tap it home.

5 Insert two new halves of oil seal in the front sump flange and the front engine cover groove (these seals should have been soaked in oil for 3 hours and should be positioned $\frac{1}{32}$ inch proud of surrounding metal surfaces in both cases. Insert the plunger and spring in the recess in the end of the camshaft. Lightly oil the plunger surface. Ensure the oil slinger disc is correctly positioned on the crankshaft, and after placing a new gasket in position, bolt the front engine cover to the cylinder block with the bolts and spring washers (note that the longer bolt screws into the boss on the lower lefthand side of the cover). Tighten to correct torque figure.

6 Fit the crankshaft pulley so that the pulley notch engages with the crankshaft key, replace the retaining bolt and spring and plain washers.

Using grease only, stick new cork sump gaskets in position and bolt up the sump. Tighten the bolts equally and evenly to the correct torque figure.

1:8 Dismantling and reassembling the oil pump

1 To dismantle the oil pump, remove the sump as described in **Section 1:6**. Unscrew the two bolts and spring washers which secure the pump to the crankcase and withdraw pump assembly. Detach screen clip and remove the screen (see **FIG 1:13**), this should be cleaned in paraffin and dried with a non-fluffy rag.

2 Unscrew the two bolts which secure the pipe flange to the pump body, remove the pipe with screen cover attached.

Unscrew and remove the oil pressure relief valve and component parts (see **FIG 1:13**) from the pump cover. Unscrew the four bolts which retain the pump cover to the pump body and remove the cover. The gear and shaft assemblies will now slide easily from their location and they should be checked for wear. If excessive side play is evident between the shaft and body, then these components should be replaced.

3 Reassembly is a reversal of the foregoing instructions. **Note that the relief valve location must be on the same side as the delivery pipe.**

Take particular care that the relief valve, spring, centralizing washer, plug and copper washer are in their correct order (see **FIG 1:14**).

When finally assembled make sure that one of the flats on the hexagon plug head lies parallel with the pump body to cover joint, this will prevent interference when fitting the delivery pipe.

Fit the delivery pipe using a new gasket. On later models a rubber O-ring is used at this point and a groove is machined to receive it. Replace filter screen and the retaining wire clip.

4 To replace the oil pump, first align the tongue and groove of the drive shafts, then fit the pump with the filter screen cover towards the front of the engine. Replace the two retaining bolts and spring washers.

Various modifications to the length have been made to the dipstick and dipstick tubes used on these engines, and if for any reason a replacement is required, then an exact type for type replacement must be made.

1:9 Removing the clutch and flywheel

1 Remove the engine from vehicle as described in **Section 1:3**.

2 Slacken the six clutch pressure plate securing bolts, equally, a little at a time. **The alternate bolts have longer threads to enable all spring pressure to be released before removing the complete plate.** Remove the friction disc.

3 Remove the sump. Withdraw the crankshaft pulley and remove the engine front cover, oil slinger, camshaft sprocket and timing chain as described in **Section 1:6**.

4 Bend back the locking tabs on the flywheel retaining bolts and unscrew them. Turn the crankshaft until the locating dowel is uppermost and lever or tap off the flywheel.

5 The starter ring gear is not serviced as a separate item and if upon examination it is found that the teeth are badly worn then a factory exchange flywheel should be fitted.

1:10 Removal of big-ends, connecting rods and pistons

1 To split the big-ends and to remove the connecting rods and pistons, the engine must be removed as detailed in **Section 1:3**. The cylinder head and sump must be dismantled as described in **Sections 1:4** and **1:8**.

The connecting rods are numbered from front to rear of the engine 1, 2, 3 and 4, and each has a corresponding number on its bearing cap. The numbers face the camshaft side of the engine (see **FIG 1:14**).

2 Unscrew the two spring locknuts and hexagon nuts from each big-end bearing cap and lift off the caps.

Remove the ring of carbon from the top of each cylinder bore and then each piston and connecting rod assembly may be pushed out **through the top of the block.**

Make sure you do not scrape or damage the bores during this operation.

3 The connecting rod small-ends are bronze bushed and two sizes of small-end are available as will be seen from **Technical Data.**

The big-end bearings are of whitemetal and under-sizes are available (see table in **Section 1:13**) but only as a complete connecting rod assembly. **Under no circumstances attempt to reduce the bearing to journal clearance by filing the bearing cap.**

1:11 Removing pistons, rings and gudgeon pins

1 To dismantle the piston from the connecting rod remove the circlip from each of the two piston bosses. Immerse the piston in very hot water and then push out the gudgeon pin. A piece of suitable diameter wooden dowel may be used in this operation. It is important to make a careful note of the particular gudgeon pin and piston which belongs to each connecting rod.

2 Pistons are available in a number of oversizes (see **Technical Data**) and the following method may be employed when fitting a new one. Insert the piston (crown first) without any piston rings into the bore. Insert a .0015 inch feeler gauge of half an inch in width between the piston skirt and the bore. Attach a spring balance to the feeler blade which should

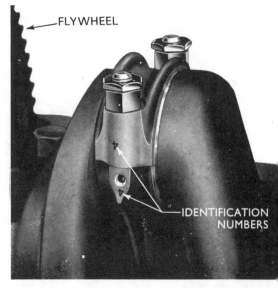

FIG 1:14 Connecting rod numbering

FIG 1:15 Removing piston rings

require a pull of 8 to 11 lbs to remove it. Mark the piston with its respective cylinder identity.

3 Piston rings should be removed and replaced by using three metal strips (see **FIG 1:15**). Even so, great care must be taken in handling the rings as any opening them beyond the diameter of the piston may cause them to fracture.

Each piston has three rings. In the top groove is fitted the chrome tapered compression ring. In the centre groove is the stepped (on the underside) compression ring. In the lower groove is fitted the oil control ring which is identified by its grooving and slots.

The two compression rings have 'TOP' marked on their upper surfaces.

4 Piston rings which have worn thin or unevenly should be replaced. Each ring should be checked for clearance in its respective groove (see **FIG 1:16**) and the following table indicates the permissible gaps between rings and grooves.

Groove	Ring to groove clearance
Top	.0015 to .0040 inch
Centre	.0015 to .0045 inch
Lower	.0010 to .0040 inch

5 Whether refitting old or new rings, check the end gaps with the piston rings actually fitted in the bores (see **FIG 1:17**. Make sure that the ring is perfectly square within the cylinder bore and see that the gap clearance is as shown below:

Ring	End gap clearance
Top	.007 to .015 inch
Centre	.008 to .017 inch
Lower	.007 to .015 inch

Too small a clearance may be increased by careful grinding of the piston ring gap end surfaces.

1:12 Refitting rings, pistons and connecting rods

Subject to the inspection and measurements described in the previous section, the pistons may be refitted to the connecting rods. Remember that the connecting rods are numbered in sequence and each piston is marked with an arrow on its crown. When assembled, this arrow should face the front of the engine whilst the connecting rod numbers face the camshaft.

1 Using the hot water method to heat the piston, push in the gudgeon pin and fit new circlips.
   Under no circumstances attempt to drive out or insert a gudgeon pin with the piston cold.
2 With the piston now fitted to its connecting rod, slide on the rings in their correct order, using the metal strips. **The piston ring gaps should be equally spaced around the piston.**
3 Oil the piston and rings and then compress the ring with a suitable compressor (a flat strip of sheet metal suitably bent to shape is a good substitute), see **FIG 1:18.**
4 Enter the big-end into the top of the cylinder bore until the ring compressor is resting on the cylinder block. Carefully push the piston through the compressor into the bore taking care not to score either the cylinder walls or the crankshaft journals with the big-end studs.
5 Check that the arrow on the piston crown points to the front and is in-line with the engine block.
   Carefully locate the big-end bearing on the crankshaft journal, replace the bearing cap and two nuts which should be tightened to the correct torque of 20 to 25 lb ft. Two new spring locknuts should be fitted, tightening them finger tight plus one third of a turn.
   The end float between the connecting rod and crankshaft web, measured with a feeler gauge should be between .004 and .010 inch.
   Repeat the procedure on the other three pistons and connecting rods.

1:13 Removing crankshaft and main bearings

1 The engine will have been removed from the vehicle as

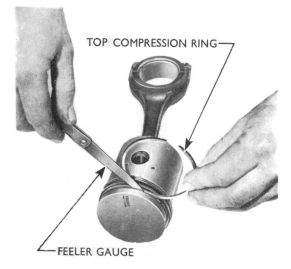

FIG 1:16   Measuring ring gap in groove

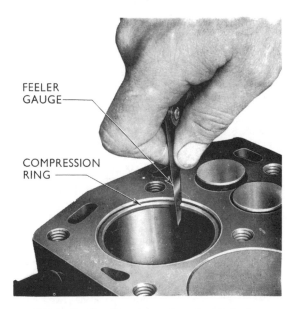

FIG 1:17   Checking ring end gap in cylinder bore

detailed in **Section 1:3.** Remove the cylinder head (see **Section 1:4**) and timing gear (see **Section 1:6**), the oil pump and the sump (see **Section 1:8**). Dismantle the clutch and the flywheel (see **Section 1:9**) and remove each of the four connecting rod big-end bearings (see **Section 1:10**). Push the pistons and rods upwards out of the way taking particular care not to damage the cylinder bores with the big-end studs.

2 Withdraw the crankshaft sprocket and remove the key. Unscrew the main bearing cap bolts and remove the main bearing caps and their respective liners. Keep

them in strict order as both the caps and liners must be replaced in the same way round and location from which they were removed.

Examine the main bearing liners and renew if necessary. If the original liners are being replaced in their cylinder block locations, ensure that they are perfectly clean and return them to their original locations. (Notice locating tabs.)

The main bearing liners may be removed and replaced with the crankshaft in position. Proceed by removing the bearing caps and the lower halves of the liners. Then with a curved strip of aluminium or brass approx. $\frac{3}{32}$ inch in thickness, rotate the upper liners in a direction opposite to that of normal engine rotation (rotating the crankshaft in the same direction will assist extraction of these liners).

To insert new upper liners, repeat the procedure but all movement will now be in the direction of normal engine rotation.

3 The crankshaft big-end and main journals may be reground if ovality exceeds .001 inch in accordance with the table below:

Size	Big-end journal	Main journal
Standard	1.698 to 1.699 inch	2.0010 to 2.0015 inch
.010 inch u/s	1.688 to 1.689 inch	1.9910 to 1.9915 inch
.020 inch u/s	1.678 to 1.679 inch	1.9810 to 1.9815 inch
.030 inch u/s	1.668 to 1.669 inch	1.9719 to 1.9715 inch

Main bearing liners are available in undersizes of .010, .020 and .030 inch.

Big-end bearings (complete rod) are available in undersizes of .010, .015, .020, .030 and .040 inch.

4 Crankshaft end float is controlled by thrust washers located on each side of the rear main bearing. Check the end float thrust washer and crankshaft web with a feeler gauge, as shown in **FIG 1 : 19,** but first tap the crankshaft forward. The end float clearance should be between .002 and .015 inch. Thrust washers are available in oversizes of .0025, .005, .0075 and .010 inch.

The thrust washer on each side of the rear main bearing is in two halves, one located in the block, the other in the bearing cap. Each washer has two oil grooves which should face the crankshaft web. The halves which fit in the bearing cap have tabs to prevent them rotating (see **FIG 1 : 20**).

On engines made between February 1957 and April 1958 (numbers 351441 to 535001) an alteration in design was made to the crankshaft rear oil seal, see next paragraph. For these engines only, two halves of the rear bearing thrust washers were used only and these, without tabs, were located in the lower bearing cap positions.

5 Before replacing the main bearing liners, examine the crankshaft rear oil seal, the top half of which is fitted in a retainer in a groove in the crankcase (not 1957–8 engines where the seal is fitted direct into the crankcase groove, the retainer having been deleted) and the lower half of the seal is fitted in a groove in the rear wall of the sump.

The packings used as oil seals should be a firm fit in their grooves and their ends should stand proud of their surrounding surfaces by not more than $\frac{1}{32}$ inch.

New packings should be soaked in oil for at least three hours.

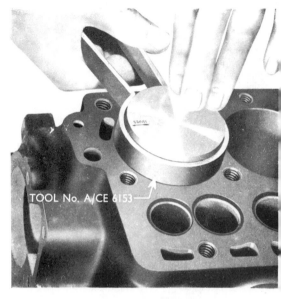

FIG 1 : 18 Using a compressor to fit a piston

1 : 19 Checking crankshaft end float

6 Replace the main bearing liners in the block locations, replace the crankshaft, thrust washers, cap liners and caps, observing scrupulous cleanliness and strict location of components. Bearing caps have a locating dowel in the cylinder block.

Replace the bearing cap bolts and tighten them evenly to 55 to 60 lb ft.

Where bearing liners are being replaced due to the bearings having run because of lack of lubrication, pressure clean the crankshaft oil passages before reassembling.

1:14 Engine oil filter

1 This is of the bypass type and is situated on the left side, lower front of the crankcase. To remove the filter element, unscrew the centre bolt at the base of the filter element casing, withdraw the bolt and the casing complete and remove the element which is of the disposable type.

Note, three types of filter elements are available; one has a $\frac{7}{8}$ inch (22 mm) diameter bore and is fitted with the flat end downwards; the other two have a $1\frac{1}{8}$ inch (31.7 mm) diameter bore and may be fitted either way up.

Two types of element seats are available. The single stepped seat can only be used with the smaller bore element; the double stepped seat can be used with all three elements and may be substituted for the former to enable a larger bore element to be fitted if required.

If a U-shaped retaining clip is incorporated, this must be replaced by a circlip if it is required to fit a $\frac{7}{8}$ inch diameter bore element.

2 When fitting a new filter element, clean out the filter case thoroughly and examine the rubber sealing ring on the underside of the filter bracket (gasket on early models) and renew if necessary. Offer up the filter case complete with element and centre bolt and tighten the bolt but do not overstrain. Run the engine for ten minutes and examine the filter for leaks.

A new element will absorb nearly one pint of oil so recheck oil level.

1:15 Reassembling stripped engine

All dismantling and reassembling operations have been given in detail in the various sections so that the purpose of this one is to remind the reader of the correct sequence of operations and give some general observations.

Commence by fitting the cylinder block main bearing liners, followed by the crankshaft, main bearing liners and caps, piston rings, pistons and connecting rods. The oil pump, camshaft, timing gear and distributor gear should follow, then with the engine the right way up, install the valves, tappets and components. Fit the cylinder head, engine side and front covers, then assemble the flywheel and clutch.

The flywheel and crankshaft mating flanges should be carefully cleaned, then with the crankshaft flange dowel at the top of the flange mount the flywheel in position ensuring the dowel pin engages in its hole in the flywheel. Use a new retaining plate and insert the four retaining bolts tightening them to 21 to 23 lb ft. Bend the locking tabs.

Full reassembly instructions for the clutch are given in **Chapter 5, Section 5:7**.

Clean the mating faces of both the fuel pump and the cylinder block, install a new gasket and fit the pump. The rocker arm lever of the fuel pump should rest against the camshaft eccentric.

Finally replace the crankshaft pulley.

Having made a final check, replace the sump. Remember never put back a suspect gasket. It is surprising how helpful a dab of grease or oil can be to fix components in place and provide you with that extra pair of hands.

Never bolt on to the main unit any ancilliary part (manifolds, carburetters, starter motor, etc) which may get in the way when replacing the engine in the car.

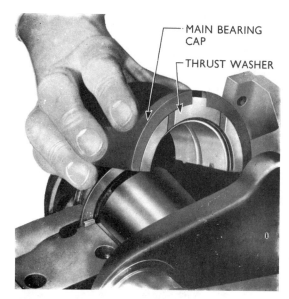

FIG 1:20 Installing crankshaft rear main bearing thrust washer

MAIN BEARING CAP

THRUST WASHER

SELF LOCKING NUT

MOUNTING FOOT

RUBBER INSULATOR ASSEMBLY

FIG 1:21 Engine mounting (righthand)

Torque wrench settings are listed in **Technical Data**. Valve clearance adjustment and ignition timing procedure are given in **Section 1:5** and **Section 1:7**.

1:16 Replacing engine in the car

Before this operation is attempted, the clutch driven plate must be aligned so that the gearbox first-motion shaft will pass easily through it on reassembly and engage in the pilot bearing which is pressed into the centre of the flywheel. Full details of the method of aligning the clutch driven plate are given in **Chapter 5, Section 5:7**.

1 Once the clutch driven and pressure plates have been assembled and aligned, **then in the case of early models** (see **Section 1:3**) the gearbox should be bolted to the flywheel housing and the combined engine/gearbox unit lowered into the frame.

2 **Early cars.** To fit the gearbox to the engine before installing the complete unit, engage the main drive gear spigot in the flywheel bush after passing the main drive shaft through the aligned driven plate (see **Chapter 5, Section 5:7**). The weight of the gearbox must be supported throughout this operation to prevent any strain upon the main drive shaft.

3 Enter and tighten evenly the eight clutch to flywheel housing bolts and their spring washers, at the same time locating the clutch operating cylinder bracket under the heads of the two bolts on the righthand side of the housing.

4 The engine/gearbox unit may now be lowered and moved backwards in the frame. Assemble the rear mounting insulator to the frame crossmember and fit the two self-locking nuts finger tight. Fit the two bolts and flat washers which secure the extension housing to the insulator. Tighten them and fit a new locking wire. Now tighten fully the insulator self-locking nuts after the engine front mounting feet have been engaged with their rubber insulators and the self-locking nuts screwed down tight.

5 Engage the front universal joint sleeve with the main shaft in the rear gearbox extension housing at the same time making sure that the rear universal joint flange alignment mark (made before dismantling) coincides with the mark on the pinion driving flange. Replace the four coupling bolts and self-locking nuts, reconnect the earthing strap. Fill the gearbox with oil.

Replace the speedometer drive in the extension housing. Tighten clutch cylinder pinch bolt.

6 **Later cars** (where the gearbox was left in position). Lower and move the engine to engage the gearbox main drive shaft spigot in the flywheel bush by sliding the aligned driven plate and pressure plate over the shaft. Although the gearbox will be supported on a jack, the greatest care must be taken to prevent the weight of the engine bearing upon the gearbox main drive shaft during this operation.

Once engagement is completed, make sure that the engine front mounting feet are engaged with their rubber insulators and screw on the self-locking nuts.

Enter and tighten evenly the eight clutch to flywheel housing bolts and their spring washers, at the same time locating the clutch operating cylinder bracket under the heads of the two bolts on the righthand side of the housing.

7 **All cars.** Reassembly is a reversal of dismantling procedure given in **Section 1:3** but the sequence is given as follows:

8 Remove lifting eye bolt or sling and replace sparking plugs. Replace the distributor and set the timing index to original position. Reconnect LT and HT wires.

9 Replace the manifolds, carburetter and connect the exhaust pipe with two-piece clamp. Fit the choke and accelerator controls, replace the wiper tube to the manifold and the air cleaner to the carburetter.

10 Replace the radiator and connect the top and bottom and heater hoses. Refit the temperature gauge unit.

Remove the plug and the connect fuel line to the fuel pump.

11 Replace the starter motor and cable. Connect the oil warning switch wire. Refit the generator and connecting wires. Replace the fan belt, adjusting it to the correct tension (see **Section 4:2**). Connect the battery.

12 Replace the engine splash shield, fill radiator and sump.

13 Fit the gearbox inspection cover and its sealing gasket and replace the gearchange lever.

14 Check clutch linkage adjustment (see **Chapter 5, Section 5:2**).

15 Check that all wires and controls have been replaced, start the engine, check for leaks.

1:17 Engine mountings

Both the front engine and rear gearbox mountings or insulators are of the metal to rubber bonded type (see **FIG 1:21**).

On early models oil leakage could occur from the cylinder block mounting foot bolt holes and gasket cement should be used on the bolt threads. On later models, blind holes or studs have been used to obviate this problem.

The condition of the rubber insulators should be checked and if deterioration has taken place, they should be replaced. This work may be carried out with the engine in place by first placing a wooden protector under the sump and jacking-up only far enough to take weight off the mountings.

Remove the rubber insulator assembly bolts which retain it to the suspension crossmember and then unscrew the single self-locking nut, withdraw the assembly downwards.

Replacement is a reversal of the dismantling procedure but allow the engine to take up its normal position by removing the jack before tightening the self-locking nut securely.

1:18 Modifications

A useful modification which owners of cars may like to carry out is the addition of a starting handle.

Estate car and commercial versions may already be so fitted, if not the following parts are required.

Starting handle 300E.17036.

Crankshaft pulley starter dog E93A.6319 (replaces the pulley retaining bolt).

The radiator presents the biggest problem for this modification and whilst it may be possible to exchange the existing one for an alternative with a starting handle hole (300E.8005) most radiator repairers will be able to carry out the appropriate modifications to provide the required opening.

The radiator grill shield will be found to have a suitable opening but **on cars** the front bumper bar will need drilling and slotting to accept the handle.

Be careful if a four bladed fan is fitted that the blades do not foul the starter dog during rotation.

1:19 Fault diagnosis

(a) Engine will not start

1 Defective coil
2 Faulty distributor capacitor (condenser)
3 Dirty, pitted or incorrectly set contact breaker points
4 Ignition wires loose or poor insulation
5 Damp sparking plug leads
6 Battery discharged, terminals corroded
7 Faulty or jammed starter
8 Sparking plug leads wrongly connected
9 Vapour lock in fuel pipes
10 Defective fuel pump
11 Overchoking or underchoking
12 Blocked petrol filter or carburetter jets
13 Leaking valves
14 Sticking valves
15 Valve timing incorrect
16 Ignition timing incorrect

(b) Engine stalls

1 Check 1, 2, 3, 4, 5, 10, 11, 12, 13, 14 in (a)
2 Sparking plugs defective or gaps incorrect
3 Retarded ignition
4 Mixture too weak
5 Water in fuel system
6 Petrol tank vent blocked
7 Incorrect valve clearances

(c) Engine idles badly

1 Check 2 and 7 in (b)
2 Air leaks at manifold joints
3 Carburetter jet setting wrong
4 Air leak in carburetter
5 Over-rich mixture
6 Worn piston rings
7 Worn valve stems or guides
8 Weak exhaust valve springs

(d) Engine misfires

1 Check 1, 2, 3, 4, 5, 8, 10, 12, 13, 14, 15, 16 in (a); and 2, 3, 4 and 7 in (b)
2 Weak or broken valve springs

(e) Engine overheats (see Chapter 4)

(f) Compression low

1 Check 13 and 14 in (a); 6 and 7 in (c); and 2 in (d)
2 Worn piston ring grooves
3 Scored or worn cylinder bores

(g) Engine lacks power

1 Check 3, 10, 11, 12, 13, 14, 15 and 16 in (a); 2, 3, 4 and 7 in (b); 6 and 7 in (c); and 2 in (d). Also check (e) and (f)

2 Leaking joint washers
3 Fouled sparking plugs
4 Automatic advance not operating

(h) Burnt valves or seats

1 Check 13 and 14 in (a); 7 in (b); and 2 in (d). Also check (e)
2 Excessive carbon around valve seats and head

(j) Sticking valves

1 Check 2 in (d)
2 Bent valve stem
3 Scored valve stem or guide
4 Incorrect valve clearance

(k) Excessive cylinder wear

1 Check 11 in (a); and see Chapter 4
2 Lack of oil
3 Dirty oil
4 Piston rings gummed up or broken
5 Badly fitting piston rings
6 Connecting rod bent

(l) Excessive oil consumption

1 Check 6 and 7 in (c); and check (k)
2 Ring gaps too wide
3 Oil return holes in piston choked with carbon
4 Scored cylinders
5 Oil level too high
6 External oil leaks

(m) Crankshaft and connecting rod bearing failure

1 Check 2 in (k)
2 Restricted oilways
3 Worn journals or crankpins
4 Loose bearing caps
5 Extremely low oil pressure
6 Bent connecting rod

(n) Internal water leakage (see Chapter 4)

(o) Poor water circulation (see Chapter 4)

(p) Corrosion (see Chapter 4)

(q) High fuel consumption (see Chapter 2)

(r) Engine vibration

1 Loose generator bolts
2 Mounting rubbers loose or ineffective
3 Exhaust pipe mountings too tight
4 Fan blades out of balance
5 Misfiring due to mixture, ignition or mechanical faults

CHAPTER 2

THE FUEL SYSTEM

2:1 Description

The system consists of a fuel tank, a mechanically operated pump driven by an eccentric on the camshaft, a downdraught carburetter and the necessary fuel lines. A two-stage carburetter is fitted to early vehicles while later cars have a carburetter which incorporates a progressive starting device.

The fuel tank fitted to Anglia and Prefect cars is within the lefthand portion of the luggage boot. The tank in the 5 and 7 cwt vans is beneath the floor behind the driver's seat and on Escort and Squire estate cars it is beneath the floor at the rear. The filler cap is of vented type. The fuel gauge registers when ignition is switched on.

2:2 Routine maintenance

Occasionally the fuel tank may be drained to remove accumulated sediment and water produced by condensation. A drain plug is provided on estate cars, whilst on cars and vans the fuel pipe union at the base of the tank should be undone and a small quantity of petrol drawn off.

The fuel pump will require attention every 5000 miles when the filter screen and bowl should be cleaned out. Dismantling instructions are given in the next section.

2:3 Dismantling the fuel pump

1 Disconnect fuel inlet pipe and plug it to prevent petrol loss.
2 See **FIG 2:1.** Remove the cover screw and the fibre washer. Lift off the cover and carefully remove the gasket. Withdraw the filter screen and wash it in petrol. Flush out the sediment from the pump body. This is the extent of normal maintenance, reassembly being a reversal of the dismantling procedure. The filter screen is installed with the reinforcement strips uppermost. Do not overtighten the cover bolt. Reconnect the fuel inlet pipe.
3 For complete overhaul, remove the fuel pump to carburetter fuel pipe taking care not to twist the pipe when loosening the unions. Disconnect and plug the fuel inlet pipe.
4 Unscrew and remove the two nuts and lockwashers which secure the pump to the cylinder block. Detach the pump, tilting it slightly so that the operating lever (rocker arm) clears the camshaft.
5 Refer to **FIG 2:2.** Unscrew the cover bolt with washer, remove the cover and the filter screen. Remove the five screws and lockwashers securing the upper and lower

pump bodies. Separate the two halves, taking care not to damage the diaphragm. Now turn the diaphragm a quarter turn which will free the diaphragm rod from the operating lever. Detach the diaphragm.

The diaphragm and pullrod are rivetted together, do not dismantle. Remove the diaphragm spring, oil seal washer and the oil seal.

6 **On cars produced after April 1956,** the inlet and outlet valves are both retained by a spring steel plate and two screws (see **FIG 2 : 2**). Remove the screws and plate and lift the two valve assemblies together with the 'figure eight' gasket from the upper body.

7 **On cars produced before April 1956,** the inlet and outlet valves are retained by a plate and three screws (see **FIG 2 : 3**). Remove the three screws and lift the plate and the gasket. Detach each valve and its spring and the inlet valve retainer.

8 The rocker arm is removed from all pumps by detaching the two circlips and pin. The two washers must be positioned one either side of the rocker arm on reassembly.

2 : 4 Reassembling the fuel pump

1 Assemble the spring, oil seal washer and oil seal to the pullrod. (On very early model pumps the original seal was unsatisfactory and it should be replaced with the later type of seal which has an elongated hole.) Insert the end of the rod in the slotted end of the link and engage by turning the diaphragm a quarter turn. The smaller tab on the diaphragm must align with the mating mark on the lower body flange.

2 Hold the upper body with the valve locations uppermost, and in the case of pumps made after April 1956 fit the 'figure eight' gasket first, then the two valve assemblies followed by the retainer plate and two screws (see **FIG 2 : 4**).

3 In the case of pumps made prior to April 1956, assemble the inlet valve, spring and retainer in the inlet valve port and fit the outlet valve spring and valve in the outlet port. Carefully fit the gasket and plate over the valves using the three securing screws (see **FIG 2 : 5**).

4 Position the fuel pump upper body over the diaphragm on the lower body so that the inlet and outlet unions are directly opposite the pump to crankcase mounting flange. Depress the rocker arm until the diaphragm rises level with the body flange and fit the five screws and lockwashers finger tight.

5 Work the rocker arm several full strokes to centralize the diaphragm and tighten the five screws evenly.

6 Replace the filter screen (reinforcement uppermost). Fit the cover and gasket (may require replacement if over-compressed) and screw down the retaining bolt with fibre washer. **Do not overtighten** but ensure a good seal is made.

2 : 5 Refitting fuel pump to engine and testing

1 Ensure that all ports and threads are clean, fit a new fuel pump to crankcase gasket (in the case of later models, a thick type of insulating gasket is used and if this is substituted on earlier models, longer crankcase holding studs and a modified rocker arm will be required). Part Nos. 88386.S and 9376.A.

2 Hold the fuel pump with its cover uppermost and insert

FIG 2 : 1 Routine servicing of the pump

the rocker arm through the slot in the crankcase so that the arm locates on the camshaft eccentric and lies between the camshaft and the crankcase wall.

Fit the retaining nuts and lockwashers and tighten evenly.

3 Connect the fuel inlet pipe **only** at this stage, crank the engine using the starter motor when a well defined spurt of petrol should be seen coming from the outlet port.

Any deviation from the foregoing may be due to incorrectly assembled fuel pump valves or unions, or the pump cover not being sufficiently tight.

Connect the fuel pump to the carburetter pipe.

2 : 6 The carburetter

This is of the single-choke downdraught type but differing in starter device according to the date of vehicle manufacture. Early models are fitted with Type 26Z1C (marked on the bowl) which gives a predetermined mixture strength in each of the two choke control positions (see **FIG 2 : 6**).

Later models are fitted with Type B26ZIC.2 which gives a progressive mixture strength up to the intermediate position of the choke control (see **FIG 2 : 7**).

Operation (early models Type 26ZIC):

The starter device consists of a shaft passing through the centre of a mixing chamber formed by the starter device body and cover. There are two disc valves fitted on the shaft, the inner valve being held against the side of the carburetter body by a large coil spring and the outer valve against the face of the starter cover by a smaller coil spring (see **FIG 2 : 8**).

When the choke control is fully withdrawn, i.e. for starting from very cold, the starter shaft turns so that an elongated hole in the inner disc valve lines up with a

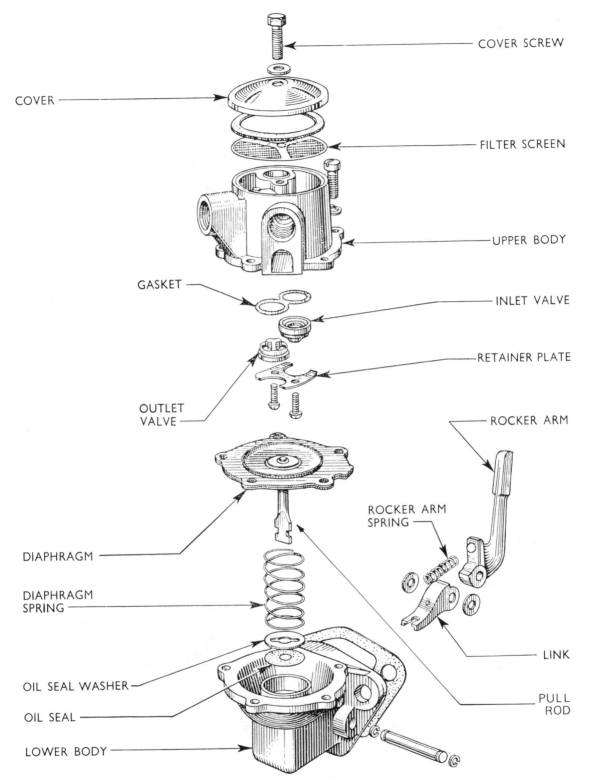

COVER SCREW

COVER

FILTER SCREEN

UPPER BODY

GASKET

INLET VALUE

RETAINER PLATE

OUTLET VALVE

ROCKER ARM

ROCKER ARM SPRING

DIAPHRAGM

DIAPHRAGM SPRING

LINK

OIL SEAL WASHER

OIL SEAL

PULL ROD

LOWER BODY

FIG 2:2   Fuel pump components (showing valve assembly after April 1956)

passage in the carburetter body through which engine vacuum is transmitted to the starter device mixing chamber. A smaller hole in this valve lines up with a passage in the carburetter body connected to the top of the starter petrol well. **FIG 2 : 6** indicates the conditions prevailing with the choke control fully withdrawn preparatory to starting the engine.

The starter motor is operated, and with the throttle butterfly closed, the engine creates depression or suction at the starter supply outlet channel below the throttle butterfly; this is transmitted to the starter mixing chamber via the outlet channel and the hole in the starter disc valve. The suction further takes effect via the top hole in the disc, on the fuel induction channel, and is finally transmitted to the float chamber well supplied by the starter petrol jet. Thus, petrol for initial starting is drawn from the well above the starter jet to the starter mixing chamber.

Simultaneously the suction acting on the surface of the starter outer valve disc draws it inwards along the shaft against the predetermined strength of the seating spring. Air is consequently admitted through the air jets, restricted however by the space forming a clearance between the disc and its original seating (**FIG 2 : 6** illustrates the disc valves in the intermediate position and not the extreme cold position of the choke control.)

By this means it will be seen that a very rich mixture is provided for extreme cold starting. **In consequence the choke needs to be returned to the intermediate position as soon as possible.**

When the choke control is returned to the intermediate position, i.e. halfway in, two holes in the starter outer disc valve register with the channel leading to the air jets, so allowing free passage of air to the full capacity of the starter air jets. At the same time the starter inner disc valve has, in its new position, presented a smaller hole to the petrol induction channel thereby reducing the quantity of petrol entering the mixing chamber. A much weaker mixture is therefore drawn in by the engine, and after a few minutes the engine will be warm enough to keep running without the aid of the starter unit, and the dashboard control should be pushed right home.

Operation (later models Type B.26Z1C.2):

This starter device is similar to that previously described though the location of the ports on the starter device mounting face of the carburetter casting differ to give a more progressive control of the starting mixture between the fully returned and intermediate position of the control.

When the starter device control is in the extreme cold weather starting position, i.e. fully out, the function is identical with Model 26Z1C (see **FIG 2 : 7**).

In the intermediate position, where the starter lever is located by a spring-loaded ball, the small dished hole in the inner disc valve is put into circuit together with the partly reduced area of the larger hole. At the same time two holes in the starter outer disc valve register with the casting channels leading to the air orifices, allowing free passage of air. This together with air drawn into the starter box through the channel drilled to connect the carburetter venturi (see **FIG 2 : 7**), gives more volume and a weaker mixture.

Removable starter air jets are not fitted to this particular carburetter starting device.

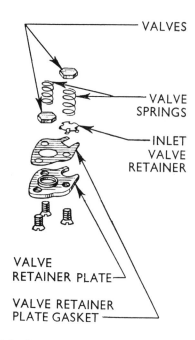

FIG 2 : 3   Fuel pump valve assembly (prior to April 1956)

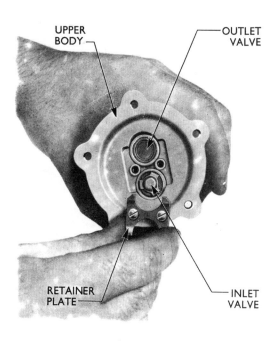

FIG 2 : 4   Fitting fuel pump valves (after April 1956)

28

Rotation of the inner disc, as the choke control is returned, progressively reduces richness and volume through the dished hole and the area of the mixture outlet, slowing the engine down as it warms up until the starting device is out of action, a blank face of the inner disc finally coming opposite the mixture inlet and outlet channels.

On opening the throttle with a comparatively cold engine (see **FIG 2:7**), extra enrichment is provided by suction then being brought directly onto the channel connecting the carburetter venturi and the starter mixture chamber, drawing mixture out from the starter box through the dished hole. Enrichment decreases to nothing as the inner disc valve is rotated from the 'intermediate' to the 'fully returned' position of the choke control.

The carburetter design provides the correct mixture for idling when the engine is warm.

It also provides through the progression orifice, the mixture required as the throttle is first opened, but before it opens sufficiently for the main spraying holes to begin to discharge. This ensures smooth transfer from the idling circuit on to the main supply circuit.

Petrol is supplied from the reserve well to the idling jet, the idling jet air bleed providing pre-emulsion.

When idling, emulsifying air is also drawn into the progression orifice, the volume of all this mixture being controlled by the volume control screw (see **FIG 2:9**).

On leaving the idling orifice the emulsion is mixed with air passing round the throttle butterfly, this being held slightly open by an adjustment screw on a bracket at the end of the throttle spindle. As the throttle is progressively opened, engine suction is directed to the progression orifice which discharges the richer mixture required to balance with the increased volume of air passing the throttle.

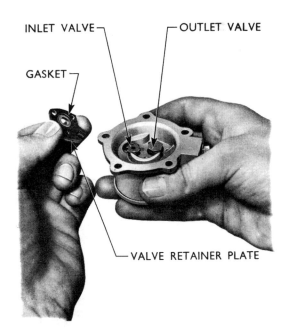

INLET VALVE — — OUTLET VALVE

GASKET —

— VALVE RETAINER PLATE

FIG 2:5 Fitting fuel pump valves (prior to April 1956)

The main supply is provided, for all speeds above idling, by the choke tube, the main spraying assembly comprising the main jet correction bleed, the emulsion tube, and the main jet, screwed into its carrier on the side of the carburetter.

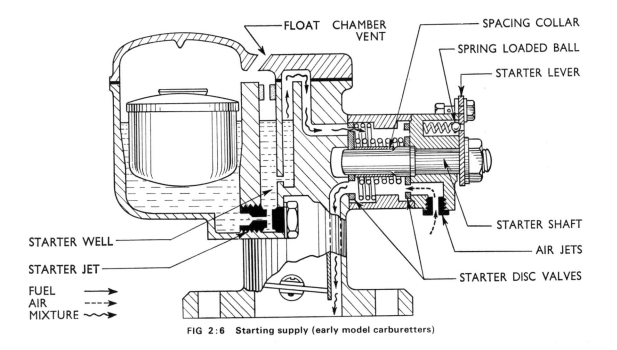

— FLOAT CHAMBER VENT

— SPACING COLLAR

— SPRING LOADED BALL

— STARTER LEVER

STARTER WELL

STARTER JET —

FUEL →
AIR ---→
MIXTURE ～～→

STARTER SHAFT

AIR JETS

STARTER DISC VALVES

FIG 2:6 Starting supply (early model carburetters)

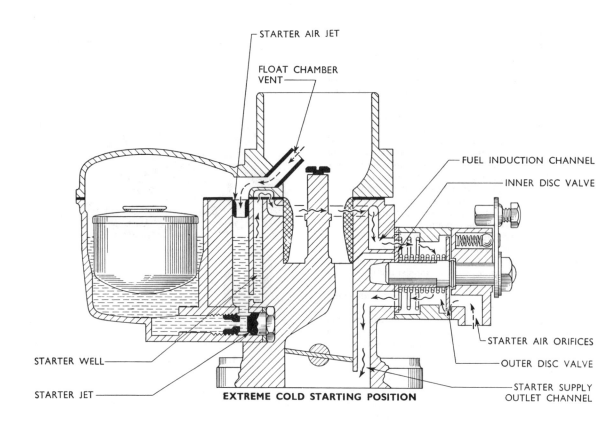

STARTER AIR JET

FLOAT CHAMBER VENT

FUEL INDUCTION CHANNEL

INNER DISC VALVE

STARTER AIR ORIFICES

OUTER DISC VALVE

STARTER SUPPLY OUTLET CHANNEL

STARTER WELL

STARTER JET

EXTREME COLD STARTING POSITION

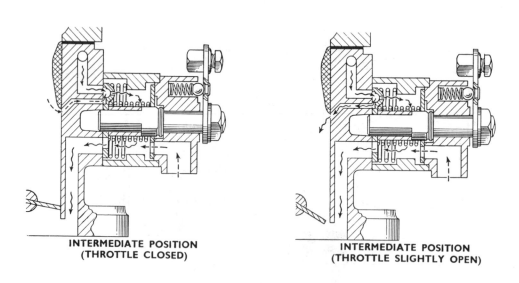

INTERMEDIATE POSITION (THROTTLE CLOSED)

INTERMEDIATE POSITION (THROTTLE SLIGHTLY OPEN)

FIG 2:7 Starting supply (later model carburetters)

Petrol passes from the float chamber through the main jet, filling the reserve well and rising to the predetermined level in the spraying well.

As the throttle butterfly is opened, air is drawn downwards to the engine, its increasing velocity creating suction at the holes in the spraying well.

Petrol, in the annulus formed by the emulsion tube and the spraying well, is drawn upwards and at the same time is emulsified by air passing down the main jet correction bleed and through the holes in the emulsion tube. The resultant emulsion emerges from the holes in the spraying assembly located in the waist of the choke tube, there to be absorbed by the main air current and thence to the engine, past the throttle butterfly.

As the engine speed increases the larger hole in the bottom of the emulsion tube is rapidly uncovered, and balancing air to weaken off the mixture is increasingly supplied through the correction bleed (see **FIG 2:9**).

2:7 Tuning and maintenance

Routine maintenance consists of cleaning out the carburetter bowl and clearing the jets by blowing through them with a hand pump (**do not use wire**). Full details for access to these components are given in the next section.

The only adjustments required to be carried out are to the volume control screw and to the slow-running screw (see **FIG 2:9**).

1 When the engine is at normal operating temperature, screw in the slow-running adjustment screw until a fast-idling speed is obtained (ignition warning light just stays on).

2 Unscrew the volume control screw until the engine begins to 'hunt' then screw in again until the engine runs evenly. Readjust the slow-running screw again until the desired tick-over is obtained and then readjust the volume control screw. Do not aim at too low an idling speed as this will tend to cause excessive rocking of the engine and tend to cause stalling until the engine has reached full working temperature.

2:8 Dismantling the carburetter

1 Remove the air cleaner (or cover plate in the case of the Popular). Disconnect the fuel pipe union at the carburetter. Detach throttle control link and disconnect the choke control cable. Unscrew flange retaining nuts, remove the lockwashers. Lift off the carburetter and gasket.

2 Remove the three retaining screws and lockwashers from the float chamber cover and lift off the cover and gasket. Lift out the float lever and spindle, remove the float and check that it is unpunctured. Unscrew the needle valve from the float chamber cover and remove its fibre washer.

3 See **FIG 2:9** and remove the four long brass screws holding the starter assembly to the side of the carburetter body and remove the assembly.

Remove the jets from their locations, as shown in **FIG 2:9**.

4 Close the throttle plate and remove the two countersunk headed screws which attach it to the throttle spindle. (Remove the spindle seal only if renewal is required.)

5 Slacken the choke tube locking screw and remove the choke tube upwards. Unscrew the volume control screw and remove it together with its spring.

6 The starter assembly will normally only require washing in petrol to clean but if stripping is essential then

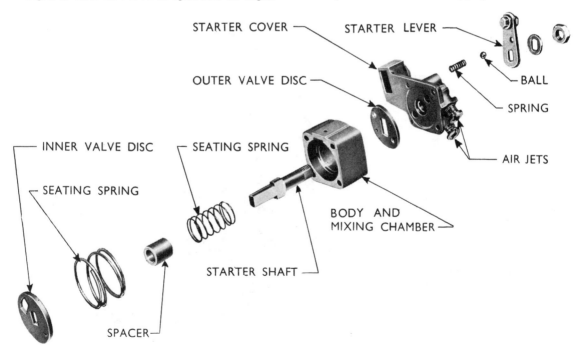

FIG 2:8 Starting device (early models)

commence by marking the two disc valves so that they may be returned to their original position on the shaft (see **FIG 2:8**).

Unscrew the two starter air jets (early models only). Unscrew the starter shaft nut, remove it together with the washer and lever but **be careful not to lose the ball and spring as the lever is withdrawn.**

File off the retaining sprags on the inside end of the starter shaft and the component parts in the order shown in **FIG 2:8** may be removed.

2:9 Reassembling the carburetter

1 Clean all parts thoroughly and check for wear. Make sure that the throttle plate and spindle are a good fit in the carburetter body. Replace any worn jets and check that the fibre washers and gaskets are sound.
2 Reassemble the starter by referring to **FIG 2:8** and reversing the order in which it was dismantled.
3 Refit the throttle plate and spindle in such a way that with the spindle in the fully open position, the No. 8 stamped on the plate faces the volume control screw.
4 Replace all jets and the emulsion tube (shouldered end uppermost). Fit the choke tube with the marked end uppermost and tighten the locking screw. Replace the volume control screw and spring.

5 Screw the needle valve into the float chamber cover using the original washer or one of similar thickness (any variation will affect the petrol level in the float chamber).
6 Insert the float in its chamber and locate the float lever and its spindle. The float and lever are both marked 'TOP' to facilitate replacement.

Refit the float chamber cover, gasket and the three retaining screws and their lockwashers.
7 Fit the correct gasket* over the carburetter securing studs.
* (a) Early models (steel gasket), part EOTA.9447.B
  (b) From engine number 115846, part 100E.9447.A
  (c) From engine number 166251, part 100E.9447.B or C
8 Place the carburetter in position and tighten the retaining nuts and lockwashers evenly. Reconnect the choke control cable. Reconnect the throttle control link and remount the air cleaner on its mounting.

2:10 Air filter maintenance

Dry gauze type air filter of two different types are fitted to domestic vehicles, whilst an oil bath type is fitted to export models (the Popular has only a metal lid covering the carburetter mouth. See **FIG 2:10** for the various types.
1 **Cylindrical type.** Disconnect the front end support

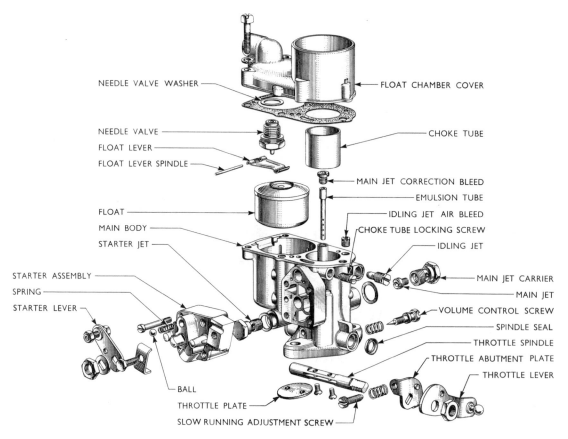

FIG 2:9 Carburetter (later type) components

strap, slacken the neck clamp and remove the filter.

Wash the element in petrol, dry and re-oil with engine oil. Replace and tighten the clamp and support strap nut.

2 **Flat rectangular type.** Slacken the neck clamp to remove. To service unscrew the centre wingnut and washer and detach lid. Lift out the gauze filter, wash it in petrol, dry and dip in engine oil, shake off surplus oil.

Replace the gauze element, lid, nut and washer.

3 **Oil bath type.** Slacken the carburetter neck clamp to remove the filter.

To service, unscrew the centre wingnut and rod and remove the lid. Lift out the filter element and wash in petrol. Dip the element in engine oil then clean out the bowl and refill to the level marked with clean engine oil. Check gaskets and refit the element, lid, centre rod and wingnut.

2:11 The exhaust manifold heat control valve

An exhaust heat control valve is incorporated in the manifold assembly of vehicles manufactured prior to June 1957 (see **FIG 2:11**).

This valve consists of a shutter welded to a spindle which passes through the manifold.

A counterweight is secured to one end of the spindle and at the other end a bi-metal spring is fitted. The free end of the bi-metal spring abuts an anchor pin located in the manifold.

When the engine is cold the counterweight holds the shutter so that it partially blocks the exhaust outlet, and fully exposes the inlet hot spot, thus allowing exhaust gases to be directed to the hot spot. A further passage from the hot spot allows the exhaust gases to return to the exhaust outlet.

As the temperature increases the bi-metal spring expands and moves away from the anchor pin. When this happens the pressure of exhaust gas overcomes the counterweight and moves the shutter until the free end of the spring again abuts the anchor pin, and the shutter partially covers the hot spot passages and exposes a larger area of the exhaust outlet.

This procedure is repeated until the hot spot passage is completely closed and the exhaust outlet fully open.

When the engine is switched 'off' and the temperature drops, the bi-metal spring contracts and the counterweight moves the shutter to its original cold starting position.

2:12 Modifications

The only modification which may be required is to the thick asbestos carburetter to manifold gasket fitted to a certain number of cars produced before engine No. 100E.166492 and this only if a whistling noise is apparent at certain speeds.

In this case cut a slot $\frac{5}{32}$ inch deep and $\frac{3}{8}$ inch wide in the gasket immediately below the cold start orifice (see **FIG 2:12**.

2:13 Fault diagnosis

(a) Leakage or insufficient fuel delivered

1 Air vent in tank or filler cap blocked
2 Fuel pipes blocked
3 Air leaks at pipe connections

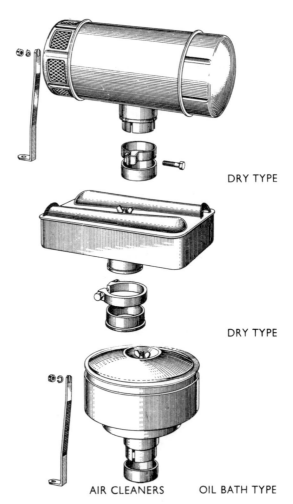

DRY TYPE

DRY TYPE

AIR CLEANERS   OIL BATH TYPE

FIG 2:10   Air cleaner types

PASSAGE OF EXHAUST GASES TO INLET MANIFOLD JACKET

RETURN PASSAGE TO EXHAUST

BI-METAL SPRING

SHUTTER

FIG 2:11   The exhaust manifold heat control valve

4 Fuel pump filter blocked
5 Pump gaskets faulty
6 Pump diaphragm defective
7 Pump valves sticking or seating badly
8 Fuel vapourizing in pipelines due to heat

(b) Excessive fuel consumption

1 Carburetter needs adjusting
2 Fuel leakage
3 Sticking choke control
4 Dirty air filter
5 Excessive engine temperature
6 Binding brakes
7 Tyres under-inflated
8 Idling speed too high
9 Car overloaded

(c) Idling speed too high

1 Rich fuel mixture
2 Carburetter controls sticking
3 Slow-running screws incorrectly adjusted
4 Worn carburetter butterfly valve

(d) Noisy fuel pump

1 Loose mountings
2 Air leaks on suction side and at diaphragm
3 Obstruction in fuel pipe
4 Clogged pump filter

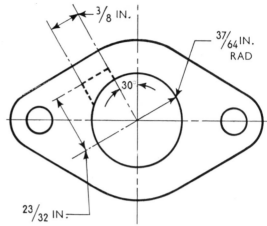

FIG 2:12   Modification to certain carburetter gaskets

(e) No fuel delivery

1 Float needle stuck
2 Vent in tank or filler cap blocked
3 Pipeline obstructed
4 Pump diaphragm stiff or damaged
5 Inlet valve in pump stuck open
6 Bad air leak on suction side of pump

34

CHAPTER 3

THE IGNITION SYSTEM

3 : 1 Description

The normal coil ignition system is employed on all engines and the distributor incorporates an automatic advance and retard mechanism based upon springs and weights which operate due to centrifugal force. No vacuum assistance is provided in the design.

The coil (oil-filled on later models marked LA.12) is mounted on the engine compartment rear bulkhead. Keep all terminals tight and the insulated end clean.

3 : 2 Distributor maintenance

Normal maintenance consists of keeping the insulated cover and HT wires clean and cleaning and adjusting the contact points. Refer to **FIG 3:1**.

1 Lift the distributor cap after disengaging the body clips. Pull the rotor from the distributor cam. Slacken the two nuts on the LT terminal screw and disengage the (spring metal) contact breaker arm. Remove the arm together with the fibre washer from the pivot post. The adjustable contact is removed by unscrewing the two retaining screws from the plate together with their spring and plain washers.

2 The two contact points should have all burning and pitting removed by rubbing them on an oilstone. Make sure the faces are kept square and true. Clean the contact faces with petrol before fitting. When the contacts have worn very thin, replace them.

3 Replace the adjustable contact and enter the two retaining screws and their spring and plain washers and screw them up finger tight only. Locate the fibre washer on the pivot post and refit the contact breaker arm so that the points are together. Connect the spring end of the breaker arm to the LT terminal **so that it is held between the head of the terminal screw and the insulator plate.** Tighten the two terminal nuts.

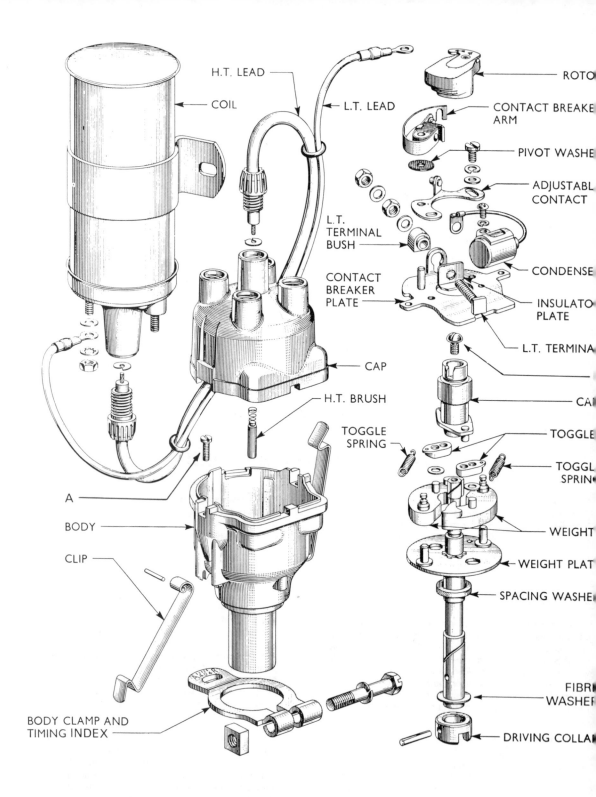

FIG 3:1 Component parts of distributor (showing coil)

COIL

H.T. LEAD

L.T. LEAD

ROTO

CONTACT BREAKE
ARM

PIVOT WASHE

ADJUSTABL
CONTACT

L.T.
TERMINAL
BUSH

CONTACT
BREAKER
PLATE

CONDENSE

INSULATO
PLATE

CAP

L.T. TERMINA

H.T. BRUSH

CA

TOGGLE
SPRING

TOGGLE

TOGGL
SPRIN

A

WEIGHT

BODY

WEIGHT PLAT

CLIP

SPACING WASHE

FIBR
WASHE

BODY CLAMP AND
TIMING INDEX

DRIVING COLLA

4 Turn the engine so that the heel of the contact breaker is on a high point of the cam. Move the adjustable contact until the points gap is between .014 and .016 inch (see **FIG 3:2**). Fully tighten the contact retaining screws. Recheck the gap. Put a smear of petroleum jelly on the high points of the cam and **two drops only** of thin oil down the cam centre screw.

5 Wipe the rotor clean and replace it on the cam. Wipe the inside of the distributor cap with a clean dry rag and replace it and the two retaining springs.

The capacitor (condenser) cannot readily be checked for efficiency but difficult starting and badly burned points are indications of failure. Ensure the capacitor retaining screw to the base plate is kept tight.

3:3 Removal and dismantling of the distributor

1 Refer to **FIG 3:1**. Disconnect the leads from the sparking plugs. Disconnect the LT lead from the distributor terminal and remove the HT lead from the centre of the distributor cap. Unscrew the index plate to cylinder head retaining screw, noting the position of the index and lift the distributor from the head.

2 Release the two clips retaining the distributor cap and remove the cap complete with sparking plug leads. Pull the rotor from the cam. Remove the contact breaker points as described in the previous section.

3 Unscrew the retaining screw and remove the capacitor from the contact breaker plate. Remove the contact breaker plate which is held by two screws 'A' (see **FIG 3:1**) which screw down vertically into the distributor body.

4 Unscrew the cam to distributor shaft screw 'B' (see **FIG 3:1**) and pull the cam from the shaft. Lift the weights off their pivot posts complete with toggles and springs, which may be detached if required. Clean and check all parts for wear.

5 Check the shaft end play, as shown in **FIG 3:3**, and also side play which should not exceed .005 inch where the shaft runs in its bush. Should you now need to remove the driving collar, drive out the pin which retains the collar to the distributor shaft. There is a spacer washer below the weight plate and a fibre washer above the driving collar (see **FIG 3:1**).

3:4 Reassembly and refitting of distributor

1 If the distributor shaft has been dismantled, refit the shaft to the body. Position the two washers correctly (see **FIG 3:1**), fit the driving collar and enter the retaining pin (small-end first). Check the shaft end float, as shown in **FIG 3:3**, and if correct drive the retaining pin home and peen over.

2 Reassemble the toggles and weights. The larger eye of each spring fits round the pivot post on the weight, the smaller one engages the toggle (see **FIG 3:4**). The toggle nearest the spring fits over the pivot post and remember that the washer goes on first.

3 Replace the cam assembly engaging the two cam yoke pegs in the two toggle holes. **The cut-out in the cam must be fitted to be on the same side of the distributor body as the small segment on the driving collar at the bottom of the shaft.**
Replace the cam securing screw.

4 Refit the contact breaker plate and the two retaining

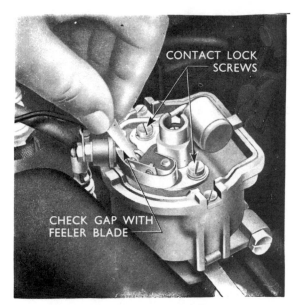

FIG 3:2 Checking contact breaker points gap

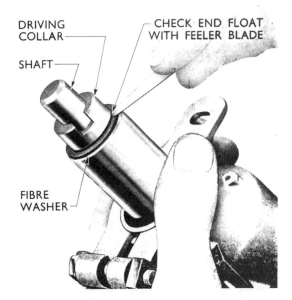

FIG 3:3 Checking distributor shaft end float

screws. Replace the capacitor and both contact breaker components, the LT terminal and LT wire from the capacitor.

Set the contact breaker points as described in **Section 3:2**. Replace the rotor on the cam.

5 Refer to modification of cylinder head instruction (see **Section 3:8**). Grease the body shank of the distributor then insert it gently into its hole in the cylinder head. Turn the rotor until the driving collar engages with the

slotted driving shaft when the distributor will push right home. Replace the index retaining screw first ensuring that the index is set to its original mark. Replace the coil and plug leads.

6 After ensuring all its interior metal contacts and the central carbon pickup brush are clean and in good order, replace the distributor cap and retaining clips.

3:5 Timing the ignition

1 Check the contact breaker gap is correct as described in **Section 3:2**. Remove the sparking plugs and turn the engine whilst placing a thumb over No. 1 sparking plug hole until compression is felt indicating that No. 1 piston is approaching TDC. Now continue turning the engine carefully until the notch on the crankshaft pulley is in alignment with the mark on the engine front cover (see **FIG 1:11**). (With the sparking plugs removed it will be found easy to rotate the engine by means of the fan blades, assuming that the belt tension is correct.)

2 Slacken the screw which retains the distributor index plate to the cylinder head and line-up the 'O' mark on the index with the line on the cylinder head. Tighten the index retaining screw.

3 Give a gentle clockwise twist to the rotor arm to take up any backlash and then slacken the distributor body clamp bolt (see **FIG 3:1** and turn the distributor until the contact points are just about to open (a 12-volt bulb connected between the LT terminal and the distributor body will indicate this position. With the ignition switched on the bulb will light when the contact points are just open). Tighten the clamp bolt.

In this position, the ignition gives a setting of 5 deg. BTDC and is suitable for regular fuels.

4 Should premium fuels be used, slacken the index plate retaining screw and rotate the distributor in the advance (clockwise) direction a further threequarter of a division, tighten the retaining screw.

3:6 High-tension cables

The HT cables which run from the distributor cap to the coil and to the sparking plugs should be kept clean and free from oil. The screwed terminal collars in the distributor cap should be kept tight.

When cables are to be renewed, use the old ones as patterns for length. The insulation at the sparking plug end should be cut back $\frac{1}{2}$ inch and the wire core bent to lie underneath the metal sparking plug connectors which should be firmly crimped in position.

The other end of each cable should have the insulation cut back $\frac{1}{8}$ inch. Slip on the screwed connector, followed by the split brass washer and peen over the strands of the core evenly in all directions.

The cable sequence between the distributor cap and the sparking plugs is 1, 2, 4, 3. The centre HT cable leads to the coil.

3:7 Sparking plugs

There is nothing to be gained by experimenting with types of plug different from those originally fitted (L10). It is worth checking the type number when buying new ones however, as from time to time the vehicle manufacturer does recommend a change in specification in the light of operating experience.

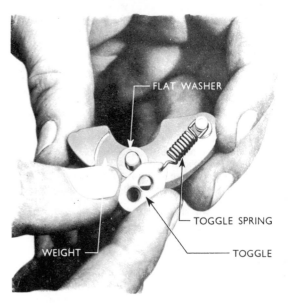

FIG 3:4 Fitting weights, toggles and springs

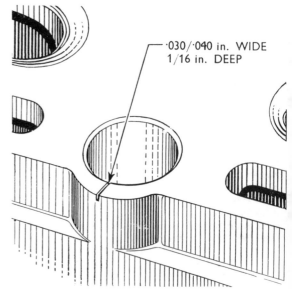

FIG 3:5 Distributor ventilation slot

Normal maintenance consists of wire brushing all deposits from the sparking surfaces, keeping the insulators clean and maintaining the gaps at .025 inch by bending the **outer contact** with a plug tool.

The plug washers should be in good condition and not flattened.

3:8 Modifications

Later model engines incorporate a slot in the cylinder head distributor seat (see **FIG 3:5**). This is provided for ventilation purposes and earlier engines may be modified to advantage by following the dimensions given in **FIG 3:5**.

3:9 Fault diagnosis

(a) Engine will not fire

1 Battery discharged
2 Distributor contact points dirty, pitted or maladjusted
3 Distributor cap dirty or cracked
4 Carbon brush inside cap not making contact with rotor
5 Faulty cable or loose connection in LT circuit
6 Rotor arm cracked
7 Faulty coil
8 Broken contact breaker spring
9 Contact points stuck open

(b) Engine misfires

1 Check 2, 3, 5 and 7 in (a)
2 Weak contact breaker spring
3 HT leads cracked or perished
4 Sparking plugs loose
5 Sparking plug insulation cracked
6 Sparking plug gaps incorrectly set
7 Ignition timing too far advanced

CHAPTER 4

THE COOLING SYSTEM

4:1 Description

All models covered in this manual have the same type of impeller-assisted, thermosyphon cooling system.

Water which is cooled in the radiator, enters the bottom of the cylinder block through the lower hose and is then drawn into the pump which is bolted to the front face of the cylinder block. The pump forces water to the rear and through the internal water passages of the engine until the now partially heated water passes through the thermostat and the top hose to reach the header tank. The cooling cycle is continuous and water now flows down the radiator tubes which are cooled by air flow and fan assistance.

A weekly check on the water level in the header tank should be made, but as the system is pressurized great care must be exercised when removing the spring-loaded radiator cap when the coolant is hot shortly after stopping the engine.

4:2 Maintenance

1 Check the water level and see that all hose clips are kept tight. The water pump has sealed bearings and requires no lubrication. The only other check to be carried out is to maintain the correct fan belt tension. This is important for if the belt is too tight, strain will be put upon the bearings in both the water pump and the generator, and if it is slack then the belt may burn and the engine may overheat whilst the battery is not efficiently charged.

2 The correct fan belt tension is **a total movement** of $\frac{1}{2}$ inch when it is pushed and pulled at a point midway between the water pump and crankshaft pulleys (see **FIG 4:1**). To vary the tension of the belt, slacken the two generator mounting bolts and the adjustment locking bolt on the slotted bar beneath the generator. Move the generator towards or away from the engine until the correct fan belt adjustment is obtained, then

tighten the three bolts.

3 Should the fan belt have stretched or deteriorated to a point where a replacement is necessary then loosen the three bolts as described in the previous paragraph and slide off the old belt by turning the fan blades in a clockwise direction and pulling the belt so that it rides up and over the water pump pulley front rim.

Replace the new belt round the crankshaft and generator pulleys and again prise it over the water pump pulley whilst turning the fan blades. Always slacken the generator before fitting a new belt and **do not use levers or tools to fit.** Adjust the tension as previously described.

4 To drain the system, allow the coolant to cool and remove the radiator cap. Open the drain tap at the base of the radiator and if a heater is fitted make sure that the heater valve on the cylinder head is open. Antifreeze solutions may be retained for twelve months use but should be replaced at yearly intervals. The system should be flushed when changing the coolant and to do this a hose should be placed in the radiator filler neck and allowed to flow for 15 minutes with the heater control valve and radiator drain taps open. If the radiator should be choked with sediment (in extreme cases), it should be removed and reverse flushed by

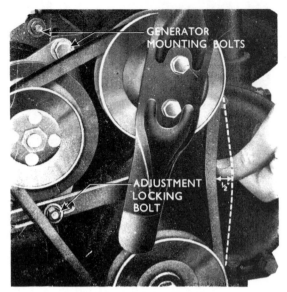

FIG 4:1   Fan belt adjustment

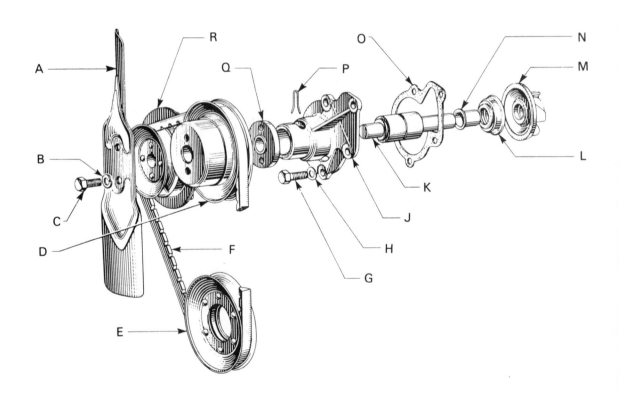

FIG 4:2   Water pump components

Key to Fig 4:2   **A** Fan   **B** Lockwasher   **C** Bolt   **D** Water pump pulley   **E** Crankshaft pulley
F Fan belt   **G** Bolt   **H** Lockwasher   **J** Water pump body   **K** Shaft/bearing assembly   **L** Seal
M Impeller   **N** Copper slinger   **O** Gasket   **P** Retainer clip   **Q** Pulley flange   **R** Generator pulley

inserting the hose in the lower water outlet and then inverting the radiator.

The following will give a guide to antifreeze protection:

10 per cent ($1\frac{1}{4}$ pints antifreeze) solution protects to 17°F (15° Frost).

15 per cent (2 pints antifreeze) solution protects to 7°F (25° Frost).

20 per cent ($2\frac{1}{2}$ pints antifreeze) solution protects to —3°F (35°Frost).

25 per cent (3 pints antifreeze) solution protects to —20°F (52° Frost).

4:3 Water pump removal and dismantling

1 Drain the cooling system and remove the fan belt as described in the previous section. Refer to **FIG 4:2** and unscrew the two retaining bolts with their lock-washers and remove the fan and water pump pulley. Unscrew the five water pump retaining bolts and lock-washers, detach the pump and gasket.

In the event of the pump requiring new bearings and a seal and perhaps the impeller is corroded, it will be advantageous to exchange the pump for a factory reconditioned unit. Where only one component is to be renewed, proceed to dismantle as follows:

2 Using a suitable extractor, withdraw the pulley flange 'Q', withdraw the retainer clip 'P', tap or press the shaft, bearing and impeller assembly from the pump body using a suitably sized piece of tubing to bear upon the **outer** race of the bearing assembly.

3 With a suitable extractor, withdraw the impeller from the end of the shaft, remove the seal and gently tap off the copper slinger 'N '. The shaft bearing assembly 'K' is supplied as a complete grease sealed unit and cannot be dismantled.

4:4 Water pump reassembly and replacement

1 See **FIG 4:2**. Locate a new copper slinger 'N' on the longer part of the shaft 'K' with the lip towards the bearing, then carefully push or tap the slinger onto the shaft so that the rim of the slinger is 1.5 inch from the end of the shaft.

2 Refit the bearing shaft assembly in the pump body and press into position until the larger groove round the bearing lines-up with the corresponding one in the pump body.

Tap the retaining clip into position.

3 Fit a new seal 'L' with the carbon face towards the impeller. Press on the impeller 'M' sufficiently far to give a clearance between the rear face of the impeller and the machined face of the pump of .100 inch (it is unlikely you will have a feeler gauge of this thickness so use something of thickness a tenth of an inch or 2.75 mm).

4 Press the pulley flange on to the shaft until the end of the shaft is flush with the face of the flange boss.

5 Thoroughly clean the mating faces of the water pump and the cylinder block and locate a new gasket (Part No. 100E.8507). Screw in the five retaining bolts with lockwashers, **first smearing the threads with jointing compound.** Fit the fan pulley and the fan to the pump flange using the two retaining bolts and lockwashers.

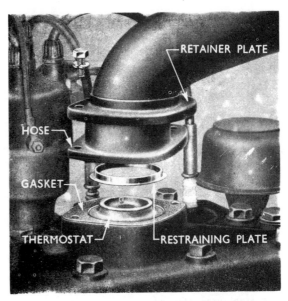

FIG 4:3 Thermostat housing (early models)

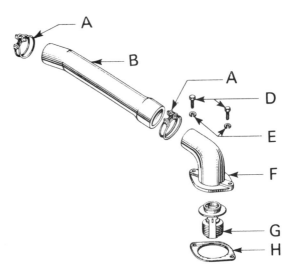

FIG 4:4 Thermostat housing (later models)

Key to Fig 4:4 **A** Hose clip **B** Hose **D** Securing bolt **E** Lockwashers **F** Water outlet casting **G** Thermostat **H** Gasket

6 Refit the fan belt and adjust the tension as described in **Section 4:2.** Tighten the adjusting nuts securely and refill the system **slowly** to avoid air locks.

4:5 The thermostat

This is fitted at the cylinder head water outlet to restrict the circulation in the cooling system until normal operating temperature is reached.

To remove the thermostat, drain the cooling system as previously described then.

1 **On early models** (see **FIG 4:3**) unscrew the two bolts with lockwashers which secure the retainer plate. Remove the moulded rubber hose in the bottom end of which is fitted the restraining plate. Lift the gasket and withdraw the thermostat.

2 **On later models** a metal elbow is used to connect the hose to the cylinder head (see **FIG 4:4**). Dismantling is similar to that for early models except of course no restraining plate is fitted.

3 To test the thermostat, suspend in water and check its opening against appropriate temperatures as given in **Technical Data.** If faulty, renew.

Replacement is a reversal of dismantling procedure, always use a new gasket.

4:6 Fault diagnosis

(a) Internal water leakage

1 Cracked cylinder wall
2 Loose cylinder head nuts
3 Cracked cylinder head
4 Faulty head gasket
5 Cracked tappet chest wall

(b) Poor circulation

1 Radiator core blocked
2 Engine water passages restricted
3 Low water level
4 Loose fan belt
5 Defective thermostat
6 Perished or collapsed hoses

(c) Corrosion

1 Impurities in the water
2 Infrequent draining and flushing

(d) Overheating

1 Check (b)
2 Sludge in crankcase
3 Faulty ignition timing
4 Low oil level in sump
5 Tight engine
6 Choked exhaust system
7 Binding brakes
8 Slipping clutch
9 Incorrect valve timing
10 Retarded ignition
11 Mixture too weak

CHAPTER 5

THE CLUTCH

5:1 Description

The clutch is of the single dry plate type operating on the rear face of the flywheel. The component parts are shown in exploded form in **FIG 5:1**. The driven plate is pressed against the flywheel by the spring-loaded pressure plate. The clutch disc which has a spring-cushioned hub 'S' is free to slide along the splines of the gearbox main drive shaft gear, the front end of which fits into the spigot bearing fitted in the centre of the flywheel.

When the clutch is fully engaged, the pressure springs 'P' exert a powerful pull on the pressure plate through lugs and setscrews. This pressure nips the driven plate by its friction linings 'D' between the flywheel and the pressure plate faces. When the engine is rotating, the driven plate is revolving with the flywheel and turning the gearbox main shaft gear to which its spring-cushioned hub is splined. The main shaft gear transmits the drive to the transmission.

To disengage the clutch, a lever which is hydraulically connected to the clutch pedal causes a release bearing (see **FIG 5:7**) to press on the thrust plate which in turn moves the pressure plate away from the driven plate and so disconnects the drive. The driven plate and the main shaft gear are then free to revolve on the crankshaft or come to rest without transmitting any driven even though the crankshaft may continue to turn.

5:2 Maintenance and adjustment

To prevent clutch slip under load, it is essential to maintain one-tenth inch clearance between the clutch release arm and the hydraulic operating cylinder pushrod (see **FIG 5:2**).

1 Disconnect the retracting spring and slacken the operating cylinder pinch bolt. Slide the cylinder until the required clearance is obtained between the end of the pushrod and the release arm. Tighten the pinch bolt and reconnect the spring. **During the adjustment operation do not give undue movement to the release arm as it is possible to detach it from its spring clips on the release bearing and it is difficult to re-engage.**

2 Adjustment to the clutch pedal is carried out by

adjusting the length of the clutch master cylinder pushrod (see **FIG 5:3**). The procedure applies also to the brake pedal and both clutch and brake pedals should be adjusted to give the same operating height.

Slacken the locknut which secures the clevis to the pushrod and screw the rod in or out of the clevis until the required measurement (see **FIG 5:3**) is obtained. Tighten the locknut.

On early model vehicles (identification black or aluminium painted pressure plate springs) the effective clutch pedal operating length is $4\frac{9}{16}$ inch. Should a later type pressure plate assembly be fitted (identification blue or gold painted springs) to early vehicles then the master cylinder pushrod may have to be shortened by $\frac{1}{8}$ inch to provide the modified pedal operating length of $4\frac{7}{16}$ inch.

3 Sluggish operation of the clutch may indicate air in the hydraulic system. First check the fluid level in the master cylinder reservoir which should be $\frac{5}{8}$ inch below the rim. Secondly ensure that the vent hole is clear. Check the tightness of all unions and the condition of flexible hoses. Any sign of leakage at the master cylinder rubber boot will indicate the need for overhaul of the unit (see **Section 5:3**).

4 To bleed the system, thoroughly clean round the bleed valve (see **FIG 5:2**) and remove its dust cap. Attach a bleeder tube to the bleed valve and insert the free end in a jar submerging it in a quantity of approved type of hydraulic fluid. Unscrew the bleed valve about half a turn and press the pedal down to its full extent but allowing it to return by itself to its normal position after each stroke. Continue pumping until the fluid coming from the end of the tube is quite free of air bubbles.

During this operation make sure that the bleeder tube is always kept below the surface of the fluid in the jar and that the master cylinder reservoir is kept topped up.

It is not advisable to use the fluid bled from the system for replenishing the reservoir.

Tighten the bleed screw **without undue force** and with the clutch pedal in the fully released position. Remove the bleeder tube and replace the bleed screw dust cap.

Never replenish the hydraulic system with anything other than the recommended fluid. Never clean metal or rubber components in anything except methylated spirit or clean hydraulic fluid.

5:3 Dismantling, servicing and reassembling the hydraulic system

(a) Removing and dismantling the master cylinder

1 See **FIG 5:3** then disconnect the clutch pedal retracting spring, remove the splitpin and clevis pin which secure the pushrod to the pedal arm. Unscrew the fluid pipe from the cylinder, unscrew the two nuts and lockwashers which hold the cylinder to the bulkhead. Remove the cylinder and empty the reservoir. **Extreme cleanliness is essential during all operations, both with components and containers used for hydraulic fluid storage.**

2 See **FIG 5:4**. Unscrew the clevis locknut and remove the clevis, withdraw the rubber boot. Remove the circlip, washer and pushrod.

Tap the rear end of the cylinder on a block of wood and pull out the piston assembly. The piston may now

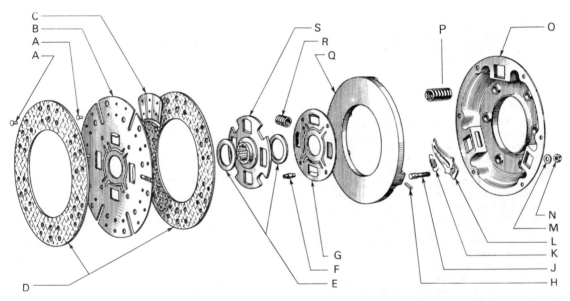

FIG 5:1   Component parts of the clutch

Key to Fig 5:1   **A** Rivet   **B** Driven plate   **C** Cushioning   **D** Friction linings   **E** Washers
F Clutch disc stop pin   **G** Driven plate washer   **H** Release lever pin   **J** Release lever stud   **K** Release lever tension spring
L Release lever   **M** Release lever washer   **N** Release lever stud nut   **O** Clutch pressure plate cover   **P** Pressure plate spring
Q Clutch pressure plate   **R** Driven plate hub cushion spring   **S** Driven plate hub

be removed from the spring retainer by lifting a tab as shown in **FIG 5:5**.

Compress the return spring and move its retainer to one side which will release the valve stem from the retainer. Slide the valve spacer and shim off the stem and remove the valve and piston seals.

3 All components should be washed in hydraulic fluid or methylated spirit and examined for wear or scoring. Renew the rubber seals and any worn parts.

(b) Reassembling the master cylinder

1 Fit the piston seal with the lip towards the narrow end of the piston. Should two annular grooves be apparent in the design of the piston, fit the seal in the groove nearest the end of the narrow part of the piston.

Fit the valve seal with the lip away from the spring. Slide the shim, spacer and spring over the valve stem, as shown in **FIG 5:4**. Now insert the retainer in the rear end of the spring and after compressing the spring locate the valve stem in the retainer by means of the offset hole.

2 Insert the narrow end of the piston in the spring retainer and secure it by locating the retainer tab under the front shoulder of the piston (see **FIG 5:5**).

Smear the inside of the master cylinder with clean brake fluid and carefully enter the piston assembly valve seal end first.

Refit the pushrod, retaining washer and circlip. With the piston fully rearwards, the end float between pushrod and piston should be .003 inch.

3 Replace the rubber boot, locknut and clevis. Check the distance between the mounting face of the cylinder

FIG 5:2 Clutch release arm clearance (operating cylinder)

and the centre of the clevis eye in accordance with type as described in **Section 5:2**, paragraph 2, and adjust accordingly.

4 Replacement to the vehicle is a reversal of dismantling procedure given in **Section 5:3 (a)**, paragraph 1.

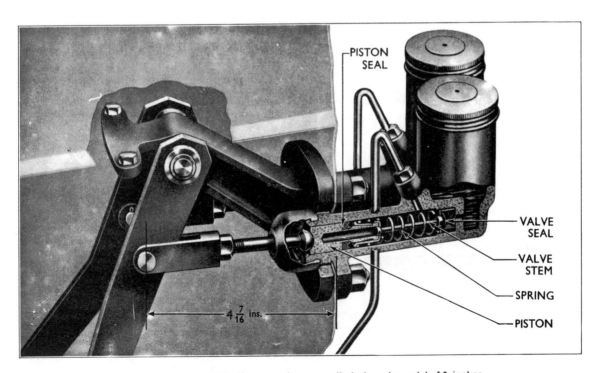

FIG 5:3 Clutch pedal adjustment (master cylinder), early models $4\frac{9}{16}$ inches

(c) Removing and dismantling the operating cylinder

1 Disconnect the retracting spring from the clutch release arm (see **FIG 5:2**. Slacken the pinch bolt and withdraw the cylinder from its bracket. Disconnect the flexible hose from the rigid pipe and drain the fluid into a clean vessel. Disconnect the flexible hose and washer from the cylinder.

2 See **FIG 5:6,** pull the pushrod from the rubber dust cover and remove the cover from the cylinder. Remove the piston and seal from the cylinder by blowing air into the fluid union or tapping the cylinder on a block of wood. Remove the bleed valve and dust cap **(do not loose the small ball—early models only).** Pull the rubber seal off its piston spigot.

3 Wash all components in hydraulic fluid or methylated spirit and examine for wear and scoring. **Maintain absolute cleanliness during all operations.** Renew the rubber seal and replace any worn components.

(d) Reassembly and replacement of the operating cylinder

1 Locate the new seal on the piston spigot (recessed face to enter cylinder). Lubricate piston and seal with hydraulic fluid and carefully enter this component into the cylinder with a twisting motion. Refit rubber dust cover. Replace bleed valve (and ball if fitted) finger tight. Insert the plain end of the pushrod through the dust cover to engage with cupped end of the piston.

2 Screw in the shorter screwed end of the flexible pipe (with washer) to the cylinder. Reconnect the other end

to the rigid pipe in accordance with instructions given regarding pipes in **Section 10:4.**

Replace the operating cylinder in its mounting bracket and tighten the clamp bolt to give an adjustment as previously described in **Section 5:2,** of one-tenth inch between the pushrod and the release lever arm.

3 Reconnect the retracting spring and fill the reservoir with fluid. Bleed the system as described in **Section 5:2,** paragraph 3. Finally recheck the pushrod to release lever arm clearance.

5:4 Removal of the clutch

Access to the clutch is gained by removal of the gearbox and on early models (prior to August 1954) the engine complete with gearbox must be removed for the reasons and by the procedure described in **Section 1:3.**

On later vehicles adopt the following procedure:

1 Drain the gearbox, retaining the oil for further use. Remove the floor covering, gearchange lever, propeller shaft, clutch operating cylinder, speedometer drive gearbox earthing strap, rear engine mounting bolts all as described for early vehicles in **Section 1:3.**

2 Place suitable supports under both the engine and the gearbox. Unscrew the eight clutch to flywheel housing bolts and remove the rear engine mounting.

3 Ease the gearbox to the rear until the main drive gear shaft is clear of the driven plate hub splines. Lower the front of the gearbox and withdraw it so that the gearbox extension housing clears the frame crossmember during a forward movement.

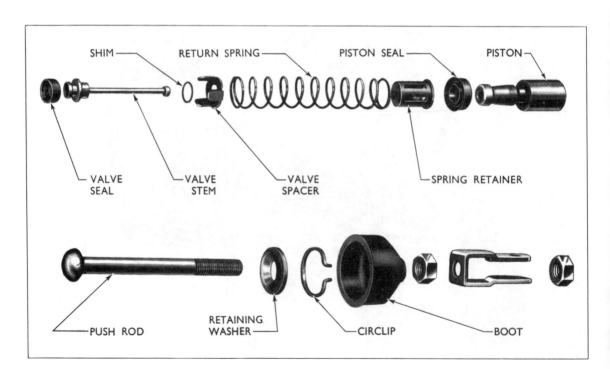

FIG 5:4   Components of the master cylinder

48

During removal of the gearbox, at no time must the weight of this unit be allowed to hang upon the main drive gear shaft whilst its spigot is still engaged with the flywheel bush or the shaft is still engaged with the splined hub of the driven plate.

5:5 Dismantling the clutch (see FIG 5:1)

1 With the gearbox removed from the vehicle (later models) or the gearbox separated from the engine (complete unit removed, early models) unscrew the six clutch assembly securing bolts, equally, a little at a time. Alternate bolts have longer threads to enable all spring pressure to be released before removing the pressure plate cover assembly completely. Remove the driven plate.

2 Inspect the condition of the driven plate friction linings. If oil stained or worn almost level with the rivet heads, renew the plate complete, do not attempt to fit new linings yourself. Excessive oil present in the clutch housing may indicate a faulty gearbox main drive gear oil seal and replacement is dealt with in **Chapter 6, Section 6:5.**

  Should the driven plate linings have been so worn away that the flywheel and pressure plate are scored then both these components too will need to be renewed. Check the splines in the centre boss for wear.

3 Check the pressure plate springs, and if they are discoloured, renew the complete pressure plate and cover assembly (available on an exchange basis) **do not attempt to dismantle the pressure plate assembly yourself.**

  Refer to the colour coding of pressure plate springs previously mentioned in **Section 5:2**, and when reassembling carry out the necessary adjustment to the operating cylinder pushrod according to the type of pressure plate being installed.

5:6 Release bearing

The clutch release bearing (see **FIG 5:7**) is a grease-packed ball thrust race, and although requiring no maintenance may need to be renewed after a considerable mileage. To withdraw the bearing, pull the forked end of

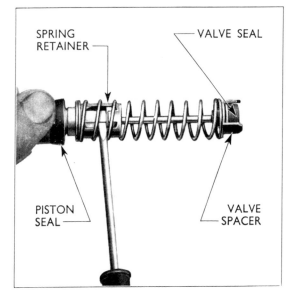

FIG 5:5   Master cylinder piston dismantling

the release arm out of the spring clips at the rear of the bearing hub. Pull the bearing and hub forward at the same time disengaging the release arm from the fulcrum pin. Separate the bearing from its hub.

The hub should be pressed squarely into the new bearing and all components replaced in reverse order of dismantling, carefully checking the condition of the spring clips.

The clutch pilot bearing which is pressed into the centre of the flywheel is self-lubricating and should not require attention.

5:7 Reassembling the clutch

1 The alignment of the driven plate is essential to this operation and as an alignment tool you should acquire an old main drive gear shaft or a mild steel round

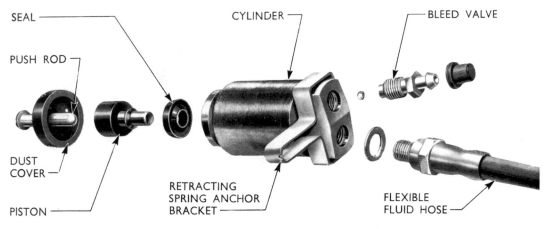

FIG 5:6   Components of the operating cylinder

suitably turned down in steps, the end to fit the flywheel pilot bearing and the larger diameter to fit the bore of the driven plate splined hub.

2 Mount the driven plate on the alignment tool so that the larger boss which contains the cushion springs is towards the pressure plate. Ensure that the paint spots (heavy points) on the flywheel and the pressure plate are diametrically opposite **(not together)** and offer up the complete clutch assembly to the flywheel so that the end of the alignment tool engages with the flywheel pilot bearing.

Screw in the retaining bolts and lockwashers (longer threads alternate) and tighten evenly to 12 to 15 lb ft. Withdraw the alignment tool.

3 The gearbox may now be replaced **taking great care that its weight does not hang upon the main drive gear** during engagement with the engine or before the clutch to flywheel housing bolts are secured. Complete replacement is a reversal of removal instructions given in **Section 5:4** according to early or late vehicle model.

5:8 Fault diagnosis

(a) Drag or spin

1 Oil or grease on driven plate linings
2 Leaking master cylinder, operating cylinder or piping
3 Driven plate binding on splines
4 Distorted driven plate
5 Warped or damaged pressure plate
6 Broken driven plate linings
7 Air in the hydraulic system

(b) Fierceness or snatch

1 Check 1, 2, 4 and 5 in (a)
2 Worn clutch linings

(c) Slip

1 Check 1 in (a) and 2 in (b)
2 Weak pressure springs
3 Seized piston in operating cylinder
4 No clearance between pushrod and release lever arm

(d) Judder

1 Check 1 and 4 in (a)
2 Pressure plate not parallel with flywheel face
3 Bent main drive shaft
4 Buckled driven plate

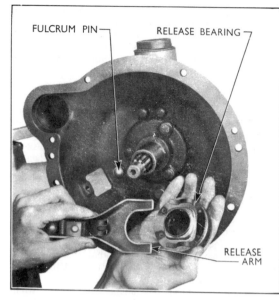

FIG 5:7   Clutch release bearing

5 Faulty engine mountings
6 Worn suspension shackles
7 Weak rear springs
8 Loose propeller shaft bolts
9 Loose rear spring clips

(e) Rattle

1 Check 2 in (c)
2 Broken driven plate cushion springs
3 Worn release mechanism
4 Excessive backlash in transmission
5 Wear in transmission bearings
6 Release bearing loose on fork

(f) Tick or knock

1 Worn main drive shaft bearing
2 Worn splines in driven plate hub
3 Loose flywheel

CHAPTER 6

THE GEARBOX

6:1 Description and maintenance

The design of the gearbox provides for three forward gears and reverse. Synchromesh is provided between second and top gears only. The gearbox is of cast iron construction and an extension housing is mounted at the rear of the gearbox.

See **FIG 6:3**. The main drive gear 22 which is driven by the engine is in constant mesh with the countershaft gear (40) which in turn is in constant mesh with the second gear 48, the latter being free to rotate on its bush 47. The main drive gear incorporates dog teeth and a cone tapered to engage the synchromesh unit as well as the helical gear.

Between the main drive gear and second gear is mounted the synchronizer assembly 33-37, the inner hub of which is splined to the mainshaft and the outer sleeve is in turn splined to this hub.

When top gear is selected the synchromesh outer sleeve slides forward and engages with the dog teeth formed on the rear of the main drive gear, thus forming a direct drive from the engine, through the gearbox, to the rear axle.

When the second gear is engaged the outer sleeve 36 moves rearwards, engaging the dog teeth on the second gear, locking the gear to the mainshaft, thus providing an indirect drive through the countershaft gear and second gear.

First gear is engaged by sliding the first and reverse gear 45 forward along the main shaft until it engages with the countershaft gear, while reverse is obtained by sliding the gear to the rear where it engages with the reverse idler gear 44.

The gearbox is lubricated with extreme pressure oil (SAE.80EP) and the capacity is $1\frac{3}{4}$ pints (.95 litres). Oil is supplied to the extension housing by means of an open trough located in the gearbox casing which collects oil splashed up by the gears and allows it to run into the top of the extension housing. The correct oil level is maintained in the extension housing by means of a slot cast in the front wall, through which any excess oil can return to the gearbox casing.

A drain plug and a combined level and filler plug are fitted.

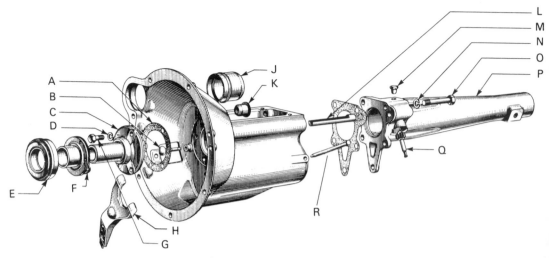

FIG 6:1   Gearbox exterior

Key to Fig 6:1   **A** Gasket   **B** Release fork pin   **C** Main drive gear bearing retainer   **D** Lockwashe
E Clutch release bearing   **F** Clutch release bearing hub   **G** Retaining bolt   **H** Clutch release for
J Starter motor drive cover   **K** Gearchange shaft hole plug   **L** Oil trough   **M** Breather   **N** Lockwashe
O Bolt   **P** Extension housing   **Q** Speedometer drive gear   **R** Countershaft and reverse idler shaft retaining pi

6:2 Removing the gearbox

On early models, remove the engine and gearbox as one unit as described in **Chapter 1, Section 1:3,** and then separate the gearbox by removing the eight clutch to flywheel housing bolts.

On later models, follow the procedure described in **Chapter 5, Section 5:4.**

6:3 Dismantling the gearbox.

(a) The gearchange mechanism

The following operations to the gearchange mechanism may be carried out with the gearbox in position in the vehicle but for convenience and for the fact that other components within the box itself will probably need attention it is recommended that work be carried out with the gearbox removed from the car.

1 The gearchange lever (in the neutral position) already having been removed so that the gearbox could be withdrawn, unscrew the four bolts and lockwashers which secure the gearchange housing to the gearbox.

Remove the gearchange housing by lifting it vertically upwards until the two selector forks disengage the synchronizer sleeve and the sliding gear. Cover the gearbox opening to prevent ingress of dirt.

On no account must the synchronizer be moved once the gearchange housing has been removed.

2 See **FIG 6:2.** File off the peened end of the guide pin 14 drive it out forward. Unscrew the spring retaining screw 15, remove the spring 16 and the ball 17. There is a duplicate assembly on the opposite side of the gearchange housing which must also be removed.

As only one shaft can be withdrawn at a time, the first and reverse gearchange shaft 6 must be in the neutral position, then rotate the second and top gear-

change shaft 7 until the selector fork pin 4 may b driven out. Withdraw the second and top gear sha at the same time sliding off the selector fork 2 and th interlock plunger 5. The latter is fitted in the centre we of the gearchange housing between the two shaf for the purpose of preventing the engagement of mo than one gear at a time.

3 Rotate the first and reverse gearchange shaft until th selector fork pin 4 may be driven from its selector fork Slide the shaft from the housing at the same tim removing the selector fork. Clean all parts thorough and check for wear or weak springs (see **Technica Data**).

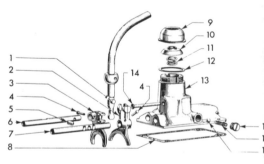

FIG 6:2   Gearchange housing

Key to Fig 6:2   **1** Gearlever   **2** Gearchange fork (secon and top)   **3** Gearchange fork (first and reverse)   **4** Fork t gearchange shaft pins   **5** Interlock plunger   **6** First an reverse gearchange shaft   **7** Second and top gearchange sha **8** Gasket   **9** Cap   **10** Gearchange lever spring sea **11** Spring   **12** Gasket   **13** Housing   **14** Gearchang guide pin   **15** Shaft lock plunger spring retaining screw **16** Shaft lock plunger spring   **17** Shaft lock plunger ba

NOTE: Parts 15, 16 and 17. Two assemblies, one each sid of housing

) The gearbox

See **FIG 6:1**. Slide the clutch release bearing hub 'F' complete with bearing 'E' off the main drive gear bearing retainer 'C'. Remove the release arm 'H' spring clips and the rubber gaiter. Remove the clutch operating cylinder bracket and the speedometer bearing and gear 'Q' from the extension housing 'P'.

Unscrew the five retaining bolts and lockwashers which hold the extension housing to the gearbox (the top left bolt is longer than the other four). Withdraw the housing carefully over the main shaft.

Unscrew the three bolts 'G' and lockwashers 'D' securing the main drive gear bearing retainer 'C' which incorporates the oil seal and remove it.

See **FIG 6:3** and check the end float of the second gear 48 by inserting a feeler blade (.010 to .020 inch) between the gear and its thrust washer 46. Excessive end float will indicate wear on the thrust washer or second gear and must be rectified by renewal of the component during reassembly.

Remove the circlip 49, the speedometer drive gear 28, its key 24 and the spacer 27. Draw the main shaft 31 to the rear and after inserting a suitable spacer between the now exposed drive shaft bearing 25 and the rear face of the gearbox housing (see **FIG 6:4**) gently tap the main shaft forward until the bearing can be removed, complete with its circlip 26.

Raise the forward end of the main shaft assembly and withdraw through the top of the gearbox.

4 At this point see **FIG 6:3** and check the end float between the countershaft gear 40 and either the front or the rear thrust washer 38 with a feeler gauge (.004 to .025 inch).

Also check the end float between the reverse idler gear face 44 and its mounting boss in the gearbox housing which should be between .004 to .025 inch. Excessive end float in respect of these components must be rectified during reassembly by appropriate renewal of the parts concerned.

5 Tap the main drive gear 22 to the rear after removal of the shaft circlip 23.

Use a hide mallet for this operation. Lift the main drive gear out through the top of the gearbox, taking off the oil thrower disc 21 as you do so.

Tap the bearing 20 complete with its circlip 19 forward out of the front face of the gearbox.

6 Remove the retainer pin which passes through holes in the countershaft and reverse idler shaft (see **FIG 6:5**).

Drive the countershaft to the rear and remove it and its two thrust washers from the gearbox housing. On no account attempt to drive the shaft forward.

Drive out the reverse idler shaft from the front using a cranked driver.

7 Dismantle the main shaft assembly by reference to **FIG 6:3**. First check that second gear 48 is a good fit on its bush 47. Remove circlip 23 and slide the synchronizer assembly off the main shaft. Withdraw the baulk ring 32 and second gear 48 from the main shaft.

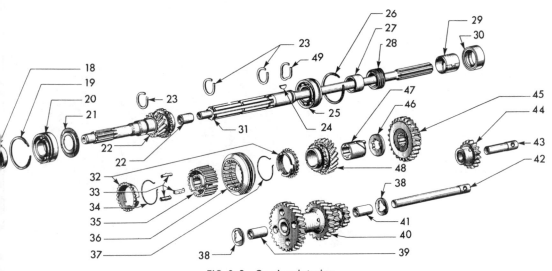

FIG 6:3 Gearbox interior

)TE: Parts 33 to 37 make up the synchronizer assembly

8 Pull the second gear bush 47 off the main shaft and then withdraw the thrust washer 46 and first and reverse gear 45, finally the circlip 23.

(c) The synchronizer

To complete the dismantling operation, the synchronizer assembly should have the two spring rings 34/37 removed. Slide out the three baulk plates 33. Check that there are mating marks on the synchronizer sleeve and hub (see **FIG 6:6**) for ease of assembly and slide the sleeve from the hub.

Now that all gearbox components have been dismantled, remember to check every part for wear and distortion particularly the teeth and splines and renew every suspect component before attempting reassembly. **Renew all the circlips.**

6:4 Reassembling the gearbox

(a) The synchronizer

Refer to **FIG 6:6** and slide the synchronizer sleeve on to the hub with the mating marks in alignment.

Slide a baulk plate into each of the three recesses in the hub and fit a new spring ring at each side so that one tag of each spring engages in one of the baulk plates while the other end locates against the inner hub face. The same baulk plate should be used for locating both spring tags.

(b) The gearbox

Ensure scrupulous cleanliness and check that all oilways are clear. Any worn components, oil seals and circlips will have been renewed in accordance with the instructions given regarding them in **Section 6:3 (b).**

1 Refer to **FIGS 6:1** and **6:3** and locate the reverse idler gear 44 in the gearbox housing with its shoulder towards the front. Fit the reverse idler shaft 43 with its shoulder to the rear, driving it home so that its hole is in correct alignment for the retaining pin 'R'.

2 Fit the countershaft gear assembly 40 with the larger pinion to the front and place a thrust washer at each end of the gear. Drive in the countershaft 42 from the rear of the gearbox making sure that its shouldered end is to the rear and its hole is in correct alignment for the retaining pin 'R'.

(A dummy shaft passed through from the front of the gearbox and maintained in contact with the countershaft will considerably ease this operation.)

3 Insert the retainer pin from the lefthand side of the gearbox to pass through the holes in the reverse idler shaft and the countershaft.

4 Now reassemble the main shaft by passing a circlip 23 over its front end and locating it in the rear groove of the splined portion. Fit the first and reverse sliding gear 45 on to the main shaft with the selector fork groove to the rear. Now pass the second gear thrust washer 46 along the main shaft so that it locates in the second groove from the front then give it a slight twist so that its teeth are covered by the main shaft splines.

5 Position the second gear bush 47 on the front (spigot) end of the main shaft with its tongues towards the thrust washer. With the internal splines of the bush engaged with the shaft splines and using a suitable

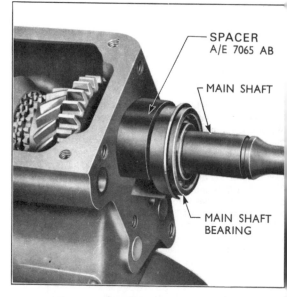

FIG 6:4 Removing main shaft bearing

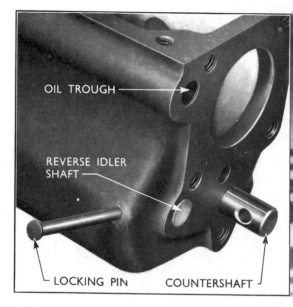

FIG 6:5 Countershaft and reverse idler shaft retaining pin

press, press on the bush until its tongues engage with two splines in the thrust washer **and it only just abuts this washer.**

6 Fit the second gear 48 on to the bush (conical face to the front) and fit the baulk ring 32 to this face. Slide the synchronizer assembly on to the main shaft (longer boss facing front) ensuring that the baulk plates fit the slots in the baulk ring. Fit a new shaft circlip 23.

7 Pass the rear end of the main shaft through the top of the gearbox and lower it into position. Locate the oil thrower disc 21 on the main drive gear 22 with the raised side facing front. Enter the gear through the top of the gearbox and through the front aperture. Fit the main drive gear bearing 20 to the main drive gear with its circlip 19 in the groove positioned nearest the forward edge of the bearing.

Tap the bearing home using great care and giving adequate support to the main drive gear during the operation. Fit a new shaft circlip 23 to retain the bearing in position.

8 Fit the main drive shaft bearing 25 to the shaft so that its circlip 26 and groove are nearest the rear face. Fit a baulk ring 32 over the conical face of the main drive gear and engage the main drive shaft spigot in the main drive gear bush.

9 Slide the speedometer driving gear spacer 27 on to the main drive shaft, fit the key 24 and the speedometer drive gear 28.

Renew the extension housing oil seal 30 (felt bush to the rear) and pass the housing carefully over the end of the main shaft so that its end does not contact either the bearing or oil seal. Fit a new gasket and replace the five securing bolts and washers O and N, remembering that the longest one goes in the top left-hand hole.

10 Fit a new oil seal 18 to the main drive gear bearing retainer 'C' so that its lip faces the gearbox. Fit a new gasket to the front face of the gearbox and secure the retainer with three retaining bolts and lockwashers.

It is most important during this operation to see that the oil passage and holes in the gasket and the gearbox housing line-up (see FIG 6:7).

11 Refit the speedometer drive gear, the clutch release bearing, the release arm, spring clips, rubber gaiter and the clutch operating cylinder bracket.

It is not recommended that the reader should attempt to fit new bushes to component parts of the gearbox, and where replacement is required this work should be left to a service station with the necessary equipment.

Speedometer gears, Escort and Squire Estate cars:

From approximately engine No. 100E.365604, a 19-tooth speedometer driven gear, Part No. 100E.17271.D, and a 5-tooth driving gear, Part No. 100E.17285.D, are fitted to these models. This gear combination gives a more accurate speedometer reading than the combination previously used (12-tooth driven gear, Part No. 100E.17271.B, 3-tooth driving gear 100E.17285.A).

These later gears are directly interchangeable with those previously fitted and are readily identified by the number of teeth on each gear, in addition, the driven gear is coloured red, the gear previously used was white.

(c) The gearchange mechanism

1 Refer to **FIG 6:2** and insert the first and reverse gearchange shaft in the hole in the housing furthest from the guide pin 14, making sure that the end of the shaft which is entered has the locking pin hole in it. Push the shaft through the end and centre webs of the housing and position the first and reverse gearchange fork 3 on the shaft so that its slotted side will line-up with the second shaft when inserted.

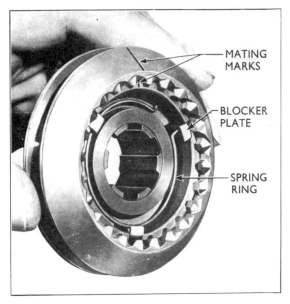

FIG 6:6 Synchronizer assembly (for blocker plate read baulk plate in text)

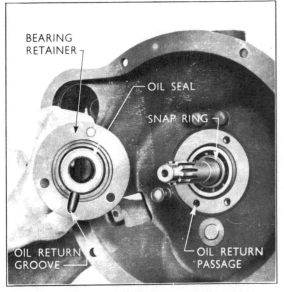

FIG 6:7 Fitting main drive gear bearing retainer

2 Position the first and reverse gearchange shaft with the three notches facing outwards to ensure engagement by the shaft lock plunger ball 17. Pin and peen the fork to the shaft. Insert the interlock plunger 5 in its location in the centre web of the housing.

3 Insert the second and top gearchange shaft 7 with the end having the three notches first but before the shaft passes through the centre web fit the gearchange

fork 2, ensuring that the gearlever notch faces inwards. Push the shaft into position with the three notches facing outwards, pin and peen the fork to the shaft.

4 Insert the guide pin 14 from the front of the housing ensuring that it passes through the slot in the second and top gearchange fork. Peen the pin.

5 Screw in the shaft lock balls (17, springs 16 and retainers 15 on each side of the housing. Insert the gearlever and check operation. Remove the lever (in neutral position). Fit a new gasket to the top of the gearbox and lower gearchange housing so that the gearchange forks engage with their respective grooves in the synchronizer sleeve and the first and reverse sliding gear. Replace the four retaining bolts, lock-washers and earthing strap.

6:5 Replacing the gearbox

Full procedure for this operation is given in **Section 5:7**. After replacement, refit the gearlever by reference to **FIG 1:3** and refill with the correct grade of oil.

6:6 Fault diagnosis

(a) Jumping out of gear

1 Broken shaft lock plunger spring
2 Worn locating notch in gearchange shaft
3 Worn synchronizer baulk plates
4 Fork to gearchange shaft securing pin loose

(b) Noisy gearbox

1 Insufficient oil
2 Excessive end float in countershaft
3 Worn or damaged bearings
4 Worn or damaged gear teeth

(c) Difficulty in engaging gear

1 Incorrect clutch pedal adjustment
2 Worn synchromesh cones

(d) Oil leaks

1 Damaged joint washers
2 Worn or damaged oil seals
3 Front, rear or gearchange covers loose or faces damaged

CHAPTER 7

THE PROPELLER SHAFT, REAR AXLE
AND REAR SUSPENSION

7:1 Description (propeller shaft and universal joints)

The propeller shaft is of the open type and has a universal joint at each end. The front universal joint assembly includes a sliding splined sleeve which fits over the rear splines of the gearbox mainshaft. The rear universal joint is attached by four bolts and self-locking nuts to the rear axle pinion flange. Before removing a propeller shaft it is advisable to mark the rear universal joint flange and the driving pinion flange to ensure that the shaft is replaced in the same relative position, to prevent any possibility of it rotating out of balance.

7:2 Dismantling and servicing (universal joints)

1 Having marked the propeller shaft flange and the rear axle pinion driving flange, unscrew the four bolts and self-locking nuts.

Separate the flanges, pull the propeller shaft downwards then rearwards to extract the front sliding joint from the gearbox extension (see **FIG 7:1**).

2 The component parts of each universal joint are serviced as a kit (Part No. 100E.7039). Extract the circlip on each spider bearing and remove the bearing cups and rollers.

Remove the spider from the yoke and detach the oil seal and seal retainer from each spider journal. Unscrew the nipple from the centre of the spider.

3 Reassemble each joint by fitting new oil seals in the retainers and locate them on the spiders (oil seals outwards).

Position the spider in the yoke then assemble the needle rollers 22 in each bearing cup and refit the bearings squarely round each spider journal. Complete one half of the joint at a time. Replace the circlips and nipple.

Replacement of the propeller shaft is a reversal of the dismantling procedure, **remember to align the flange marks.**

7:3 Description (rear axle), see FIG 7:2

The rear axle is of the three-quarter floating type employing a spiral bevel crownwheel and pinion, together with a two-pinion differential. The differential case is mounted between the two taper roller bearings carried in the split axle housing.

The pinion is supported on two adjustable taper roller bearings. Correct depth of mesh of the pinion with the crownwheel is obtained by means of a shim fitted between the rear pinion bearing cone and the pinion teeth.

The pinion and bearing assembly is mounted on the righthand side of the split axle housing.

The hub and brake drum assemblies are mounted and keyed on the taper end of each half shaft (axle shaft). The hubs run on parallel roller bearings, and must be removed and repacked with fresh grease every 5000 miles

The oil capacity of the axle is approximately $1\frac{1}{2}$ Imperial pints (.852 litres). A drain and level plug are provided on the differential housing and when filled to the level of the filler plug hole the differential gears and crownwheel and pinion assemblies will be adequately lubricated.

An extreme pressure SAE.90 gear oil is used and the unit should be drained and refilled with fresh oil every 5000 miles. It is also suggested that the level be checked by means of the level plug every 1000 miles.

When renewing hubs or brake drums, both 7 inch and 8 inch diameters are used, check replacement part before fitting.

The following operations may be carried out with the axle in position.

7:4 Dismantling hubs and brake drums

1 Securely jack-up the vehicle, release the handbrake and place the gearlever in the neutral position. Remove the road wheel.
2 See **FIG 7:2,** remove the splitpin from the axle shaft nut then unscrew the nut and withdraw the flat washer.
3 A hub puller of the type shown in **FIG 7:3** is essential for their removal and one may be loaned from a Ford service station or purchased from the British Extractor Tool Co. of Croydon, Surrey.

    With the use of the puller, draw the hub fully off the taper and key. Remove the key from the axle shaft taper.
4 Place the hub and drum assembly on a flat surface and prise the grease retainer from its location. Lift out the roller bearing. Turn the hub and drum assembly over and with a piece of tubing of suitable diameter bearing upon the thrust washer which in turn rests upon the hub bearing sleeve, drive both the sleeve and washer from their location.

7:5 Reassembling hubs and brake drums

1 Thoroughly clean the hub and brake drum assembly, removing all traces of old grease from the hub. Ensure that the brake drum surfaces are clean and completely free from grease. Examine the bearing sleeve and rollers for wear and renew if necessary.
2 Position a new thrust washer in the base of the hub and drive the bearing sleeve into position. Insert the parallel roller bearing and press a new grease retainer

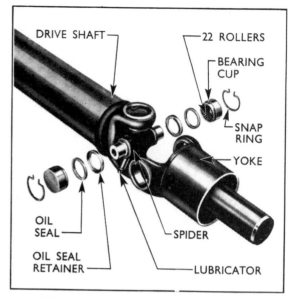

FIG 7:1   Component parts of a universal joint

Key to Fig 7:1   For 'snap ring' in illustration read 'circlip' in text

into position (lip towards bearing). Pack the hub with fresh wheel bearing grease, wiping away any surplus from around the grease retainer housing.
3 Tap the key into position in the groove on the taper end of the axle shaft. The tapered end of the key should face the inner end of the axle shaft, which must be supported when the key is fitted.

    Offer up the hub assembly to the axle shaft taper ensuring that the key engages the groove correctly. Lightly tap the hub onto the taper. Replace the flat washer and castellated nut.

    Tighten the nut securely and lock it in position with a new splitpin.

    Replace the road wheel and remove the supporting jack. Check wheel nuts for tightness and apply the handbrake.

7:6 Renewing the pinion oil seal

Before commencing this operation, the following part production modifications should be noted.

The pinion seal is located in the housing bolted to the front face of the axle throat.

Later production vehicles have an axle housing with a slot in the throat which lines up with a lip at the bottom of the pinion oil seal retainer housing. This slot connects with an oil return passage in the axle housing throat.

At the same time, the pinion oil seal retainer has been modified by introducing an O-ring rubber seal (located in a groove machined in the retainer) to supersede the gasket fitted at this point on earlier production vehicles.

This new retainer and O-ring must be used with the latest type axle housing. They must not be used with the early type axle housing.

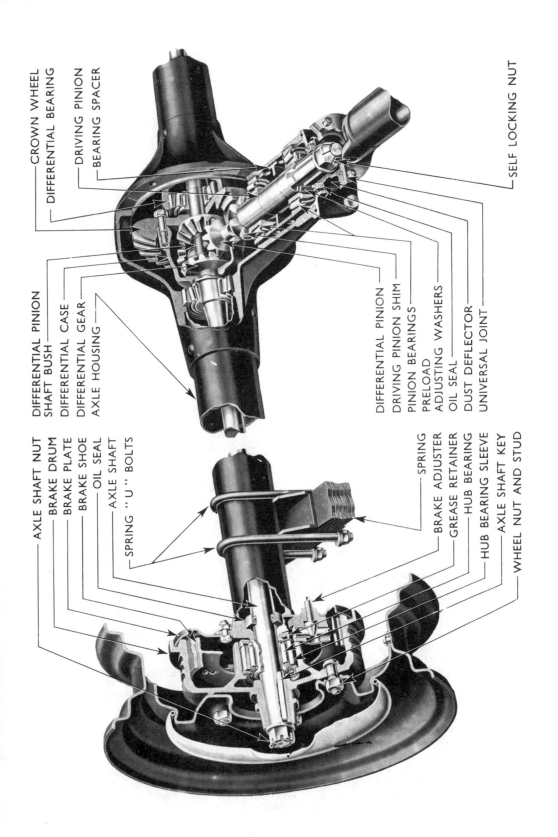

CROWN WHEEL
DIFFERENTIAL BEARING
DRIVING PINION
BEARING SPACER

SELF LOCKING NUT

DIFFERENTIAL PINION
SHAFT BUSH
DIFFERENTIAL CASE
DIFFERENTIAL GEAR
AXLE HOUSING

DIFFERENTIAL PINION
DRIVING PINION SHIM
PINION BEARINGS
PRELOAD
ADJUSTING WASHERS
OIL SEAL
DUST DEFLECTOR
UNIVERSAL JOINT

AXLE SHAFT NUT
BRAKE DRUM
BRAKE PLATE
BRAKE SHOE
OIL SEAL
AXLE SHAFT
SPRING "U" BOLTS

SPRING
BRAKE ADJUSTER
GREASE RETAINER
HUB BEARING
HUB BEARING SLEEVE
AXLE SHAFT KEY
WHEEL NUT AND STUD

FIG 7:2   The rear axle prior to approximate engine number 100E.292674

Various thicknesses of gasket are available in service for fitting between the oil seal retainer and the axle housing throat, on vehicles built prior to the later type of oil seal retainer and O-ring seal referred to above.

The approximate thickness gaskets should be selected as follows:

1 With the pinion assembly in position in the axle housing, assemble the oil seal retainer with the bolts finger tight to give an even gap between the housing and retainer.

2 Measure the gap with a feeler gauge.

3 Select the gasket, according to the gap measurement, as indicated in the following table and **make sure that the oil passage in the housing lines up with the hole in the gasket when fitted.**

Part No.	Measured gap	Free thickness of gasket
7W.4507	.0054 to .006 inch	.008 to .010 inch
100E.4507.A	.006 to .007 inch	.009 to .011 inch
100E.4507.B (2 off)	.007 to .008 inch	.005 to .007 inch
100E.4507.C	.008 to .012 inch	.0135 to .0165 inch
100E.4507.D	.012 to .016 inch	.018 to .022 inch

The oil seal itself has been increased in width from $\frac{19}{64}$ to $\frac{1}{2}$ inch on present production vehicles.

It will be necessary to replace the rear axle drive pinion oil seal assembly, deflector and retainer, with those parts listed below in order to bring the earlier type assembly into line with the later models.

Part No. 100E.4675.B—Rear axle drive pinion oil seal retainer.

Part No. 100E.4676.B—Oil seal.

Part No. 100E.4859.B—Pinion dust deflector.

1 Now jack-up the vehicle and apply the handbrake.

Mark the pinion driving flange and the mating universal joint flange so that they may be refitted in the same relative position. Unscrew the four retaining bolts and their self-locking nuts and lower the propeller shaft and its rear universal joint and flange, supporting it on a stand to prevent strain on the front universal joint.

2 Hold the pinion flange quite still with a tool made from $1 \times \frac{1}{8} \times 18$ inch long mild steel flat suitably drilled so that it may be bolted through two of the pinion driving flange holes and then with a torque wrench ascertain by trial and error the figure at which the pinion nut will just start to turn. Take a note of the torque setting.

3 By the continued use of the tool described above ensure that the pinion flange does not rotate and unscrew the pinion nut, remove the holding tool, the plain washer, pinion flange and dust deflector.

4 Unscrew the four bolts and spring washers securing the oil seal housing (see **FIG 7:4**) and remove it.

Tap the oil seal out of the housing.

5 Locate a new seal with the lip facing inwards and press home.

Refit the oil seal housing to the axle housing throat, ensuring that it is fitted with the word 'TOP' uppermost, and secure it with four bolts and lockwashers. Tighten the bolts evenly to a torque of 20 to 25 lb ft.

Note whether a gasket is used, as on earlier type vehicles, or whether the O-type sealing ring is used. Full details of the gasket or sealing ring are given at the beginning of this section.

FIG 7:3   Removing a rear hub and brake drum assembly

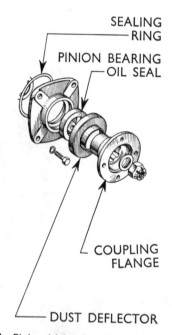

FIG 7:4   Pinion driving flange and oil seal components

6 Replace the oil seal dust deflector, check that the pinion bearing preload adjusting washers are in position on the larger diameter pinion shaft splines, and replace the drive pinion flange, plain washer and pinion nut.

7 Again using the flange holding tool to prevent the flange turning, tighten the nut to the torque noted in Operation 3.

Reconnect the propeller shaft, checking the aligning marks and fit the four securing bolts and self-locking nuts (nuts on propeller shaft side), tightening them securely and evenly to a torque of 15 to 18 lb ft.

Remove the jacks.

7:7 Rear axle removal

1 Jack-up the vehicle and place adequate support stands under the chassis frame. Remove the road wheels and drain the axle, retaining the oil for further use.

2 Disconnect the two rigid brake pipes by unscrewing the the unions from the wheel cylinders and the T-piece which is mounted on the axle casing. Carefully lever up the pipe securing clips and remove the pipes.

The T-piece connector should be removed by unscrewing the retaining bolt, the latter is drilled and serves as the axle breather. Ensure that the brake pipes and the connector are kept away from grease and dirt until required for reassembly.

3 Disconnect the handbrake cable ends from the brake levers by withdrawing the splitpins and clevis pins from the clevises. Remove the two spring clips from the cable outer casings where they abut the axle brackets. Carefully lever up the axle housing clips and then remove the rubber grommet from the axle housing web. The cables may now be detached from the axle.

4 Disconnect the rear universal joint flange as fully described in the previous section then unscrew the self-locking nuts from the U-bolts which retain the axle housing to the road springs. Lift away the U-bolts and pull aside the road spring clip plates which provide the lower mounting for the dampers.

(On Escort, Squire and 7 cwt vans, disconnect the damper links at the axle housing.) Lift the axle slightly so that the brake backplates clear the road springs and remove the axle sideways from the vehicle.

7:8 Renewing axle housing oil seals

(a) Removal

These oil seals (see **FIG 7:2**) are located inside and a short distance from, the outer end of each axle housing. Their purpose is to prevent oil escaping from the differential housing into the hub. Attention to them will only normally be required after a considerable mileage and renewal can only be carried out after splitting the housing and withdrawing the half shafts and differential assembly.

1 Jack-up the vehicle, drain the oil and remove the axle as described in the previous Section. Remove the hubs and brake drum assemblies as described in **Section 7:4**, not forgetting to withdraw the keys.

2 Remove the four bolts and self-locking nuts which secure each brake backplate to the axle housing flange and withdraw the backplates.

3 Unscrew the eight bolts and spring washers which secure the two halves of the axle housing and carefully withdraw the lefthand section over the end of its half shaft.

Lift the half shaft and differential assembly from the righthand section of the axle housing.

4 Using a suitable drift, inserted from the hub ends of the axle casings, drive out the oil seals.

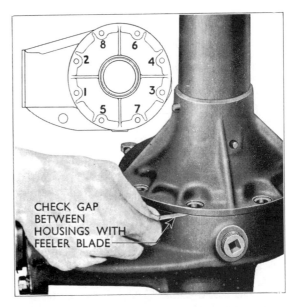

FIG 7:5 Checking differential bearing preload and nut tightening sequence

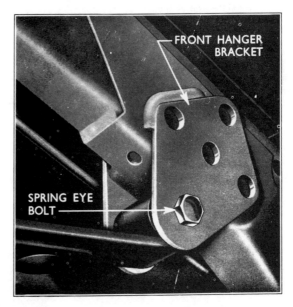

FIG 7:6 Rear road spring hanger bracket

(b) Replacement

1 Position a new oil seal (lip facing inwards) in its machined location in the axle housing and drive carefully home with a piece of tubing of suitable diameter to bear upon the outer edge of the seal (alternatively a threaded rod having appropriate nuts and thrust washers may be used to draw the seal into position but take extreme care not to damage the shaft contact surface of the seal).

Repeat the operation on the other half of the axle housing.

2 Refit the differential and half shaft to the righthand axle housing taking great care that the half shaft does not damage the new oil seal as it passes through and that the pinion and crownwheel teeth mesh correctly.

3 Lower the lefthand axle housing over the other half shaft again taking great care not to damage the new oil seal.

4 Using a feeler between the two halves of the axle housing check the clearance, as shown in **FIG 7:5.** (This clearance determines the differential bearing preload and must be between .005 and .010 inch.)

The gasket which must be fitted between the mating flanges measures between .005 and .007 inch in its compressed state so by simple subtraction from the clearance measured, the desired clearance may be calculated. More than one gasket may be used if necessary.

5 Fit the eight axle housing bolts and lockwashers and tighten in the sequence given in **FIG 7:5** to a torque of 20 to 25 lb ft.

6 Replace the brake backplates and the bolts and self-locking nuts which retain them to the axle housing flanges.

Refit the hubs and brake drums and half shaft keys as described in **Section 7:5,** paragraph 3.

Refill the axle with oil.

Any further dismantling or other operations to the rear axle require special gauges and tool and are not within the scope of the home mechanic.

The operations described in this Chapter must therefore be regarded as the limit to which the reader may go in undertaking repairs and maintenance to this unit.

7:9 Rear axle replacement

1 Lift the axle through the road springs from the side of the vehicle so that the hole in each axle spring seat locates on the respective spring assembly tie bolt. Place the two pairs of U-bolts over the axle housing so that their threaded ends engage in the holes in the rear spring clip plates. Fit the self-locking nuts and tighten to 20 to 25 lb ft (ensuring that the nuts are tightened evenly and a little at a time).

(On Escort, Squire and 7 cwt vans reconnect the damper links to the axle housing.)

2 Couple the rear universal joint flange to the pinion flange, mating the alignment marks and insert the retaining bolts and self-locking nuts (the nuts are positioned on the propeller shaft side) and tighten to 15 to 18 lb ft.

3 Pass the lefthand brake cable through the aperture in the righthand axle housing web and fit the rubber grommet. Pass the ends of the cables through the axle brackets and refit the retaining clips to the cable outer casing grooves.

Fit the cable clevises to the brake levers using new splitpins. Replace the cables in the axle housing clips which should be bent down to secure the outer casing.

4 Refit the T-piece brake pipe connector using the hollow vent bolt and then reconnect the two rigid brake pipes,

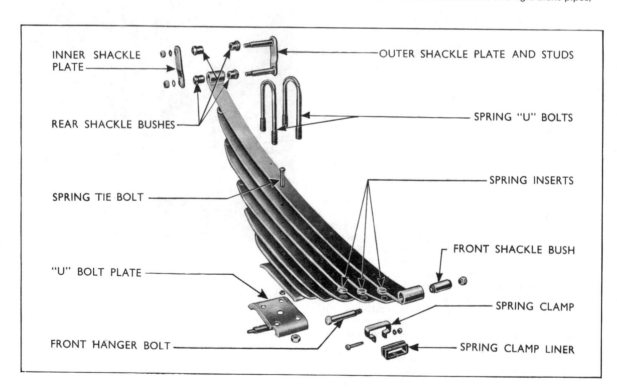

INNER SHACKLE PLATE

OUTER SHACKLE PLATE AND STUDS

REAR SHACKLE BUSHES

SPRING "U" BOLTS

SPRING INSERTS

SPRING TIE BOLT

FRONT SHACKLE BUSH

"U" BOLT PLATE

SPRING CLAMP

FRONT HANGER BOLT

SPRING CLAMP LINER

FIG 7:7   Rear road spring components

making sure that all unions are sound. Refit the pipes in their clips. Bleed the brakes as described in **Chapter 10, Section 10:7.**

5 Replace the road wheels and remove the jacks and support stands. Recheck wheel nuts for tightness. Fill the axle to the level of the filler plug hole.

7:10 Description (the rear suspension)

The rear springs are longitudinally mounted at each end of the axle housing and are supported at the rear on swinging shackles under the body sidemembers. The front end of each spring is secured to a hanger bracket welded to the body sidemember (see **FIG 7:6**).

The springs fitted to Anglia and Prefect cars (1953 onwards) are symmetrical about the centre tie bolt as were the springs fitted to early production 5 cwt vans and estate cars.

With the introduction of the 7 cwt van (1954 onwards), however, a spring with an offset bolt was introduced and this type of spring was fitted to all 5 and 7 cwt vans and estate cars.

The tie bolt is located $\frac{1}{4}$ inch forward of the centre of the main leaf so that from the spring front eye to the tie bolt is approximately $\frac{1}{2}$ inch shorter than from the spring rear eye to the tie bolt.

To facilitate identification the spring front eye is marked with a daub of yellow paint to identify the short end of the spring.

The axle is mounted on top of the springs and is secured to each spring by two U-bolts and a plate. On the Anglia, Prefect and the 5 cwt vans, this U-bolt plate also provides the lower mounting for the telescopic damper.

Each spring rear eye and swinging shackle is insulated by four detachable rubber bushes, as shown in **FIG 7:7**.

The spring front eyes are insulated by bonded type bushes.

The rear spring leaves are coated with an anti-rust lubricant prior to assembly. Rubber pads are fitted in the ends of the longer leaves to prevent squeaks and provide a bearing surface for the tips of the leaves. These rubber inserts are oil-resistant, and springs should be brushed with penetrating oil at 5000 mile intervals.

Telescopic type dampers are fitted to Anglia and Prefect cars and 5 cwt vans. Vertical-type, two cylinder dampers are fitted to estate cars and 7 cwt vans. This type of damper is mounted on the body rear sidemembers and is connected at each side to the axle housing spring seats, by rubber bushed links.

7:11 Removal and servicing of rear road springs

1 To remove the rear road springs, first jack-up the rear of the vehicle and place supports underneath the body sidemembers, then place a jack beneath the centre of the axle housing. Unscrew the rear shackle nuts and withdraw the shackle plate on the inner side of the spring. See **FIG 7:7**, adjust the height of the axle jack until the outer shackle plates complete with their studs can be withdrawn.

2 Detach the four rubber bushes from the spring rear eye and from the outer shackle plate. Unscrew the front shackle self-locking nut and tap the bolt through the shackle bush. Unscrew the nuts on each spring U-bolt and lower the spring from the vehicle.

FIG 7:8   Rear shackle assembly

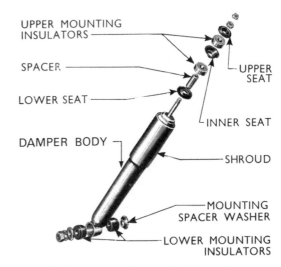

FIG 7:9   Telescopic damper Anglia, Prefect and 5 cwt Van)

3 Check the spring leaves for cracks or flattening due to fatigue. Do not attempt to replace individual leaves but fit a complete new assembly. The rubber spring inserts (see **FIG 7:7**) should be renewed if necessary.

4 The bonded type rubber shackle bush fitted to the front eye of each road spring may need renewal. The old bush should be removed by using a drift of suitable diameter or by pressing it out in a vice using distance pieces. Fit the new bush by pressing in a vice or using

a short bolt with washers and nut to draw it into position in the spring eye.

All pressure must be concentrated on the outer sleeve when fitting the new bush.

5 The rear shackle bushes are easily renewed, being of the split rubber type.

7:12 Rear road spring replacement

Ensure that the springs are correctly positioned before offering up (see **Section 7:10** regarding shorter end forward on estate cars and vans).

Locate the front spring eye complete with its bush, in the hanger beneath the body sidemember and replace the shackle bolt. Refit the self-locking nut **but do not tighten it fully.**

Locate the spring tie bolt head in the location in the axle housing spring seat. Refit the spring U-bolts, locate the U-bolt on the underside of the spring and replace the nuts, **tightening them evenly** to a torque of 20 to 25 lb ft.

Insert new rubber bushes in the outer side of the rear spring shackle eye and bracket.

Pull the rear end of the spring downwards, jacking-up the axle if necessary, until the outer shackle plate and studs can be inserted into the spring and mounting bracket bushes.

Fit the rubber bushes on the shackle studs at the inner side of the spring and bracket and replace the shackle plate with the depressions in the plate to the rubber bushes (see **FIG 7:8**). Fit the lockwashers and nuts **but do not tighten the nuts fully.**

If new rubber bushes have been fitted it may be necessary to apply a clamp across the shackle plate and bar to compress the rubber bushes before it is possible to fit the nuts.

Lower the vehicle to the ground before tightening the spring front and rear shackle nuts securely.

7:13 Description (rear dampers)

To Anglia, Prefect (1953 onwards) and 5 cwt vans (1954 onwards) a double acting telescopic damper is fitted. This is a sealed unit and requires no adjustments or maintenance in service (see **FIG 7:9**).

Periodically, it is advisable to check the rubber bushes or insulators at both the upper and lower mounting to ensure that these are in good condition and have not deteriorated in any way.

On Anglia and Prefect cars, the upper mounting of the damper passes through the under body of the car, and it is therefore necessary to remove the rear seat before the damper assembly can be detached (see next Section).

On 5 cwt vans, a bracket is welded to the underbody to which the upper mounting of the damper is secured.

The settings differ between van and passenger car dampers and a yellow line is painted on the shroud of 5 cwt van dampers for identification purposes.

To Escort, Squire and 7 cwt vans a vertical piston-type damper is fitted on each body rear sidemember above the rear axle housing (see **FIG 7:11**).

These piston-type dampers operate on the hydraulic, self regulating principle, giving a stronger resistance to the rebound of the spring than to the compression.

Dampers are set during manufacture to suit the particular operating conditions under which they may

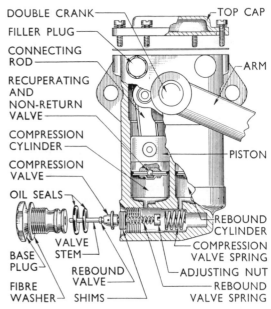

FIG 7:10 Piston type damper (Escort, Squire and 7 cwt Van)

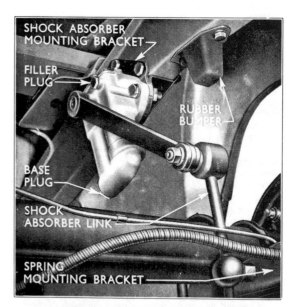

FIG 7:11 Piston type damper mounting

Key to Fig 7:11 For 'shock absorber' in illustration read 'damper' in text

normally be expected to function, and no attention should be required apart from maintaining the fluid level in the body.

The two equal diameter cylinders have steel pistons which are reciprocated by short connecting rods coupled to the double crank to which the damper arm is splined.

A recuperating ball valve, which also acts as a non-return valve, is fitted in each piston head to enable any fluid that escapes past the pistons to be replenished from the reservoir above the pistons.

The compression and rebound valve assembly is located in the base plug which acts as a seat for the conical valve.

7:14 Damper maintenance and servicing

(a) Telescopic type (replacement of rubber mounting bushes and insulators):

1 To remove the damper (see **FIG 7:9**) unscrew the nut and remove the lockwasher, flat washer and outer insulator rubber from the lower connection to the U-bolt road spring clip plate. Withdraw the damper eye and remove the remaining insulator rubber and spacer washer.

On 5 cwt vans the following operation may be carried out from beneath the vehicle but on Anglia and Prefect cars the rear seat must be removed before the upper damper mounting can be exposed. To remove the seat, withdraw the lining panel from behind the squab in the luggage compartment. This is held in position by seven press studs.

A number of hooks will be seen in the body at the base of the squab through which an elastic cord is threaded. Release the elastic cord from each hook with the exception of the extreme lefthand and righthand hooks.

From inside the car pull the rear seat forward slightly and lift the front edge upwards clear of the retaining clips. Lift the pad from above each mounting nut.

2 Unscrew the upper mounting locknut and retaining nut and withdraw the upper dished seat, the upper rubber insulator and inner dished seat. Remove the damper complete with the second rubber insulator, spacer and lower seat.

Apart from the renewal of the rubber insulating components, no other servicing is possible. **During removal and replacement, keep the damper in an upright position to avoid possible aeration to the fluid.**

Where a telescopic damper offers little or no resistance when operated by hand, it should be renewed as a complete unit.

Replacement of the damper to the vehicle is a reversal of the procedure given earlier in this section but ensure that component mounting parts are replaced in strict sequence, as shown in **FIG 7:9**.

(b) Piston type:

1 Dampers of the vertical piston-type should be inspected and topped up as necessary, at least every six months or 5000 miles.

Clean the area surrounding the filler plug to remove all traces of dirt or grit.

Remove the filler plug and top the unit up to the bottom of the filler plug orifice with hydraulic damper fluid only.

If any other fluid is used, the characteristics of the damper may be altered and damage can be caused by the use of an unsuitable fluid.

Replace the filler plug and washer and tighten securely.

When the dampers are new, a slight leakage of fluid from the gland behind the arm may be noticeable. This slight leakage may continue until the gland packing is properly bedded-in. This point should be checked to ensure that leakage diminishes as the packing beds-in. The gland is not adjustable.

Damper wear is normally caused by dirt falling into the body when the filler cap is removed for fluid replenishment. Every precaution should be taken to prevent this happening, and the filler cap should only be unscrewed after the cap and surrounding area have been carefully cleaned.

2 **To test.** Disconnect the damper link at the axle housing.

Move the damper arm up and down. More resistance should be felt on the downward stroke than on the upward stroke.

If no resistance can be felt when the arm is moved quickly, it indicates either a lack of fluid or internal damage to the valves. Top up the shock absorber with the correct fluid and retest. If there is still no resistance after topping up, the shock absorber should be replaced.

3 **To adjust.** Valve adjustment should only be attempted in extreme cases and careful adherence to these instructions is necessary, otherwise abnormal hydraulic stresses may be imposed on the mechanism. The compression setting of the damper is controlled by the position of the collar on the valve stem, the resistance of the compression valve spring and the thickness of the base plug washer (see **FIG 7:10**).

The position of the collar on the stem is determined at the time of manufacture in connection with its own valve, spring, base plug and washer, so that predetermined characteristics of the damper compression cylinder are obtained.

It is not practicable to adjust the compression setting in service. **It is essential that the thickness of the base plug washer is not altered, otherwise the compression setting will vary.** On the other hand the rebound setting may be altered to suit individual requirements providing every care is exercised when carrying out the adjustment.

(a) See **FIG 7:10**. Remove the valve assembly by unscrewing the base plug. Providing the damper arm is not moved or the filler cap unscrewed, no appreciable quantity of fluid will be lost.

(b) Float off the solder locking the valve spindle nut.

(c) To increase the resistance of the damper tighten up the rebound spring by means of the valve spindle nut. The rebound spring must not be compressed within two turns of the 'hard-up' position of the nut.

To decrease the resistance, the nut may be screwed out slightly.

(d) Before replacing the valve assembly, make sure that the valve spindle nut is secured by soldering it to the spindle.

(e) When replacing the valve assembly see the original washer is positioned on the base plug and that no dirt or grit prevents the valve seating properly. The omission of the washer or the use of a washer from another damper will affect the characteristics of the unit. Top up with fluid.

4 **To remove a piston-type damper see FIG 7:11.** Disconnect the link at the damper arm. Partly unscrew

the nut and give it a sharp tap with a copper hammer, at the same time supporting the arm. This will release the taper on the arm. Do not attempt to lever the link out of the arm as the ends of the link are rubber bushed and they may be forced out of alignment.

Remove the two bolts, flat washers and self-locking nuts holding the damper to the mounting plate on the body sidemember, and detach the unit.

Inspect the rubber bushes in the damper link and renew the link if these are excessively worn.

Bolt the new damper to the mounting plate on the body sidemember, securing it with two bolts, flat washers and self-locking nuts. Check that the mounting plate is firmly secured to the bodymember. The mounting plate is secured to the bodymember with three bolts and self-locking nuts.

Reconnect the damper link to the arm after ensuring that the tapers are clean. If the arms have worked loose on the tapers of the links, the holes may be elongated and even replacement links may not enable a satisfactory repair to be made.

7:15 Fault diagnosis

(a) Noisy axle

1 Insufficient or incorrect lubricant
2 Worn bearings
3 Worn gears

(b) Excessive backlash

1 Worn gears, bearings or bearing housings
2 Worn half shaft splines
3 Worn universal joints
4 Loose or broken wheel studs

(c) Oil leakage

1 Defective hub oil seals
2 Defective pinion oil seal
3 Defective universal joint spider seals

(d) Vibration

1 Propeller shaft out of balance
2 Worn universal joint bearings

(e) Rattles

1 Rubber bushes in damper links worn
2 Dampers loose on mountings
3 Spring U-bolts loose
4 Loose road spring clips
5 Worn bushes in spring eyes and shackles
6 Broken road spring leaves

(f) Settling

1 Weak or broken road spring leaves
2 Worn shackle pins and bushes
3 Loose road spring anchorages

CHAPTER 8

FRONT SUSPENSION AND HUBS

8:1   Description

The front suspension system, which is illustrated in **FIG 8:1,** utilizes coil springs in conjunction with vertical type dampers to form front suspension units. The suspension units are mounted between ball joints on the ends of the radius rods and thrust bearings in reinforced flanges at the top of the engine compartment side walls.

The upper mounting assemblies contain the thrust bearings which allow the unit to rotate about its vertical axis to provide the steering.

The front wheel stub axle is pressed into the lower end of the suspension unit.

The radius rods are secured at their inner ends to the suspension crossmember, and at their outer ends to the base of the suspension units. The centre stud of the ball joint at the outer end of each arm passes up through the boss at the base of the unit, and through the front wheel stub axle.

Both ends of the anti-roll bar are located in the outer ends of the radius rods. Attachment feet at each side of the anti-roll bar secure it to the body sidemembers.

Each coil spring is located at the top on a seat on the suspension unit piston rod, and at the bottom on a seat welded to the body of the suspension unit.

Rubber bushes are used in most joint locations of the front suspension system, and therefore lubrication is kept to a minimum.

FIG 8:2 illustrates the linkage lubricators on the left-hand side of the vehicle in which grease should be injected at servicing periods.

The anti-roll bar and radius rod bushes can be easily renewed, without removing the assemblies from the vehicle. Castor, camber and kingpin inclination are set in production and cannot be altered, but may be checked (see **Section 8:8**).

Filler plugs have been incorporated in the front suspension units of later production vehicles (see **Section 8:5**).

Whenever repairs are to be carried out to any part of the front suspension system, it is essential that spring clips are fitted to the coil springs otherwise extreme difficulty will be experienced in dismantling and reassembling the component parts.

The wheel alignment should always be checked after carrying out repairs to the suspension units or linkage (see **Section 8:8** and **Chapter 9, Section 9:9**).

8:2 Front hub adjustment

1 Jack-up the front of the vehicle and grasp the wheel at two diametrically opposite points (the top and bottom of the tyres). If the wheel and brake drum can be rocked and moved relative to the spindle then adjust as follows:

2 Remove the hub cap from the wheel and then tap free the grease cap (see **FIG 8:4**) which is a press fit in its location.

3 See **FIG 8:3** and remove the splitpin from the adjusting nut. Turn the wheel in its usual direction of rotation and tighten the adjusting nut until severe resistance is felt then turn back the nut two castellations or until the wheel is completely free without any end float. Fit a new splitpin and replace the grease cap and the hub cap. **Do not fill the grease cap with any grease but leave dry.**

8:3 Removal and replacement of front hub bearings and seals

1 Jack-up the front of the vehicle, remove the hub cap, the road wheel, the grease cap, splitpin and adjusting nut. Withdraw the tongued thrust washer (see **FIG 8:4**) and draw the hub off the stub axle, taking care that the outer bearing race does not fall to the ground during this operation.

2 Prise out the grease retainer and lift out the inner bearing spacer, bearing and cup. Wash out all grease from the hub and its bearings and replace any worn or pitted races or cups. Do not remove the circlip type bearing retainer from the hub.

A bearing cup puller should preferably be used during these operations rather than a drift as otherwise damage to the seats may result.

3 Fitting new bearings where required will necessitate pressing new cups into position (a threaded rod with suitable nuts and thrust washers will prove adequate for this). Pack the hub between the two bearing cups with a high melting point, lithium based grease **but do not completely fill the space.**

Work the grease well into the roller races.

4 Fit the inner roller bearing in its cup and drive into place a new grease retainer (lip towards bearing), see **FIG 8:5**. Locate the inner bearing spacer on the stub axle and position the hub assembly on the stub

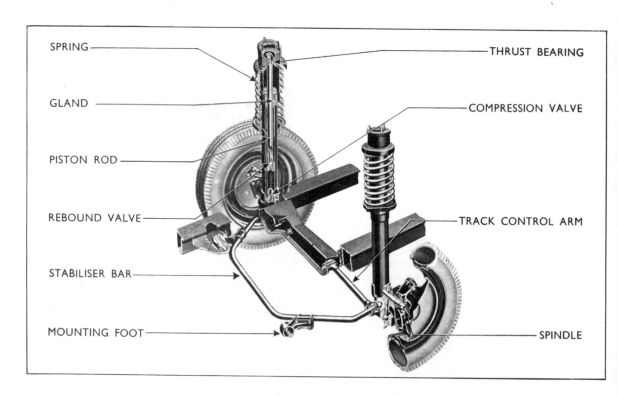

FIG 8:1 The front suspension layout

Key to Fig 8:1 For 'track control arm' in illustration read 'radius rod' in text. For 'spindle' in illustration read 'stub axle' in text. For 'stabilizer bar' in illustration read 'anti-roll bar' in text

axle. Fit the outer bearing in its cup, refit the thrust washer ensuring that its tongue engages in the slot in the stub axle. Replace the castellated nut.

The thrust washer fitted to later production vehicles is smaller in outside diameter to that previously fitted, $1\frac{1}{4}$ inch instead of $1\frac{1}{2}$ inch, ensuring that it does not have a grease seal effect between the bearings and grease cap, as it is essentially a thrust washer. This later type washer can be fitted to earlier vehicles, or alternatively the earlier type washer can be re-worked by filing two diametrically opposite flats on the outer circumference of the washer, so that the distance measured across flats is $1\frac{1}{4}$ inch.

5 Adjust the bearings as described in the previous section, then replace the grease cap, refit the road wheel, remove the jack, check the wheel nuts for tightness and replace the hub cap.

8:4 The front suspension unit (description)

A combination of both hydraulic damper and coil spring is designed into this unit which consists of (see **FIG 8:4**) an outer casing, inside which is a cylinder, located at the top by the piston rod gland cap and at the bottom by the compression valve assembly in the base of the unit.

A piston rod operates inside the cylinder and is secured to the thrust bearing at its upper end. The piston and rebound valves are located in the bottom of the piston rod.

In operation the piston rod remains stationary and the suspension unit body moves up and down on the rod.

The piston valve operates inside the cylinder and is mounted on the rebound valve assembly. The rebound valve seat is inside the piston valve body which seats on the piston valve screw. Compression springs are fitted to both these valves.

The compression valve, located at the base of the cylinder, also incorporates the recuperating foot valve assembly. The seat for the compression valve is provided in the foot valve nut and the pressure of the compression valve spring is set during manufacture and should not be adjusted. The foot valve is located inside the cylinder and is held on to the face of the body by a compression spring. A leak path is cut across the face of the body under the foot valve.

When the vehicle hits a bump, the body of the suspension unit moves upwards on the piston rod, and the fluid between the end of the piston and the compression valve assembly forces the compression valve off its seat, which allows fluid to flow into the annular space between the cylinder and the outer casing of the suspension unit (see **FIG 8:6**).

At the same time the piston valve is forced off its seat on the piston valve nut, and fluid flows past the valve, through the ports in the piston rod, to fill the space above the piston between the piston rod and the cylinder.

When the vehicle moves over a bump, the body of the suspension unit is forced downwards by the coil spring.

This compresses the fluid above the piston, closes the piston valve and forces the rebound valve off its seat, so controlling the rebound rate of the unit.

The flow of fluid from above the piston is not sufficient to fill the space below the piston, so a partial vacuum is set up.

This vacuum lifts the recuperating foot valve off its seat against the pressure of the light spring, so that fluid

FIG 8:2 Steering linkage lubricator location (lefthand side only)

Key to Fig 8:2 For 'track control arm ball joint' in illustration read 'radius rod ball joint' in text

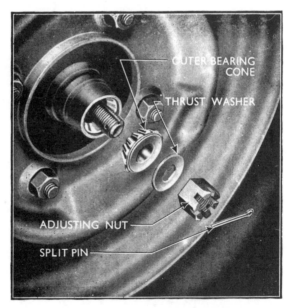

FIG 8:3 Front wheel outer bearing

may then flow back into the cylinder from the annular space between the outside of the cylinder and the suspension unit body (see **FIG 8:7**).

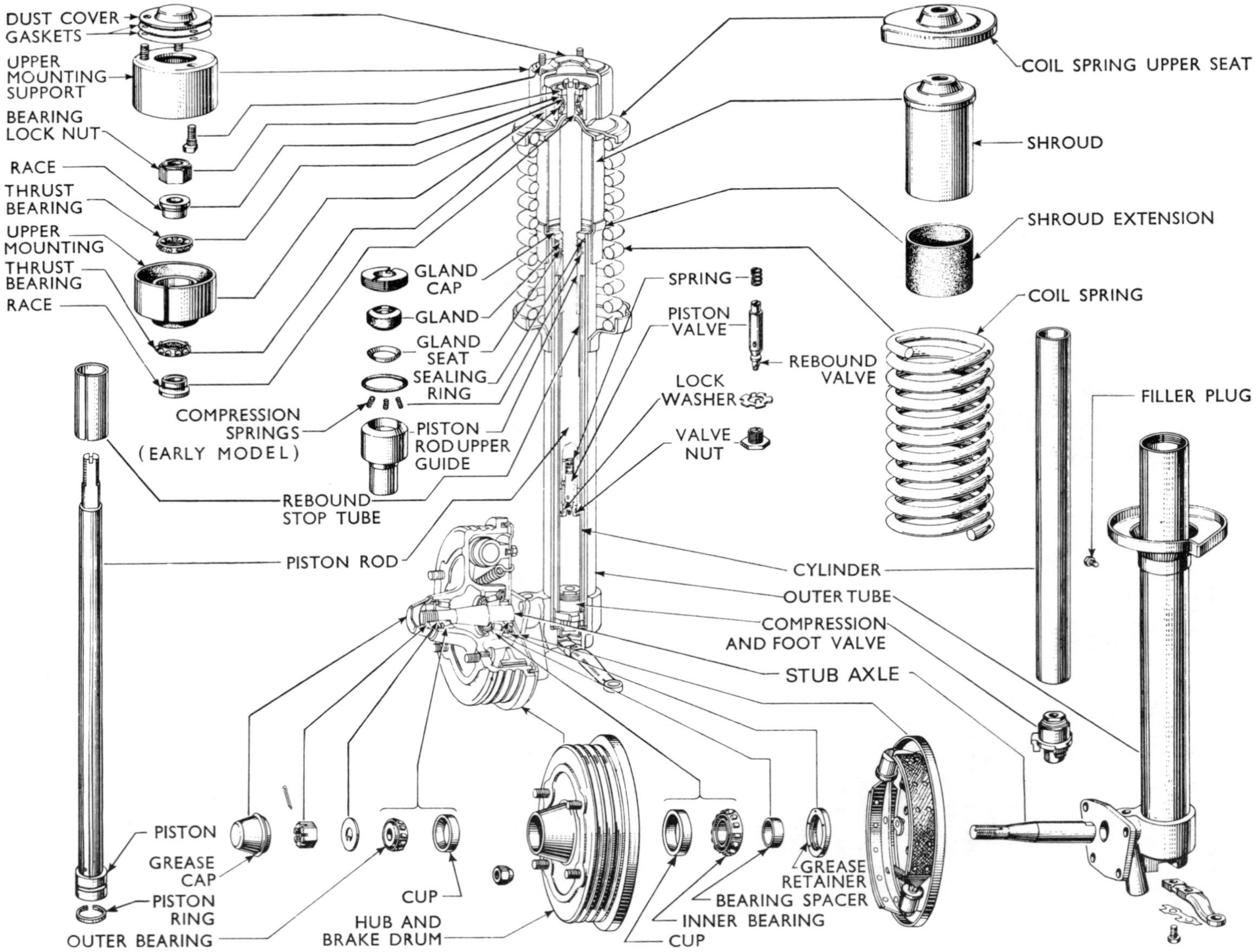

COIL SPRING UPPER SEAT

SHROUD

SHROUD EXTENSION

COIL SPRING

FILLER PLUG

REBOUND VALVE

SPRING

PISTON VALVE

LOCK WASHER

VALVE NUT

CYLINDER

OUTER TUBE

COMPRESSION AND FOOT VALVE

STUB AXLE

GREASE RETAINER

BEARING SPACER

INNER BEARING

CUP

GLAND CAP

GLAND

GLAND SEAT

SEALING RING

PISTON ROD UPPER GUIDE

COMPRESSION SPRINGS (EARLY MODEL)

REBOUND STOP TUBE

PISTON ROD

CUP

HUB AND BRAKE DRUM

PISTON

GREASE CAP

PISTON RING

OUTER BEARING

DUST COVER

GASKETS

UPPER MOUNTING SUPPORT

BEARING LOCK NUT

RACE

THRUST BEARING

UPPER MOUNTING

THRUST BEARING

RACE

FIG 8:4 Front suspension components

70

8:5 Maintenance of suspension unit

Later-type vehicles have a filler plug located in the body of the suspension unit below the coil spring lower seat.

The suspension units fitted to earlier vehicles were of the sealed-type and did not incorporate a filler plug. These units do not require topping up.

When topping up the suspension units on vehicles fitted with a filler plug, the vehicle must be standing unladen on level ground.

Remove the filler plug and add approved hydraulic shock absorber fluid until the fluid level reaches the bottom of the filler plug hole.

After topping up, replace the filler plug securely but do not overtighten.

On no account should fluid be added to the suspension unit under pressure.

No other adjustment is required to the unit.

8:6 Removing and replacing the suspension unit

Apart from the replacement of the suspension unit on a factory exchange basis or the renewal of the coil spring, further dismantling of the unit is not within the scope of the home mechanic due to the specialized tools required.

(a) Removal:

1 Either make up suitable clips or obtain them and a retaining strap (Tool No. A/E.5310) from your dealer and place in position over five coils of the spring (see **FIG 8:8**). Jack-up the front of the vehicle.

2 Detach the hub cap and grease cap and withdraw the splitpin, wheel bearing nut, thrust washer and outer bearing, and pull the wheel and brake drum assembly from the stub axle. Remove the bearing spacer. Remove the brake plate after unscrewing the four self-locking nuts and bolts securing the brake plate to the flange on the bottom of the suspension unit. Provided the brake plate is suitably supported by a block, it is not necessary to disconnect the fluid pipe. Do not stretch or distort the flexible brake pipe, and ensure that the brake pedal is not depressed, otherwise the wheel cylinder pistons may be displaced and fluid lost.

3 Withdraw the splitpin and unscrew the castellated nut securing the trackrod to the steering arm. The ball joint stud is a taper fit in the steering arm, and a rubber dust cover and two metal caps (see **Section 8:10**) are fitted over this ball joint (see **FIG 8:12**). See **Section 8:7** and bend back the tabs of the locking washer, unscrew the nuts and detach the anti-roll bar U-bolts at each attachment mounting foot (see **FIG 8:11**).

4 Remove the splitpin and unscrew the castellated nut on the radius rod ball joint stud where it passes through the boss at the base of the suspension unit (see **FIG 8:12**). Tap the stud to free the taper, using a copper drift. Press down the radius rod and anti-roll bar to free the ball joint stud from the suspension unit (see **FIG 8:13**).

5 Raise the vehicle bonnet and unscrew the three nuts on the upper mounting studs, which pass through the mudguard apron reinforcement. Lift the unit from its location, withdrawing it from beneath the vehicle.

6 See **FIG 8:4** and unscrew the self-locking nut at the top of the unit which retains the upper thrust bearing at the same time stopping the piston rod from rotating

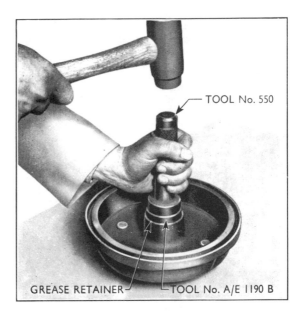

FIG 8:5   Fitting a new hub grease retainer

Key to Fig 8:5   A tubular drift and an old bearing cup may be used instead of the tools illustrated

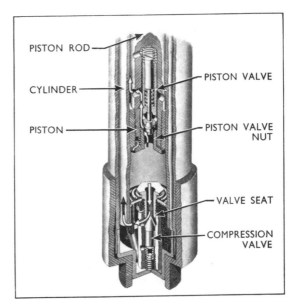

FIG 8:6   Suspension unit operation (compression)

by means of its centre slot. Withdraw the upper thrust bearing races and mounting assembly carefully over the piston rod.

Lift off the upper spring seat and withdraw the piston rod shroud. Draw the coil spring (still in its clips) over the end of the suspension unit.

7 Remove the steering arm from the base of the suspension unit by bending back the locking tabs and unscrewing the two retaining bolts.

The unit may now be exchanged for a replacement or if a new coil spring is required, have the retaining clips removed from the old one and fitted to the new by a service station who have the required compressor for this work.

(b) Replacement:

1 Refit the coil spring (compressed and with retaining clips in position). Springs are graded according to pressure (see **Technical Data**) and have one or two notches marked on the end coil. **Ensure that the new spring is of similar pressure to that of the one removed and springs of equal rating are fitted to each side of the vehicle.**

Fit the spring with its notches at the bottom.

2 Pull the piston rod up to the top of its stroke and refit the shroud; note that the flat on the internal bore of the shroud cap engages with the corresponding flat on the piston rod.

Replace the spring upper seat (see **FIG 8:9**), ensuring that the spring is seating correctly. Refit the upper mounting assembly (see **FIG 8:10**).

The bearings and bearing races should be inspected carefully and new parts fitted if required.

Place the lower bearing race on the piston rod, together with the lower half of the thrust bearing. Smear the bearing with a thin film of grease to hold it in position on the race whilst the upper bearing is assembled.

3 Position the upper mounting over the piston rod so that the tapered rubber face is towards the spring upper seat, making sure that it locates correctly on the lower half of the thrust bearing. Keep the piston rod pulled to the top of its stroke and locate the top half of the upper thrust bearing inside the upper mounting assembly. Refit the upper bearing race.

Replace the thrust bearing retaining locknut and prevent the piston rod rotating by means of its centre slot. The correct tightening torque for this locknut is 45 to 55 lb ft.

4 Position the unit in its location, from beneath the vehicle, fitting two thrust bearing dust cover gaskets on top of the suspension unit mounting, locating the three mounting studs in the holes in the mudguard reinforcement. Place a rubber gasket in position on the three studs and refit the circular dust cover. Fit the three self-locking nuts, tightening them securely to a torque of 15 to 18 lb ft.

Check to see there is a metal cap and a rubber dust excluder on the radius rod ball joint stud when fitting the earlier-type rods (see **Section 8:10**), then reconnect the radius rods to the suspension unit. Later type radius rods have two metal caps as well as the rubber dust excluder.

Locate the stud in the hole in the boss at the base of the suspension unit and refit the castellated nut, tightening it to a torque of 20 to 25 lb ft and secure it with a new splitpin.

See **Section 8:7** and refit the anti-roll bar U-bolts, ensuring that the bolts engage in the notches machined in the anti-roll bar. Refit the U-bolt locking plates and

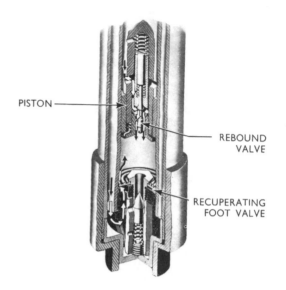

PISTON

REBOUND VALVE

RECUPERATING FOOT VALVE

FIG 8:7 Suspension unit operation (rebound)

TOOL No. A/E 5310

FIG 8:8 Coil spring clips

retaining nuts. Tighten the four U-bolt nuts evenly on each attachment mounting foot to a torque of 15 to 18 lb ft then turn over the tabs of each locking plate to prevent the nuts working loose.

Locate a plain conical washer, a lipped conical washer (lip uppermost) and the rubber dust excluder on the track rod end ball stud. Connect the ball joint stud to the steering arm and tighten the ball stud nut securely, locking it with a splitpin (see **FIG 8:12**).

Bolt the brake plate to the suspension unit, using the four brake plate bolts and self-locking nuts, tightening them evenly to a torque of 15 to 18 lb ft.

Replace the inner bearing spacer, wheel and brake drum on the stub axle, packing the hub bearings with wheel bearing grease, as described in **Section 8:3**.

Adjust the wheel bearings, then refit the grease cap and hub cap. Remove the jack. Remove the spring clips when the weight of the vehicle is taken up on the springs.

On later-type units, top up the suspension unit, filling it to the level of the filler plug hole, as described in **Section 8:5**.

8:7 The anti-roll bar, removal and replacement

The anti-roll bar is connected to the outer ends of the radius rods and is secured at the front by rubber bushed mountings beneath the body sidemembers.

The front mountings of the anti-roll bar consist of U-bolts which engage in slots in the bar and pass through the attachment mounting feet to ensure positive location of the suspension units.

Incorrect fitting of the U-bolts in the slots will affect the castor angle (see the next Section).

(a) Removal:

1 Fit spring clips (see previous Section) on each coil spring and jack-up the vehicle as high as possible without allowing the wheels to come clear of the ground.
2 Remove the anti-roll bar U-bolts (see **FIG 8:11**) by straightening the tabs of the lock plates and removing the four nuts from each U-bolt attachment mounting foot. Slacken the nuts evenly to prevent distortion of the U-bolts.
3 Remove the splitpin and castellated nut from each end of the anti-roll bar and withdraw the washer and the outer flanged rubber bush. Pull the anti-roll bar forward out of the radius rods and slide the second flanged rubber bush from the anti-roll bar. Remove the anti-roll bar.
4 The attachment mounting feet are secured in the mounting brackets on steel-lined rubber bushes by bolts (see **FIG 8:11**).

It is possible to renew an attachment mounting foot with the anti-roll bar in position, though it will be necessary to turn the mounting through 90 deg. to clear the anti-roll bar.

As previously described, fit clips to the coil springs and jack-up the vehicle then remove the U-bolts.

Unscrew the nut on the bolt 'A', withdraw the bolt and pull the attachment mounting foot from the bracket.

Note that two flanged conical rubber bushes are used for mounting purposes at this point, these bushes being steel-lined.

Inspect and renew the bushes if necessary.

(b) Replacement

Fit the conical rubber bushes one at each side of the mounting foot bore, with the flanges outermost (see **FIG 8:12**). Locate the assembly between the mounting brackets, using soapy water as a lubricant. Insert the bolt 'A' through the bracket and the steel liners of the bushes, refit the nut, but do not fully tighten it at this stage. Place a rubber bush on each end of the anti-roll bar with the flanged ends of the bushes against the shoulders of the bar.

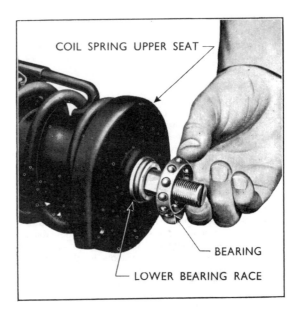

FIG 8:9 Fitting lower bearing and race

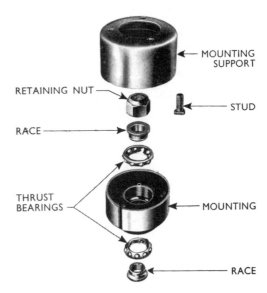

FIG 8:10 Upper mounting assembly

Re-insert the anti-roll bar through each radius rod. Reassemble another rubber bush to each end of the bar with its flanges to the rear.

Replace the washer and castellated nut on each end of the bar, tightening the nuts to a torque of 50 to 60 lb ft. Lock the nuts with a new splitpin in each. Refit the U-bolts in the notches machined in the bar. Position the locking plates over the threaded end of the U-bolts and replace the nuts, tightening them to a torque of 15 to 18 lb ft. Bend over the tabs of the locking plates to prevent the nuts loosening in service. Lower the vehicle to the ground, and remove the spring clips from the coil springs.

Tighten the attachment mounting foot bolt 'A' nut to a torque of 15 to 18 lb ft.

8:8 Wheel alignment

Correct wheel alignment is vital to accurate steering and even tyre wear. The following measurements should be checked after first ensuring that the vehicle is unladen and standing on a level surface and that the tyres are correctly inflated. Modern equipment at a service station will provide precise calculation but the home mechanic can carry out his own check particularly as the inclination figures are set during manufacture and are not subject to adjustment. Any variation found will therefore indicate damage, to or looseness in, the parts concerned.

A suitable gauge may be made up from a piece of wood about 6 inches wide and of sufficient length to enable it, when acting as a straightedge, to contact both upper and lower wheel rims. A cut-out to allow for the hub cap should be made and then with a plumb line mark a central vertical line on the gauge and segments radiating in degrees from the top.

When the gauge is positioned either against the road wheel for camber or against the suspension leg for castor, the inclination in the plumb line will indicate visually any escessive deviation from the correct angles.

(a) The castor angle:

This is the angle at which the kingpin (front suspension leg) is tilted from the vertical when viewed from the side of the vehicle and should be between 1 and 3 deg.

If the angle is incorrect, check that the anti-roll bar U-bolts are engaging in their slots in the anti-roll bar and that the securing nuts are tight. Also check that the anti-roll bar attachment foot nuts are tight and that the rubber bushes are not worn (see **FIG 8:11**).

(b) The camber angle:

This is the angle at which the road wheel is tilted from the vertical when viewed from the front of the vehicle and should be between 0° 30' and 2° 15'.

In the design of this steering and suspension layout, the kingpin inclination angle is closely allied to the camber angle as the stub axle is connected to the foot of the suspension unit. If the camber angle therefore is incorrect the stub axle should be checked for distortion, also the radius rod and its mounting bushes and stud for distortion or wear (see **FIG 8:14**).

8:9 Adjusting the steering lock

The steering stops consist of a bolt and locknut, passing through a bracket on each body front sidemember (see **FIG 8:2**).

1 To check the adjustment, raise the vehicle and turn the steering to maximum lock on either side. The lock should be limited by the idler arm or drop arm contacting their respective stop bolts but if this is not the case then loosen both locknuts and screw the bolts fully in.

2 Turn the steering to full lock, gently, when the steering box rocker arm will be limiting the lock by contact with

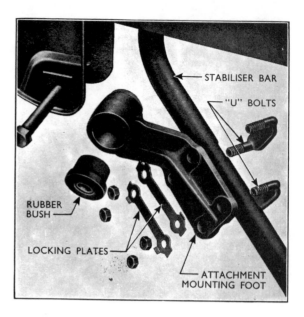

FIG 8:11   Anti-roll bar attachments

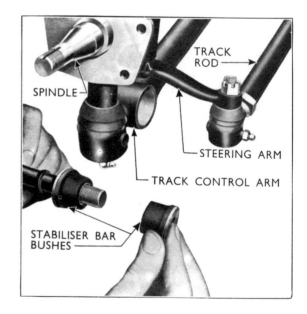

FIG 8:12   Fitting the anti-roll bar

Key to Fig 8:12   For 'spindle' in illustration read 'stub axle' in text. For 'stabiliser bar bushes' in illustration read 'anti-roll bar bushes' in text. For 'track control arm' in illustration read 'radius rod' in text

the internal wall of the steering box. Now screw out the stop bolt until it just contacts the drop arm.

Repeat the operation with opposite lock and screw out the stop bolt until it just contacts the idler arm.

3 Turn the steering to the straight-ahead position and screw out each stop bolt a further $\frac{3}{16}$ or $\frac{1}{4}$ inch. Tighten the locknuts.

8:10 The radius rods

The radius rods connect the lower ends of each suspension unit to the front suspension crossmember (see **FIG 8:2**. The inner end of each rod is rubber bushed and the outer end is secured to the base of the suspension unit by the radius rod ball joint stud passing through its location adjacent to the brake plate support. The ends of the anti-roll bar are held in the outer ends of the radius rods.

On early production vehicles, a single radius rod ball stud cap was fitted. From approximate engine number 100E.56123, two caps were fitted to each stud, the movement of the lower cap being restricted by a machined step on the ball joint. The drilled hole in the outer end was also increased from $\frac{13}{16}$ to $\frac{29}{32}$ inch diameter thus increasing the angular movement by 5 deg.

From approximate engine number 100E.320894, the earlier tubular type radius rods were superseded by rods of forged section, Part Nos. 100E.3078C (righthand) and 1000E.3079B (lefthand).

These assemblies are interchangeable with the previous design, the righthand and lefthand designation being due to the location of the lubricator on the ball joint housing pointing towards the front of the vehicle.

(a) To remove:

The method to be adopted when removing a radius rod will depend on whether further work is to be carried out on the front suspension system.

1 Remove either the front suspension unit (see **Section 8:6**) or the anti-roll bar (see **Section 8:7**).

2 If the anti-roll bar has been removed, withdraw the splitpin and unscrew the castellated nut behind the brake plate, securing the radius rod ball joint stud. Tap down the stud with a copper drift to release the taper (see **FIG 8:13**).

3 If the suspension unit has been removed, withdraw the splitpin and unscrew the castellated nut at the end of the anti-roll bar. Withdraw the washer and the rear conical bush.

4 Unscrew the self-locking nut and remove the bolt securing the radius rod to the front suspension crossmember. Withdraw the radius rod together with its bushes.

5 Inspect the rod and the rubber bushes and renew as necessary if wear or distortion has taken place.

(b) To replace:

1 If the suspension unit has been removed, first refit the radius rod to the anti-roll and crossmember (see operations 3 and 4, also **FIGS 8:13** and **8:11**). Then replace the unit as described in **Section 8:6**.

2 If the anti-roll bar has been removed, fit the track control arm to the crossmember and unit (see operations 3 and 4). Check to see that there are one or, on later

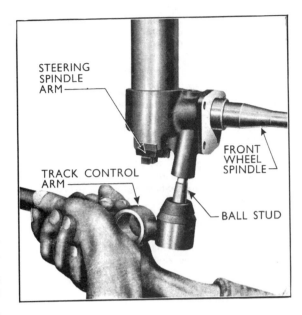

FIG 8:13 Fitting or removing radius rod to suspension unit

Key to Fig 8:13 For 'track control arm' in illustration read 'radius rod' in text. For 'front wheel spindle' in illustration read 'stub axle' in text

FIG 8:14 Fitting inner radius rod bushes

Key to Fig 8:14 For 'track control arm' in illustration read 'radius rod' in text models, two metal caps and a rubber dust excluder positioned on the radius rod ball joint stud before locating the stud in the boss in the base of the suspension unit. Refit the castellated nut, tightening it to a torque of 20 to 25 lb ft and securing it with a new splitpin.

Refit the anti-roll bar as described in **Section 8:7.**

3 Replace the two conical rubber bushes, flanges outwards, to the inner end of the radius rod (see **FIG 8:14**). Each rubber bush is fitted with a steel liner.

4 Push the end of the radius rod into the front suspension crossmember, lining up the holes in the bushes with the bolt hole in the crossmember. Applying soapy water to the bushes will assist in this operation.

Insert the retaining bolt and tighten the self-locking nut securely.

5 Check that the anti-roll bar castellated nuts are tightened to a torque of 50 to 60 lb ft and secured with new splitpins.

6 Also check that the anti-roll bar U-bolts are tightened and locked with the locking plates.

8:11 Fault diagnosis

(a) Wheel wobble

1 Worn hub bearings
2 Broken or weak front coil springs
3 Unevenly worn tyres
4 Worn suspension linkage
5 Loose wheel nuts

(b) 'Bottoming' of suspension

1 Check 2 in (a)
2 Lack of fluid in suspension unit
3 Failure of internal components of suspension leg

(c) Heavy steering

1 Neglected lubrication
2 Incorrect suspension inclination angles

(d) Excessive tyre wear

1 Check 4 in (a), 2 and 3 in (b) and 2 in (c)

(e) Rattle

1 Check 2 in (a)
2 Upper suspension unit mounting stud nuts loose
3 Anti-roll bar mountings loose or rubber bushes worn

(f) Excessive rolling

1 Check 2 in (a) and 3 in (b)
2 Anti-roll bar broken, mountings loose or rubber bushes worn

CHAPTER 9

THE STEERING GEAR

9:1 Description

The steering gear (see **FIG 9 : 1**) is of the worm and ball peg type. The worm is an integral part of the steering shaft and is carried on ballbearings at each end. The upper end of the steering shaft is supported by a felt bush located in the steering column, below the steering wheel.

Adjustment for steering shaft end float is effected by reducing the number of shims between the steering box and end plate.

The ball peg, which engages in the worm, fits into the upper end of the rocker shaft and is secured by a lockwasher and circlip. Ballbearings in the top of the rocker shaft permit the ball peg to rotate.

To eliminate rocker shaft end float, an adjuster screw and thrust button are located in the housing cover.

The lower end of the rocker shaft is splined and carries the steering drop arm which is secured in position by means of a spring washer and nut.

The steering shaft is hollow to permit the direction indicator and horn switch wires to pass down the column. The stator tube which carries these wires is secured by a clamp bracket, located by one of the end plate bolts.

On earlier model Prefect cars, a steering wheel shroud, secured to the instrument panel housing by two countersunk knurled nuts, was fitted.

Later de luxe vehicles have a two-piece shroud secured by four cross-headed screws, or a one-piece shroud secured to the underside of the instrument panel by a clamp and two bolts.

9:2 Maintenance and adjustment
(without removal of steering box from vehicle)

(a) Lubrication:

The only lubrication required is to keep the steering box filled to the level of the filler plug and occasionally apply a little thin oil to the steering shaft upper (felt) bush.

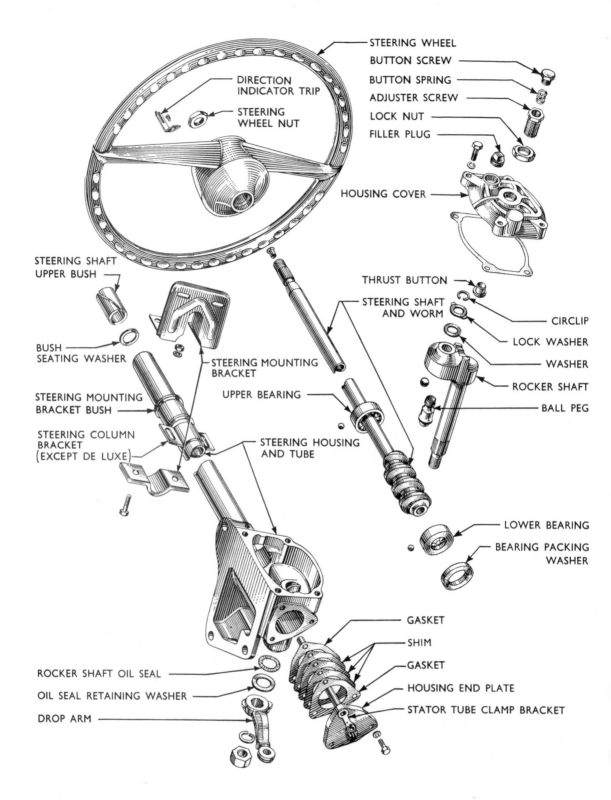

FIG 9:1 Exploded view of the steering gear

Labels (clockwise from top):

- STEERING WHEEL
- BUTTON SCREW
- BUTTON SPRING
- ADJUSTER SCREW
- LOCK NUT
- FILLER PLUG
- HOUSING COVER
- DIRECTION INDICATOR TRIP
- STEERING WHEEL NUT
- THRUST BUTTON
- CIRCLIP
- LOCK WASHER
- WASHER
- ROCKER SHAFT
- BALL PEG
- STEERING SHAFT AND WORM
- STEERING SHAFT UPPER BUSH
- BUSH SEATING WASHER
- STEERING MOUNTING BRACKET
- STEERING MOUNTING BRACKET BUSH
- UPPER BEARING
- STEERING COLUMN BRACKET (EXCEPT DE LUXE)
- STEERING HOUSING AND TUBE
- LOWER BEARING
- BEARING PACKING WASHER
- GASKET
- SHIM
- GASKET
- HOUSING END PLATE
- STATOR TUBE CLAMP BRACKET
- ROCKER SHAFT OIL SEAL
- OIL SEAL RETAINING WASHER
- DROP ARM

Regular application of the grease gun to the linkage nipples shown in **FIG 8 : 2** is also of great importance.

(b) Adjusting rocker shaft end float:

1 Check that the steering shaft cannot be moved up and down as such movement will indicate the need for steering shaft end float adjustment (see the next **Section (c)**). Assuming the steering shaft end float adjustment is correct then:

2 Disconnect the drop arm to idler arm rod at the drop arm, (see **FIG 9 : 13**), using a suitable forked tool Bring the steering gear to the straight-ahead position. Remove the button screw from the steering gear housing cover (see **FIG 9 : 2**). It is important that the button and spring are removed from the adjuster screw before commencing the adjustment.

3 Slacken the adjuster screw locknut and turn the adjuster screw in or out, until a light resistance can be felt at the straight-ahead position as the steering wheel is rotated from lock to lock (see **FIG 9 : 3**). This will ensure that the ball peg is in contact with the high point on the rocker shaft thrust face in the straight-ahead position. Take care not to overtighten the adjuster screw, otherwise the ball peg will bind on the high point of the thrust face.

4 Lock the adjuster screw in this position by tightening the locknut and bending over the flange of the lock-washer if one is fitted. When the adjustment is correct, refit the button spring and screw, tightening the screw securely. Reconnect the idler arm rod to the drop arm. Top up the steering gear with the correct grade of oil, if necessary, see **Section 9 : 4**.

(c) Adjusting steering shaft end float:

This is carried out by removal of shims which are fitted between the steering box and the end plate (see **FIG 9 : 1**).

1 Loosen the stator tube clamp bracket on the steering box end plate (see **FIG 9 : 4**).

2 Remove the drop arm with a puller similar to the one shown in **FIG 9 : 5**.

3 Unscrew the four bolts securing the steering housing top cover and remove the cover and rocker shaft adjuster screw assembly; tap the lower end of the rocker shaft upwards, which will lift the ball peg clear of the worm. Now place a receptacle beneath the steering gear to collect the oil, and unscrew the three bolts securing the steering box end plate to the housing. Carefully detach the end plate and shims, holding the worm lower bearing up to prevent the balls falling out.

A thick packing washer is fitted beneath the lower bearing, between the end plate shims and the bearing cup. This washer must not be lost.

4 Remove only one shim at a time, cutting it with a pair of scissors to allow it to pass over the indicator wires. Each shim is .004 to .005 inch thick (see **FIG 9 : 6**).

To check the adjustment, replace the steering box end plate and tighten the three screws securely. **The three screws used to secure the end plate are not of equal length, the shortest bolt must be used in the top hole (nearest the oil filler plug). If one of the longer bolts is used in this location, the bolt may foul the rocker shaft and prevent full lock from being obtained.** Check for end float at the steering wheel. If all end float has now

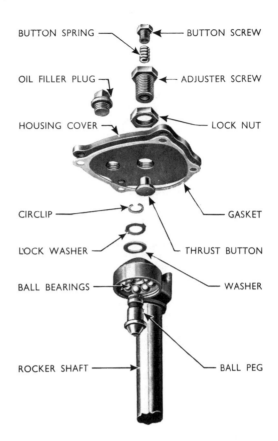

FIG 9 : 2 Steering rocker shaft and cover assembly

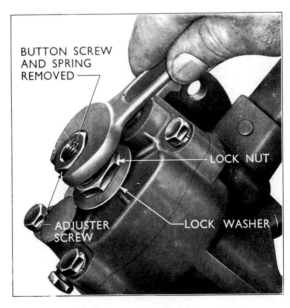

FIG 9 : 3 Adjusting rocker shaft end float

been removed and there is no tendency for the steering shaft to bind, press the rocker shaft down to engage fully in the worm and refit the housing cover and gasket with the adjuster screw fully unscrewed. Tighten the four bolts securely with a lockwasher under the head of each.

5 Refit the drop arm, ensuring that the master splines, which indicate the correct fitting position, engage.

6 Check that the indicator switch is correctly aligned and tighten the stator tube clamp bracket securely. Also check that the indicators cancel correctly. Adjust the rocker shaft end float as previously described and refill the box with oil.

9:3 Removal of steering gear from the vehicle

1 Disconnect the battery as a safety measure, and disconnect the horn and direction indicator wires at their junctions in the engine compartment (see wiring diagrams in **Appendix 2**). Slacken off the stator tube clamp at the steering gear end plate (see **FIG 9:4**) and provide a receptacle to catch any oil drainage. Ease the horn and indicator switch assembly from the steering wheel hub by pushing the stator tube up into the steering gear housing and withdraw the assembly, including the stator tube and wires, from the steering column.

2 Unscrew the steering wheel nut and with a puller similar to the one shown in **FIG 9:7**, withdraw the steering wheel from the shaft splines.

3 Unscrew the two countersunk screws securing the instrument panel and lower housing on the early standard Anglia and the instrument panel and shroud on the earlier Prefect. Suitably support the instrument panel to avoid straining the wiring connections. On early de luxe vehicles the shroud is secured by four screws. On later models, unfasten the wire clip located at the inside top of the shroud, and lift off. Remove the clamp from the steering column mounting bracket. This is retained in position by two bolts, lockwashers and nuts (see **FIG 9:8**).

4 Lift up the floor mat and slacken off the self-tapping screws securing the weatherpad retaining plate to the floor. Remove the weatherpad. Jack-up the front end of the car and fit stands at each side of the vehicle. Disconnect the drop arm to idler arm rod. Unscrew the three self-locking nuts securing the steering gear housing to the frame (see **FIG 9:4**).

The steering gear can now be withdrawn downwards and removed from the car.

9:4 Dismantling the steering gear

1 Drain the oil from the box and remove the drop arm (see **FIG 9:5**).

Unscrew the four housing cover bolts, detach the cover and gasket and push the rocker shaft out of the steering box. Unscrew the adjuster screw and locknut from the housing and extract the thrust button. Remove the button screw and spring from the adjuster screw. Dismantle the rocker shaft assembly by detaching the circlip on the end of the ball peg, remove the lockwasher and flat washer and extract the ball peg complete with eight ballbearings (see **FIG 9:9**).

FIG 9:4   Stator tube exit clamp

FIG 9:5   Removing the drop arm

2 See **FIG 9:1** and remove the steering shaft end plate, together with the oil retaining tube, gaskets and shims, after unscrewing the three securing bolts.

3 Remove the steering shaft by pushing it gently towards the lower end of the steering gear housing. The lower bearing cup, ballbearings and packing washer will thus be pushed from the steering gear housing. Prise out the upper bearing cup with a suitable thin tool after removing the shaft. Each bearing assembly

consists of fourteen ballbearings and care should be taken that none of these is lost (see **FIGS 9:10** and **9:11**).

4 The felt bush in the top of the steering shaft can now be removed. This bush is located in position by a seating washer, which should not be removed. If this washer moves in its locating counterbore, care should be taken to ensure that it is replaced squarely.

5 Remove the rocker shaft seal by prising out the retaining washer and the seal (see **FIG 9:12**).

Careful attention must be given to the date of manufacture of the steering box when replacing the oil seal as the following part modifications have been made during vehicle production.

A synthetic rubber square-sectioned rocker shaft oil seal with a tapered bore was introduced in November 1955, instead of the O-sectioned oil seal previously fitted. These seals are directly interchangeable, and the later type should be fitted with the smaller inside diameter towards the steering box to produce a lip seal action. With the introduction of a modified steering box in January 1956 a U-section type oil seal is fitted. This is a spring-loaded type and the open side of the 'U' should face inwards. This type of box should be filled with SAE.90.EP oil.

On earlier boxes, no identification paint spot on the top cover indicates that the steering box is filled with an SAE.90.EP oil, and fitted with the early type O-sectioned oil seal.

A yellow paint spot on the top cover denotes that the steering box is filled with an SAE.140.EP oil, and fitted with the early type O-sectioned oil seal.

A white paint spot on the top cover denotes that the steering box is filled with an SAE.140.EP oil, and fitted with the later type square-sectioned oil seal.

After January 1956, the steering gear housing and tube assembly was redesigned to accommodate a longer steering gear rocker shaft.

The rocker shaft is supported in a replaceable bush at the end adjacent to the steering gear drop arm.

On later models a redesigned drop arm is used, which is straight as opposed to the slight crank which was provided in the drop arms used with the earlier steering gear.

The later steering gear is directly interchangeable with the earlier type used prior to January 1956, and is readily identified by the straight drop arm, and elongated rocker shaft housing.

9:5 Reassembly

1 Inspect all components for wear and damage and renew as required. Replace the rocker shaft oil seal after reference to the previous Section.

2 Fit a felt bush so that it abuts the seating washer (see **FIG 9:1**) in the top of the steering shaft, soaking the bush in hot heavy grease before assembly.

Insert the upper bearing cup in the housing and replace the fourteen $\frac{7}{32}$ inch diameter ballbearings, retaining them in position in the cup with a smear of grease.

Enter the steering shaft through the housing into the steering column. Refit the lower bearing cup, together with the fourteen $\frac{7}{32}$ inch diameter ballbearings, also retaining them in position with a smear of grease. Replace the thick bearing packing washer.

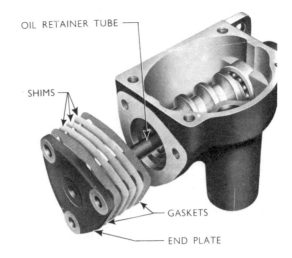

OIL RETAINER TUBE

SHIMS

GASKETS

END PLATE

FIG 9:6 Steering box end plate shims

TOOL No. AT2/CDEVY-3600-A

FIG 9:7 Removing the steering wheel

3 Adjust the steering shaft end float as described in **Section 9:2**. Use new gaskets when reassembling the end plate, and when the adjustment is correct, tighten the three end plate bolts securely, ensuring that a lockwasher is under the head of each. Remember that the stator tube clamp bracket also locates under the head of one of these bolts.

4 Assemble and replace the rocker shaft by first checking the ball peg bearing locations for pitting and position eight $\frac{3}{8}$ inch diameter balls in the cup, holding them in place with the ball peg.

Turn the rocker shaft over and fit the flat washer, lockwasher and circlip whilst retaining the ball peg in position in **FIG 9:9**. The tabs of the lockwasher should point away from the rocker shaft.

5 Refit the housing cover plate, using a new gasket, and tighten the four securing bolts evenly and securely, using a spring washer under the head of each.

Replace the adjuster screw, locknut and thrust button in the housing cover plate. Do not fit the button screw and spring at this stage. Fit the drop arm on the rocker shaft splines, ensuring that the master splines are engaged and that with the steering gear in the straight-ahead position the drop arm is in-line with the steering shaft. Replace the lockwasher and nut, tightening it securely. Temporarily fit the steering wheel and adjust the end float of the rocker shaft as described in **Section 9:2**. It is important that the button screw and spring have been removed from the adjuster screw before commencing this adjustment. When the adjustment is correct, refit the spring and button screw and tighten them down fully.

9:6 Refitting to vehicle

1 Pass the steering column up through the hole in the car floor. Attach the steering box to the frame by means of the three bolts and self-locking nuts. Use new self-locking nuts but do not tighten them fully at this stage. Replace the rubber weatherpad and tighten down the self-tapping screws securing the retaining plate.

2 Replace the rubber mounting bush on the steering column. Refit the clamp to the mounting bracket.

Refit the instrument panel and lower housing (or shroud, whichever is applicable) to the steering column on early vehicles.

On later vehicles, lower the shroud into position and tighten the wire clip located at the inside top of the shroud.

3 Replace the steering wheel by turning the front wheels to the straight-ahead position, i.e. with the drop arm pointing downwards and in-line with the steering column, and locate the steering wheel on the steering shaft splines so that the spokes are horizontal. (Very slight resistance can be felt at the straight-ahead position when the steering wheel is rotated from lock to lock).

Replace the steering wheel nut and tighten it securely. Pass the horn and stator tube assembly down the centre of the steering shaft, fitting the anti-rattle bush around the stator tube at the top. Ensure that the direction indicator trip lever engages in the notch in the indicator body, and press the assembly fully into the steering wheel hub. Secure the lower end of the stator tube in its clamp at the steering box end plate.

Check that the indicator switch lever is in the central position and vertical, then tighten this clamp.

Reconnect the indicator and horn switch wires, then the battery and check that the direction indicator switch and horn function satisfactorily.

4 Tighten the self-locking nuts on the steering gear housing securing bolts. Reconnect the drop arm to idler arm rod, to the drop arm, securing it with a castellated nut and new splitpin.

Check the oil level in the steering box and top up if necessary and ensure that the steering gear moves

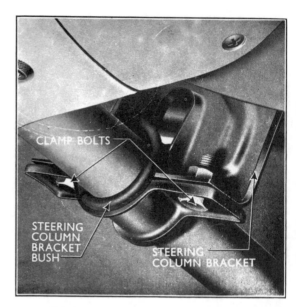

FIG 9:8 Steering column support bracket

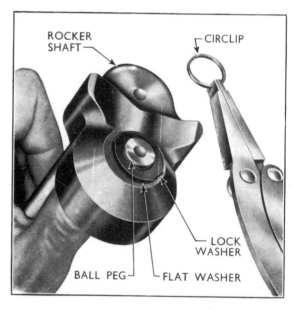

FIG 9:9 Dismantling rocker shaft assembly

freely from lock to lock. Replace the floor mat. Remove the stands and jack and lower the car to the ground.

9:7 The idler

Removal of the idler arm support bracket and stud (see **FIG 9:13**) is carried out by withdrawing the splitpin and unscrewing the castellated nut and separating the idler arm from the drop arm rod at the ball joint. Remove the two bolts and self-locking nuts which locate the idler arm bracket to the body sidemember, and lift away the bracket and stud assembly. Separate the idler arm from the stud assembly after removing the splitpin and castellated nut.

Replacement :

1 On early vehicles the idler arm stud and bush were serviced as a complete assembly. The stud and bush are now serviced separately, and to ensure that when assembled they are correctly located on later vehicles a tab washer is fitted under the idler arm stud to idler arm retaining nut.

To accommodate this tab washer the stud has been lengthened to approximately $2\frac{9}{16}$ inch. In addition a new idler arm with thicker bosses is now used to replace the original idler arm.

When fitting a tab washer, a new stud and bush assembly or a new idler arm, the following sequence of operations must be observed.

2 Check that the bush is a good fit on the stud, renewing the stud and bush assembly if wear has occurred. Screw the stud clockwise into the bush until tight, and then screw back one full turn. Ensure that this setting is not altered. Secure the idler arm bracket to the body sidemember, using two bolts and self-locking nuts. Fit a rubber dust seal to the stud and with the steering in the straight-ahead position fit the idler arm to the stud. Loosely fit a tab washer and castellated nut to the stud. Turn the tab washer until the two longest and most widely spaced tabs lie on either side of the idler arm. Bend these down to grip the idler arm.

3 Tighten the nut securely. Check that the distance between the lower face of the idler arm and the upper face of the steering drop arm to idler arm rod is approx. $\frac{35}{64}$ inch. This dimension should also exist between the upper face of the other end of the idler arm and the lower face of the idler arm support bracket. Splitpin the nut and turn up one of the two remaining tabs of the tab washer against a flat of the nut to prevent the stud and nut assembly from rotating. Attach the other end of the idler arm to the drop arm to idler arm rod, ensuring that a rubber dust cap is fitted over the idler arm to drop arm rod ball joint stud. Secure the idler arm with a castellated nut and splitpin.

4 Remember that the idler has a lubrication point, as shown in **FIG 8 : 2.**

9 : 8 Steering joints and track rods

(a) Removal :

1 The ball joints at the ends of each track rod should be removed with care. After first removing the splitpin and castellated nut the ball joint taper should be removed from its location by one of two methods, either :

(i) by use of a suitable forked tool of wedged section or

(ii) by the application of sharp blows to the outside of the eye in which the taper fits. Adequate support must be given during either removal process to the steering or idler arms in which the ball joint tapers locate.

FIG 9 :10 Steering shaft bearings (lower)

FIG 9 :11 Steering shaft bearings (upper)

(b) Replacing :

1 Place the inner and outer caps over the track rod inner ball joint stud; the inner cap has a larger internal diameter. Place the rubber dust cap over the stud and pass the stud through the drop arm to idler arm rod, engaging the tapers. Secure the stud with a castellated nut and splitpin.

2 Fit the inner and outer caps, together with the rubber dust cap to the track rod outer ball joint stud, then pass the stud through the steering arm, securing it with a castellated nut and splitpin. Ensure that the wheels are in the straight-ahead position, and that each track rod end ball joint is in the middle of its 'throw' before locking and both joints are in the same plane. Always tighten the clamps in the pendant position with the slots in the clamps in-line with the slots in the track rod and the clamp bolts located beneath the track rods, both to avoid any possibility of fouling adjacent parts and for ease of assembly.

Two methods of tightening the track rod ends have been used. On earlier models, the ends were retained in position by a locknut abutting the end of the trackrod tube.

On later models, a slot and clamp are included at each end of the track rod (see **FIG 9:13**).

The track will of course need adjusting once the track rods and ends have been dismantled, and this operation is fully described in the next Section.

9:9 Adjusting the track

The distance measured between the insides of both front road wheel rims should be between $\frac{1}{16}$ and $\frac{1}{8}$ inch less when measured at the forward edge than when measured between the wheels at the rear edges. This is known as the toe-in and is essential to even tyre wear and accurate steering.

The toe-in can be quite accurately measured by the use of a length of steel tubing, cranked to clear the sump, and having one fixed end and the other end incorporating a setscrew and locknut.

Carry out the following sequence of operations:

1 Check each front road wheel for runout of the rim and position the wheel with maximum runout at the top. Ensure the wheels are in the straight-ahead position and that the vehicle is standing on level ground.
2 Make a chalk mark on the front side wall of each tyre level with the hub retaining nut.
3 Slacken the locknut or clamp (dependent on type, see **FIG 9:13**) at the end of each trackrod and ensure that each rod and its ball joints are of equal length to the other.
4 Place the measuring tool between the front inside wheel rims at the height of the chalk mark and turn the setscrew until the width is accurately set on the tool. Remove the tool carefully so not to alter the setting.
5 Roll the vehicle backwards until the chalk mark on the tyre now appears level with the hub retaining nut but on the rear side wall.

Place the measuring tool between the rear inside wheel rims again at the height of the chalk mark and the distance should now be between $\frac{1}{16}$ and $\frac{1}{8}$ inch **greater** than that to which the tool is set.

Should the desired toe-in not be apparent then rotate each track rod equally (turning the track rod so that the top moves to the rear, decreases the toe-in, turning so that the top moves forward, increases the toe-in) until the adjustment is correct. Now pull the vehicle forward and repeat the checking procedure.
6 When the toe-in adjustment is correct, tighten the track rod locknuts or clamps securely, first ensuring

FIG 9:12 Rocker shaft oil seal retainer (prior to January 1956)

that the ball joint ends are in the middle of their 'throw' and in the same plane.

9:10 Fault diagnosis

(a) Wheel wobble

1 Unbalanced wheels and tyres
2 Slack steering connections
3 Incorrect steering geometry
4 Excessive play in steering gear
5 Broken or weak front coil springs
6 Worn hub bearings

(b) Wander

1 Check 2, 3 and 4 in (a)
2 Front suspension and rear axle mounting points out of line
3 Uneven tyre pressures
4 Uneven tyre wear
5 Weak dampers or springs

(c) Heavy steering

1 Check 3 in (a)
2 Very low tyre pressures
3 Neglected lubrication
4 Wheels out of track
5 Steering gear maladjusted
6 Steering column bent or misaligned
7 Steering column bushes tight

(d) Lost motion

1 End play in steering column
2 Loose steering wheel, worn splines
3 Worn steering box and idler
4 Worn ball joints
5 Worn suspension system

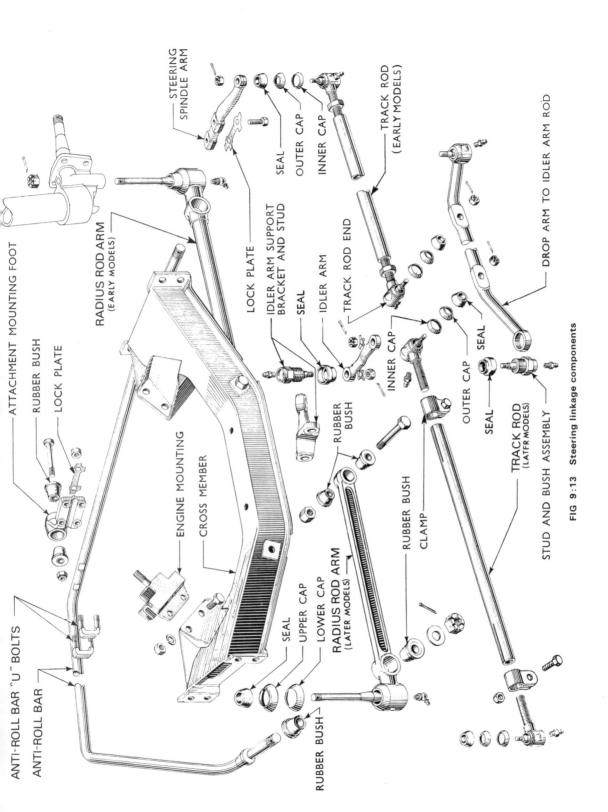

ANTI-ROLL BAR "U" BOLTS

ANTI-ROLL BAR

RUBBER BUSH

ATTACHMENT MOUNTING FOOT

RUBBER BUSH

LOCK PLATE

LOCK PLATE

RADIUS ROD ARM
(EARLY MODELS)

STEERING
SPINDLE ARM

SEAL

OUTER CAP

INNER CAP

TRACK ROD
(EARLY MODELS)

LOCK PLATE

IDLER ARM SUPPORT
BRACKET AND STUD

SEAL

IDLER ARM

TRACK ROD END

DROP ARM TO IDLER ARM ROD

INNER CAP

OUTER CAP

SEAL

SEAL

TRACK ROD
(LATER MODELS)

STUD AND BUSH ASSEMBLY

RUBBER BUSH

ENGINE MOUNTING

CROSS MEMBER

SEAL

UPPER CAP

LOWER CAP

RADIUS ROD ARM
(LATER MODELS)

RUBBER BUSH

CLAMP

RUBBER BUSH

FIG 9:13   Steering linkage components

CHAPTER 10

THE BRAKING SYSTEM

10:1 Description of layout

The brakes are hydraulically operated by means of a pedal beneath the instrument panel, connected to the master cylinder through a short pushrod.

The front brakes are of the two leading shoe type, with an independent cylinder for each shoe; the rear brakes have, for each pair of shoes, a single cylinder which also incorporates a mechanical expander operated by the handbrake.

The mechanical linkage, operated by the handbrake lever, is connected only to the rear wheels. The system is illustrated in **FIG 10:1**.

Two grease nipples are provided on the handbrake cable, for lubrication purposes.

Brakes of two different diameters have been fitted to vehicles in the Anglia and Prefect range.

Prior to January 1955, all vehicles were fitted with 7 inch diameter brake plate assemblies. After this date 8 inch diameter brakes were introduced, and a further change was incorporated during July 1955, when adjustable steady posts were fitted to the front brake plates only.

On later models the use of steady posts was discontinued, each shoe resting against three contact pads formed as part of the brake plate, and is held in contact with these pads by a coil spring. The earlier and later type brake plate assemblies are directly interchangeable but the component parts of each are not interchangeable between the two designs.

Unless reference is made to a particular brake system, the procedures and information contained in this section will apply to brakes of both diameters.

Should the reader wish to convert 7 inch diameter brakes to 8 inch, the procedure is fully described in **Section 10:11**.

The master cylinder is connected to a five-way union to which are connected the stoplight switch and distributing pipelines for both front and rear brakes. A pipe is led to each front brake plate, connection being made by a flexible hose to the upper wheel cylinder on each brake plate. From the rear of the five-way union a single pipe is connected with a flexible hose to a three-way union mounted on the rear axle housing. Pipes run from this union to each rear brake plate wheel cylinder.

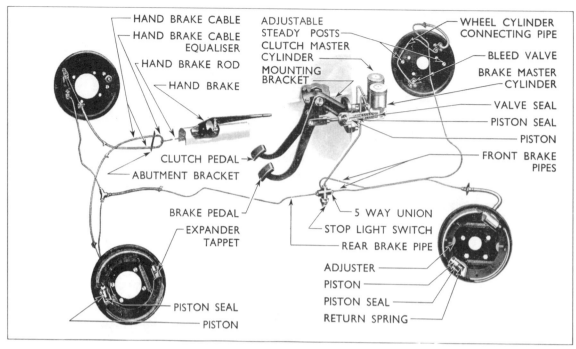

FIG 10:1   The braking system layout (8 inch diameter)

The brake fluid reservoir is part of the master cylinder. The handbrake linkage operates on the rear wheels only.

A rod connects the handbrake lever to the equalizer (see **FIG 10:2**). The cable is free to slide in a slot formed in the equalizer, and the conduits or outer casings abut a bracket welded to the floor pan and the rear spring seats on the rear axle housing. Clevises complete the cable linkage to each operating lever, which is pivoted in the end of its respective wheel cylinder expander housing.

Applying the handbrake lever pulls the equalizer forward, the cable is placed in tension, applying an equal pull to each handbrake operating link, owing to the compensating action of the cable which is free to slide in the equalizer, giving an equal brake action to each rear wheel.

10:2 Routine maintenance and adjustment of shoes

1 Regular inspection of the fluid lines both rigid and flexible, should be carried out to ensure that all unions are tight and that the metal brake pipes have not been damaged by flying stones or careless driving over obstacles nor that the flexible pipes have perished. The latter should be kept clean and free from oil or grease which will otherwise cause rapid deterioration.

The master cylinder reservoir must be checked regularly and the fluid level maintained to the mark indicated on the outside of the reservoir. **It is of the utmost importance that only hydraulic brake fluid of approved type is used in the system.**

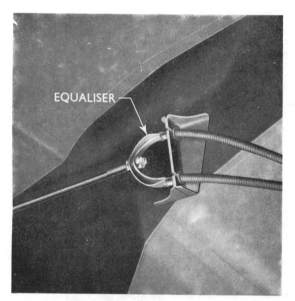

FIG 10:2   The handbrake equalizer

Carry out regular greasing of the handbrake cable nipples and apply a few drops of engine oil periodically to the brake clevises and brake pedal clevis pins. Grease the cable channel in the handbrake equalizer.

2 Brake shoe adjustment

(a) Front brakes:

Adjust each front brake shoe individually, on vehicles fitted with 7 inch diameter brakes there are two hexagonal snail-cam adjusters for each drum (see **FIG 10:3**). Vehicles with 8 inch diameter brakes have two small square-headed adjusters (see **FIG 10:4**).

With both types proceed to adjust by raising the front wheels clear of the ground then:

(i) Turn the adjuster of one shoe anticlockwise to bring the lining away from the drum. Turn the other shoes adjuster clockwise until the drum is locked, and slacken back until the wheel is just sufficiently free to rotate without binding.

(ii) Repeat this procedure on the first shoe, rotating the wheel steadily during the operation.

(iii) Adjust the shoes of the other front wheel in a similar manner.

This adjustment must be performed accurately to obtain minimum clearance between the linings and the drums. This will give minimum pedal clearance and maximum braking efficiency when the brake pedal is operated.

(b) Rear brakes:

On early models, a single square-headed adjuster is provided on each rear brake backplate, as shown in **FIG 10:5** for vehicles fitted with 7 inch diameter brakes, and **FIG 10:6** for those with 8 inch brakes. For both types adjust by first raising the rear wheels clear of the ground then turn the adjuster in a clockwise direction until the shoes bind in the drum, then slacken back until the linings are just free, to obtain minimum running clearance. Repeat the operation on the other brake plate.

On later models, a snail cam adjuster is incorporated on each brake backplate, operating on the leading shoe. Here the procedure for rear brake adjustment is as follows:

1 Raise the rear wheels clear of the ground.

2 Turn the **threaded** square-headed wedge adjuster, (**A**) as shown on **FIG 10:7** (positioned on the brake plate in front of and above the axle housing) clockwise until both shoes are held firmly against the drum.

3 Gently turn the **plain** square-headed snail-cam adjuster 'D' clockwise until the cam 'B' can be felt to touch the leading shoe.

4 Slacken off the wedge adjuster two 'clicks' and then slacken back the snail cam adjuster a fraction of a turn. Repeat on the other brake plate and rotate each wheel in turn when no binding should be evident. If a shoe is binding, the snail cam adjuster should be slackened back just sufficiently to free this shoe. If movement of the snail cam adjuster has no effect on the binding shoe, return the snail cam to its original position and slacken back the wedge adjuster until the shoe is free.

10:3 Removing the master cylinder

At the rear end of the cylinder, a ball-ended pushrod is located in the cupped end of the piston by a retaining washer and circlip (see **FIG 5:4**).

The front end of the piston is counterbored to accommodate the valve stem, and carries the spring retainer. A return spring is fitted under compression

FIG 10:3 Adjusting one shoe of a 7 inch diameter front brake

FIG 10:4 Adjusting one shoe of a 8 inch diameter front brake

between the spring retainer and the valve spacer at the valve head.

The reservoir port drilled at the front of the cylinder chamber allows fluid to flow from the reservoir to this chamber.

In the chamber above and behind the reservoir port, is the pipeline port. The pipeline supplies fluid to front and rear wheel cylinders through the five-way union.

When the brake pedal is in the 'OFF' position, fluid is free to flow from the reservoir and pipeline into the chamber.

On depressing the brake pedal the piston moves forward, advancing the valve which closes the reservoir port, thus preventing the fluid returning to the reservoir from the chamber.

As the piston moves further forward, fluid is forced through the pipeline port developing pressure in the wheel cylinders. When the brake pedal is released the return spring pushes back the piston, reducing the pressure in the chamber, and fluid then returns from the wheel cylinders to the master cylinder by the action of the brake shoe retracting springs releasing the shoes. The valve uncovers the reservoir port and communication between the reservoir and master cylinder chamber is restored.

The rubber boot over the pushrod prevents water and dust entering the cylinder.

Complete instructions for the removal, dismantling, servicing and reassembly of the brake master cylinder are given as for the clutch pedal which is identical in construction and operation (see **Chapter 5, Section 5:3**). When the new master cylinder has been fitted, the brake pedal pushrod must be checked and adjusted in accordance with the instructions given in **Chapter 5, Section 5:2**.

Check the overall length of the pushrod, and if it is $3\frac{3}{16}$ inches, check that the distance between the centre of the clevis eye and the mounting face of the master cylinder is $4\frac{7}{16}$ inches. If the overall length of the pushrod is $3\frac{5}{16}$ inches, check that the distance between the centre of the clevis eye and the mounting face of the master cylinder is $4\frac{9}{16}$ inches. Reset the length of the pushrod if necessary, by adjusting the clevis and locknut to ensure that the exact dimension is maintained.

10:4 Dismantling brakes

Before dismantling either the front or rear brakes make a careful note of the method and points of attachment of the pull-off springs (see **FIGS 10:8, 10:9** and **10:10**) and the positioning of the shoes themselves.

The leading edge of a front brake shoe fitted to the 7 inch diameter brake may be identified by the longer space, approximately $1\frac{1}{2}$ inch between the lining and the end of the brake shoe. Both ends of the brake shoe on this brake system are tapered.

The leading edge of a brake shoe used in the 8 inch brakes can be identified by the tapering shoe web. The trailing edge of this brake shoe is not tapered.

The leading edge of a rear brake shoe may be identified by the longer space, approximately $1\frac{1}{2}$ inch between the lining and the end of the brake shoe.

When removing or replacing brake shoes, do not allow the shoes to come into contact with the wheel cylinder. If the shoe is allowed to hit the cylinder, under the action of the retracting spring, it may damage the cylinder.

Once brake shoes have been removed, it is good practice to wire or fit elastic bands to the wheel cylinders to prevent the pistons dropping out of their bores. **Never touch the brake pedal during these operations.**

Particular care must be given when uncoupling flexible

FIG 10:5 Adjusting both shoes of a 7 inch diameter rear brake

FIG 10:6 Adjusting both shoes of a 8 inch diameter rear brake

brake hoses, never try to release one by turning the ends with a spanner. Always unscrew the metal pipeline union nut from its connection with the hose. Hold the adjacent hexagon on the hose with a spanner and remove the locknut which secures the hose to the bracket. The hose can now be turned without twisting the flexible part by using a spanner on the hexagon at the other end.

(a) Front brakes:

1 Jack-up the vehicle, remove the hub cap, road wheel and grease cap. Withdraw the splitpin from the castellated hub nut and remove the nut, thrust washer and outer bearing, then withdraw the brake drums and hub assembly.

2 **On early vehicles** (see **FIG 10:8**), pull the tapered end of one shoe out of the wheel cylinder piston slot, lift the shoe away from the brake plate and detach the retracting spring. Remove the other shoe and spring in a similar manner.

3 **On later models** it will be necessary to first remove the two shoe retaining springs by rotating the top retaining washer through 90 deg. when it will pass over the spindle, allowing the spring to be lifted off. In this type of brake plate the end of the wheel cylinder piston is not slotted. The brake shoe retracting springs are of equal length and are coloured red in the case of 7 inch brakes and black in the case of 8 inch brakes.

(b) Rear brakes

Jack-up the vehicle, release the handbrake, and unscrew the axle shaft nut.

Remove the axle shaft washer and draw the wheel and hub off the axle shaft by using a hub puller as described fully in **Chapter 7, Section 7:3**. On earlier vehicles, pull the expander end of one brake shoe out of the slot in the expander piston; then disengage the other end from the adjuster tappet slot (see **FIGS 10:9** and **10:10**).

On later vehicles it will be necessary to first remove the two shoe retaining springs by rotating the top retaining washer through 90 deg. when it will pass over the spindle, allowing the spring to be lifted off. In this type of brake plate the end of the wheel cylinder piston is not slotted. Detach the shoes and return springs. The return springs are of unequal length. The spring with two sets of coils (overall free length $4\frac{27}{64}$ inches) is red in colour and fits adjacent to the expander housing. The shorter spring is coloured black and fits adjacent to the adjuster housing. This shorter spring has an overall free length $2\frac{13}{16}$ inches when 7 inch diameter brakes are concerned, and an overall free length of $3\frac{5}{8}$ inches in the case of 8 inch diameter brakes.

10:5 Servicing the wheel cylinders

(a) Front wheel:

Dismantle the brake shoes as described in the previous section then:

1 Disconnect and remove the short pipe at the rear of the brake plate, which connects the two wheel cylinders. Unscrew the two nuts and spring washers or the setscrews securing each cylinder to the brake plate, and detach the cylinders.

2 To dismantle a wheel cylinder, pull off the rubber boot and extract the piston (see **FIG 10:11**). Carefully extract the piston seal, spring seat, and return spring from the cylinder. Unscrew the bleed valve from the lower cylinder and remove the small ball valve. Later vehicles are fitted with the conical type bleed valve, identical to that fitted to the clutch operating cylinder (see **Chapter 5, FIG 5:6**).

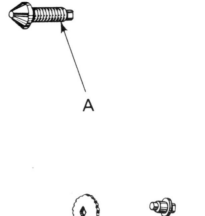

A

B   D

FIG 10:7   Rear brake wedge and snail cam adjusters exploded (late model vehicles)

FIG 10:8   Front brake shoe assembly

Never use mineral oils, or petrol, paraffin, carbon tetrachloride etc, to clean brake components, as they will cause the rubber seals to swell and become ineffective. The slightest trace of mineral oil can soon render the brakes inoperative.

Methylated spirit or brake fluid only must be used for flushing out the system, washing brake housings, components and any container that comes into contact with brake fluid.

If dirt finds its way into the system it may score the pistons or damage the seals and render the brakes either wholly, or partly inoperative.

Pistons and piston seals should be kept away from grease or oil and handled carefully.

The seals should be inspected carefully before fitting, even if they have just been purchased.

See that the sealing lips are perfectly formed, concentric with the bore of the seal, free from knife edges, surface blemishes or marks. Any seal that is not perfect, no matter how small the blemish may appear to be, should not be used.

Seals should not be turned inside out when inspecting them since this strains the surface skin and may eventually lead to failure.

All pistons and housings must be carefully inspected before assembly. Any imperfections or scores on the piston or cylinder bore may provide a track for fluid leaks under pressure and any damaged parts must be discarded. Parts should be handled very carefully to prevent any possibility of accidental scoring.

3 Reassemble the wheel cylinders by locating the return spring on the spring seat and insert them into the cylinder, spring first.

4 Dip the rubber piston seal in brake fluid and carefully insert it to locate over the spring seat, with the lip of the seal facing inwards. Take care not to damage the edges of the seal during insertion. Now refit the piston, sliding it into the cylinder, plain end first. Push the piston to the end of the cylinder to expel the air. The vacuum created by closing the fluid ports should hold down the piston. If it does not, the seal is faulty and should be renewed.

If the piston seal is in good condition, refit the rubber boot to exclude dust.

5 Fit the wheel cylinder in their locating holes in the brake plate, and secure each cylinder with two nuts and spring washers or setscrews. Refit the short connecting pipe between the two wheel cylinders and tighten the unions securely.

Replace the small ball valve and the bleed valve, or the conical type valve in the lower cylinder. **Do not overtighten.**

(b) Rear wheel

Dismantle the brake shoes as described in the previous section then:

1 Remove the adjuster unit which is secured to the brake plate by two self-locking nuts and single coil lock-washers (see **FIG 10 : 1**). Extract the tappets and screw the adjuster wedge out of the housing.

2 Remove the cylinder rubber dust cover, and in the case of 7 inch brakes, the expander housing retainer wire clip (see **FIG 10 : 12**). In the case of 8 inch diameter brakes, remove the expander housing rubber dust cover, the retainer and retainer spring (see **FIG 10 : 13**). Unscrew the bleed valve and remove the small ball valve. Later vehicles are fitted with a conical type bleed valve. The expander housing and handbrake operating link can now be detached from the brake plate slot.

3 To dismantle the expander cylinder remove the expander cylinder rubber boot, and withdraw the piston and seal as an assembly, from the housing. A boot

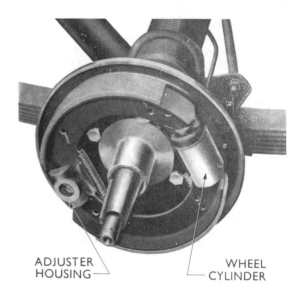

FIG 10:9 Rear brake shoe assembly (7 inch)

FIG 10:10 Rear brake shoe assembly (8 inch)

retainer, as shown in **FIG 10 : 13** is used on 8 inch diameter brakes. Air, from a tyre pump, applied at the housing fluid port, will facilitate removal of the piston and seal.

Components should be washed and inspected prior to reassembly as described for front wheel cylinders.

4 Dip the piston and seal in brake fluid to facilitate assembly in the cylinder. Reassemble the piston seal to the piston with the flat face of the seal adjacent to

the piston rear shoulder. For 7 inch diameter brakes insert the piston and seal in the cylinder, taking care not to damage the seal during insertion. Refit the rubber boot over the slotted end of the piston.

In the case of 8 inch diameter brakes fit the rubber boot to the piston with the flat side of the boot parallel to the deeper slot in the piston end. Dip the piston and seal in brake fluid to facilitate assembly and insert the piston seal in the expander housing, again taking care not to damage the seal during insertion. Locate the rubber boot on the housing and refit the boot retainer.

5 Insert the handbrake operating link and the bleed valve housing projection of the expander housing into the slot in the brake plate. For 7 inch diameter brakes, clip on the expander housing retainer (see **FIG 10:12**) and locate the handbrake operating link pivot pin in the expander housing.

6 For 8 inch diameter brakes, fit the expander housing retainer spring from the handbrake lever end of the housing, with the dimples on the end of the spring away from the back plate (see **FIG 10:14**). Ensure that it engages correctly in the slots formed in the housing. Fit the retainer in the opposite end of the housing, ensuring that the dimples on the spring are locating those formed on the plate (see **FIG 10:14**). On early types of 8 inch brakes the expander retainer spring (without dimples) should be fitted from the handbrake lever end of the housing with the tongues on the end of the spring away from the back plate. The retainer should then be fitted from the opposite end of the housing, ensuring that the tongues on the spring locate behind the end of the retaining plate. Refit the rubber dust cover.

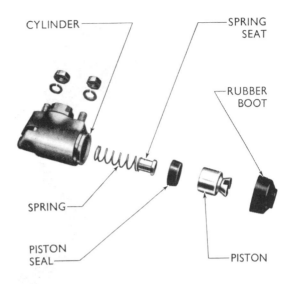

FIG 10:11 Front wheel cylinder components (early models)

10:6 Reassembling the brake shoes

(a) Front:

1 When fitting new shoes, check that the lining ends are slightly chamfered, and locate the hooked end of the return spring in the hole in the brake shoe web (see

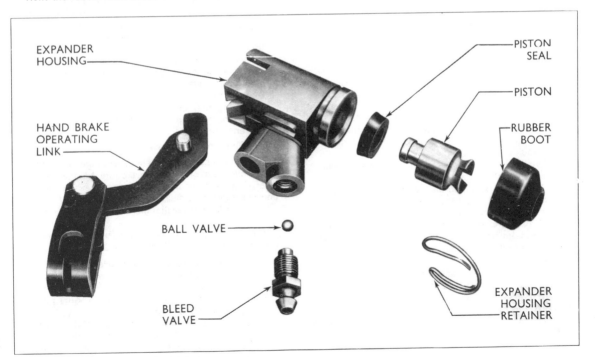

FIG 10:12 Rear wheel cylinder components (7 inch brakes)

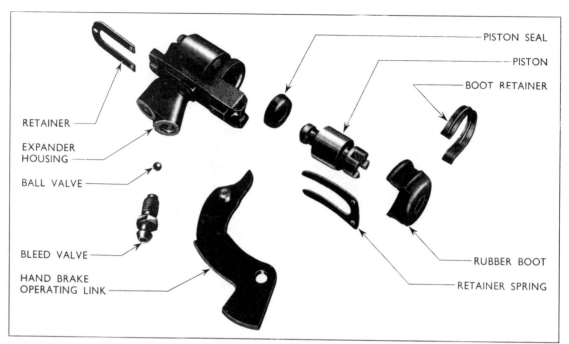

FIG 10:13 Rear wheel cylinder components (8 inch brakes)

FIG 10:8) and the other end in the brake plate hole adjacent to the wheel cylinder.

Check that the felts are in position on the steady posts if this type of fitting is used.

Where adjustable steady posts (see FIG 10:1) are fitted to the brake plates assemblies, the following procedure should be followed after fitting the shoes.

Expand the shoes by the adjuster until they are just on the point of rubbing the drum.

Slacken back the locknut on one of the steady posts and by means of a screwdriver or coin inserted in the slotted end, turn the steady post slowly in a clockwise direction, at the same time moving the brake drum to and fro over a small arc, until a definite drag is felt. Counting the number of turns, unscrew the steady post in an anticlockwise direction until the drum is again felt to be dragging.

Finally, screw in the steady post, half this number of turns, and tighten the locknut.

Repeat this operation on the other steady posts.

Recheck and adjust the brake shoes as necessary.

2 Locate the wider end of the shoe web in the slot at the closed end of the opposite shoe wheel cylinder and pull out the other end of the shoe until the web engages in the piston slot or on the plain face of the wheel cylinder.

Refit the shoe, holding down springs if fitted.

Replace the other shoe in a similar manner.

Refit the brake drum and wheel, outer bearing, thrust washer and bearing adjusting nut.

Adjust the front wheel bearings as described in **Chapter 8, Section 8:2.**

(b) Rear:

1 Reassemble the brake shoes and springs, fitting the

springs exactly as shown either in **FIG 10:9** or **10:10**, according to diameter. Fit the leading edge of one shoe in the expander piston slot if this type is fitted and the other end in the adjuster tappet slot.

2 Pull the other shoe against the action of the return springs and drop the leading edge of this shoe into the adjuster tappet slot and the other end into the expander housing slot.

3 Check the felt fitted to the steady posts and replace the shoe holding down springs if either or both of these components are fitted.

4 Replace the brake drum, thrust washer and shaft nut, tightening fully and fit a new splitpin. Fit the road wheel and hub cap and adjust the brakes as described in **Section 10:2.**

10:7 Bleeding the system

Before commencing operations, examine the vent holes in the fluid reservoir cap and make sure that they are quite clear. Check that the fluid level is up to the indicated mark and that there is no fluid leakage visible at any union or wheel cylinder and see that the flexible hoses are in good order.

Before bleeding, always adjust both front and rear brakes as described in **Section 10:2.**

Always use Ford hydraulic brake fluid.

1 Clean the bleed screws and surrounding areas on each wheel cylinder. Bleed the front brakes first, commencing at the brake having the shorter pipeline. Remove the rubber cap on the bleed valve and fit a rubber tube on the valve. Place the end of the bleed tube in a clean jar containing some brake fluid. Keep the end of the tube under the surface of the fluid during the bleeding operation (see **FIG 10:15**).

2 Open the bleed valve and quickly depress the brake

pedal fully to the floor. After slowly releasing the pedal, pause for an instant before the next depression to ensure full recuperation of the master cylinder. At each stroke of the brake pedal, some fluid or air should come out of the tube. If neither fluid nor air is pumped out, the bleed valve has not been properly opened or there is a blockage in the pipeline.

Continue making full strokes of the brake pedal, until no more air bubbles emerge from the tube.

It is important that the fluid level in the reservoir is maintained during the bleeding operation.

Do not replenish the reservoir with fluid drained from the system as it may be contaminated or aerated. If the fluid in the system is dirty, it is advisable to drain it completely and refill with fresh fluid.

3 When, with each stroke of the brake pedal, fluid without any air bubbles comes out of the bleed tube, close the valve with the pedal released in the 'OFF' position. Do not use excessive force when tightening the valve, otherwise the ball may damage the seating. Remove the tube and refit the rubber cap on the bleed valve.

Repeat the operation on the other front brake and then on the rear brakes, starting with the rear brake which has the shorter pipeline.

If a spongy pedal still exists after bleeding, recheck the front brake shoe adjustment, unequal shoe adjustment in one drum may be mistaken for air in the hydraulic system.

If difficulty is experienced in expelling air from the system, it may help to first expand the rear brake shoes by means of the wedge adjusters and then back-off both shoes in each front brake by means of the snail cam adjusters. Readjust the front and rear brakes after a satisfactory bleed has been obtained.

4 Top up the reservoir to the mark indicated and test the brakes on the road **but use your mirror.**

10:8 Adjusting the handbrake

1 Before commencing the adjustment, check that no sharp bends exist in the handbrake outer cable and that it is secured by clips in the bracket on the floor pan and in the rear spring seats on the axle housing. Check the rubber grommet supporting the lefthand cable where it passes through the web on the rear axle housing and that the rear wheel expander housings slide freely in the brake backplate slots. A faint smear of wheel bearing grease may be applied to the sliding surfaces if necessary.

2 Adjust the rear brakes as described previously in **Section 10:2,** then pull the handbrake lever fully on. If it moves through more than four or five notches on its quadrant in order to lock the rear wheels then adjust the rod (see **FIG 10:2**) by means of the nut and locknut until the desired travel of the handbrake lever is obtained.

10:9 Modifications

1 If the handbrake cable becomes very slack, then vibration may occur at the clevis hole, resulting in the possibility of the cable fraying. To overcome this a bowed spring steel washer, Part No. 118165.ES7, was later fitted between the handbrake operating link, Part No. E5.FB.1, and handbrake clevis, Part No.

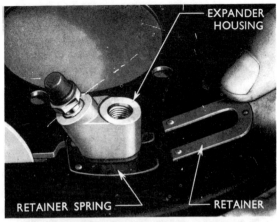

FIG 10:14 Fitting wheel cylinder retainer plates (8 inch)

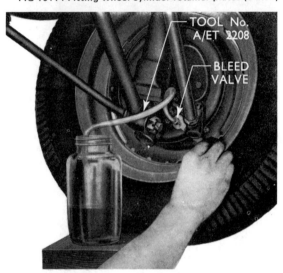

FIG 10:15 Bleeding the brakes

Key to Fig 10:15   A rubber or plastic tube will substitute for tool number shown in illustration

100E.2857, to present the clevis from vibrating. This bowed spring steel washer can be fitted to earlier model cars and one should be fitted to each of the two clevises.

2 **Fitting 8 inch diameter brakes in place of 7 inch diameter brakes.**

Vehicles having 7 inch diameter brakes may be modified so that 8 inch diameter brakes can be fitted. No other work other than assembling the larger brake plate is required when modifying the front brakes.

When modifying rear brakes however, additional work is involved in cutting and welding the spring seats but this can usually be quite easily done if the components are removed and taken to a local engineering shop.

(a) The front brakes:

1 Remove the front wheels, brake drums and hub assemblies, and brake backplate assemblies.

2 Assemble the 8 inch front brake plates as previously described, using the wheel cylinders from the 7 inch brake plate assembly and the new parts shown in the following table.

3 Refit the new brake backplate assemblies, new brake drums and original wheels.

(b) The rear brakes:

1 Detach the rear wheels and remove the rear axle as described in **Chapter 7.**

2 Remove the hubs and brake backplate assemblies.

3 It will be necessary to modify the spring seats on the rear axle housing as under:

(a) Scribe a line transversely on the rear spring seats $1\frac{3}{4}$ inch rearwards from the centre of the spring centre bolt hole (towards the handbrake cable conduit mounting hole).

(b) Cut off the rear section at this point, vertically and at right angles to the spring face of the seat.

4 The new spring seats supplied must also be modified as follows:

Mark off transversely the new spring seats (Part Nos. 100E.5793.C—righthand, and 100E.5794.C—lefthand) $1\frac{3}{4}$ inch rearwards from the centre of the spring centre bolt hole. Cut off the rear sections; these are to be used to replace the portions removed from the spring seats already on the axle housing.

5 Securely weld the portions containing the hole for the rear brake cable conduit, removed from the new spring seats, on to the seats mounted on the axle housing, in the same location as those removed in operation 3.

Ensure that the portion removed from the new lefthand spring seat is welded to the lefthand seat existing on the axle housing. Similarly, the new righthand portion should be welded to the existing righthand seat. Ensure that the portions are squarely located on the spring seats.

The distance between the centres of the spring centre bolt hole and the handbrake cable conduit mounting hole should be $4\frac{1}{8}$ inches.

6 Rebuild the brake plate assemblies, using the adjuster unit removed from the 7 inch diameter brake plate assemblies and the new parts listed below:

FRONT

Current Part No.	Previous Part No.	Description	Quantity
100E.1105.B	100E.1105.A	Hub (front) and brake drum assembly	2
100E.2012.B	100E.2012.A	Plate (front brake) assembly—righthand	1
100E.2013.B	100E.2013.A	Plate (front brake) assembly—lefthand	1
100E.2018.B	100E.2018.A	Shoe (front brake) and lining assembly—righthand	2
100E.2019.B	100E.2019.A	Shoe (front brake) and lining assembly—lefthand	2
100E.2035.B	100E.2035.A	Spring (front brake shoe return)	4
E9.FA.1	E4.FA.1	Pipe (front brake wheel cylinder connecting) assembly	2

REAR

Current Part No.	Previous Part No.	Description	Quantity
100E.1115.C	100E.1115.B	Hub (rear) and brake drum assembly	2
100E.2103.B	100E.2103.A	Lever (rear brake operating)	2
100E.2211.B	100E.2211.A	Plate (rear brake) assembly—righthand	1
100E.2212.B	100E.2212.A	Plate (rear brake) assembly—lefthand	1
100E.2261.C	100E.2261.B	Cylinder (rear brake wheel) assembly	2
100E.2220.B	100E.2220.A	Shoe (rear brake) and lining assembly	4
E14.FB.1	—	Plate (rear brake wheel cylinder retaining spring)	2
E15.FB.1	—	Plate (rear brake wheel cylinder retaining spring)	2
—	E6.FB.1	Circlip (rear wheel cylinder)	2
100E.2267.B	100E.2267.A	Pipe (rear brake wheel cylinder to 'TEE' piece assembly—righthand	1
100E.2268.B	100E.2268.A	Pipe (rear brake wheel cylinder to 'TEE' piece assembly—lefthand	1
100E.2663.C	100E.2663.A	Dust cover (rear brake wheel cylinder)	2
100E.5793.C	100E.5793.B	Seat (rear spring)—righthand	1
100E.5794.C	100E.5794.B	Seat (rear spring)—lefthand	1

10 : 10 Fault diagnosis

(a) Spongy pedal

1 Leak in the system
2 Worn master cylinder
3 Leaking wheel cylinders
4 Air in the system
5 Gaps between shoes and undersides of linings

(b) Excessive pedal movement

1 Check 1 and 4 in (a)
2 Excessive lining wear
3 Very low fluid level in supply reservoir
4 Too much free movement of pedal

(c) Brakes grab or pull to one side

1 Brake backplate loose
2 Scored, cracked or distorted drum
3 High spots on drum
4 Unbalanced shoe adjustment
5 Wet or oily linings
6 Worn or loose rear spring fixings
7 Front suspension or rear axle anchorages loose
8 Worn steering connections
9 Mixed linings of different grades
10 Uneven tyre pressures
11 Broken shoe return springs
12 Seized handbrake cable

CHAPTER 11

THE ELECTRICAL EQUIPMENT

11:1 Description

The electrical system is of 12-volt earth return type, the positive terminal of the battery being earthed.

Testing of the generator and voltage control regulator, also the cut-out may be carried out providing suitable high quality instruments are available, otherwise these checks are best left to the service station or auto-electrician with the necessary equipment.

Where major items such as the starter motor or generator have serious faults or they have seen considerable service, then these units should be exchanged on the Ford exchange plan rather than attempt extensive dismantling operations with the possibility of unsatisfactory performance after reassembly.

Wiring diagrams for all the models covered in this manual are to be found in **Technical Data** at the end of the book.

No fuses are incorporated in the electrical system with the exception of one in the direction indicator flasher circuit which protects the flasher unit.

11:2 The battery

The battery is of the lead/acid type and is mounted in the engine compartment. An aperture in the side wall allows air circulation for cooling the battery and this must not be covered during the fitting of accessories.

Always keep the exterior of the battery clean and smear petroleum jelly on the terminals to prevent corrosion.

Use distilled water only for topping up and the electrolyte level should be maintained at $\frac{1}{4}$ inch above the plastic separators. Take care when filling and mop up immediately any spilled water.

Never add neat acid to a battery. In the rare event of it being necessary to make new electrolyte due to loss by spillage, **always add sulphuric acid to distilled water and never add water to acid.**

Never bring a flame or spark near a battery particularly during or shortly after a charge, as the gases produced may be explosive.

Never add acid to the cells unless:

The specific gravity and voltage at the end of a charge

have remained constant over five successive hourly readings.

The specific gravity is more than .010 (10 points) below 1.280 at 70°F, or as given in the fully charged specific gravity table below.

Never empty acid from a battery to refill with fresh acid unless the battery is fully charged.

Never leave a battery in a discharged condition.

Avoid high temperatures as electrolyte temperatures above this tend to shorten the life of the battery.

Keep the filler plugs tight and clean. Check the vents to ensure they are clear.

The most effective way to test the condition and state of charge of a battery is by means of a hydrometer. Check the specific gravity of the electrolyte, as shown in **FIG 11:1.**

At a standard electrolyte temperature of 70°F (21°C):

          Fully charged—1.280
          Half discharged—1.196
          Discharged—1.110

When the temperature of the electrolyte varies from the standard of 70°F (21°C) a correction should be made.

Add four points (.004 specific gravity) for every 10°F (5½°C) above 70°F (21°C).

Subtract four points (.004 specific gravity) for every 10°F (5½°C) below 70°F (21°C).

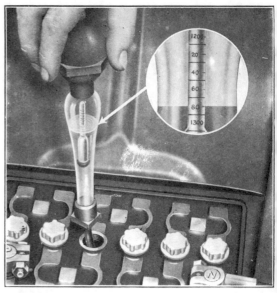

FIG 11:1 Checking specific gravity of a battery with a hydrometer

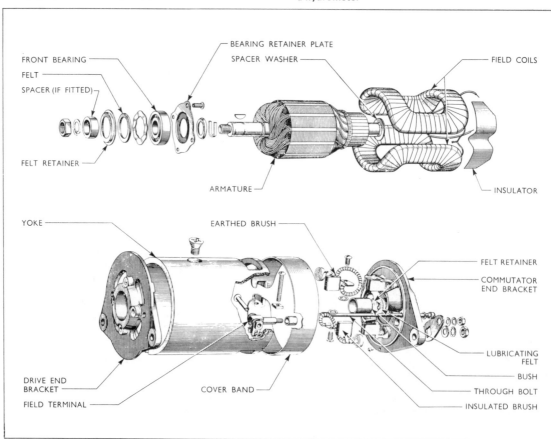

FIG 11:2 Exploded view of the generator

All cells should read approximately the same, if one differs investigate for cracks or internal fault.

Any recharging carried out from a mains operated battery charger should be done at 3 amps.

11 : 3 The generator

(a) Description:

The generator is of the two-brush type and is used in conjunction with the voltage control regulator mounted on the righthand side of the engine compartment.

Later-type generators do not incorporate brush inspection slots, and the cover band is no longer provided. When examining or replacing brushes it is necessary to remove the generator and detach the commutator end bracket (see **FIG 11 : 2**).

(b) Maintenance:

The commutator should be inspected periodically. A commutator in good condition will be smooth and free from pits or burned spots.

Clean the commutator with a petrol-moistened cloth. If this is ineffective, carefully polish it with a strip of very fine glasspaper, not emery cloth, while the armature is rotated.

On early models, generator lubrication was provided by a felt pad and grease well. Later generators have an oil hole in the end bracket in which oil is injected during normal vehicle servicing.

(c) Testing when not charging

First check tension of the fan belt as described in **Chapter 4, Section 4 : 2.**

1 Disconnect the leads from the 'D' and 'F' terminals of the generator and join the generator terminals together with a short piece of wire. Connect a 0-30 volt meter between this junction and earth. Run the engine at 1000 rev/min when the voltage reading should rise rapidly without fluctuation above 24 volts. Do not increase the engine speed above fast-idle in an endeavour to obtain this voltage, as this will give a false reading.

If there is no reading, first check the generator leads, brush and brush connections. If the reading is very low, the field or armature windings may be suspect.

2 If the output reading is incorrect, but does not indicate the cause of the trouble, remove the fan belt by slackening the generator mounting bolts and moving the generator in towards the engine. Connect a 0-30 amp meter between the joined terminals of the generator and the battery negative post.

The generator should now revolve and the current consumption should be 4 to 6 amps.

(a) A high reading on the ammeter is an indication of tight generator bearings.

(b) An excessively high reading will indicate a shortcircuit.

(c) A low reading is a general indication of bad commutation.

11 : 4 Removing, dismantling and servicing the generator

1 Slacken the three generator securing bolts and push the generator towards the engine so that the fan belt may be detached. Disconnect the electrical leads, and after

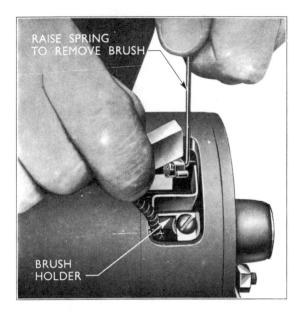

FIG 11 : 3 Removing generator brushes (early models with cover band)

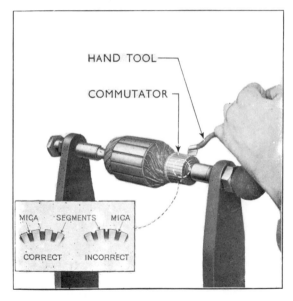

FIG 11 : 4 Undercutting commutator segments

removing the three securing bolts and nuts, lift the generator from its supports.

2 On early generators, slacken the clamp screw, slide the cover band away from the brush apertures, lift the brush springs off the brushes and draw the brushes out of their holders (see **FIG 11 : 3**).

Hold the pulley still and unscrew the pulley nut and spring washer. If the pulley is tight on the shaft, it may be removed, using a suitable puller. Detach the key and spacer (if fitted).

3 Unscrew the two through-bolts which hold the end brackets together and detach the 'D' and 'F' terminal nuts and spring washers. The commutator end bracket is now free and can be removed from the yoke. If it is a tight fit, it should be carefully levered off with a screwdriver.

It is necessary to dismantle later model generator assemblies to this extent, before the brushes can be removed.

Do not lose the spacer washer on the commutator end of the armature shaft.

The drive end bracket and armature may now be pulled from the generator yoke.

4 If the brushes are sticking, clean with a petrol-moistened rag and, if necessary, ease the sides by polishing on a smooth file.

If the brushes are worn so that they do not bear on the commutator or the brush lead is exposed on the brush face, new brushes must be fitted.

5 Unscrew the brush terminal screw, holding the brush lead, taking care not to lose the lockwasher. The brush may now be removed.

Slide the loop on the brush spring off the post and remove the spring if necessary.

FIG 11:5 Testing field coils for continuity

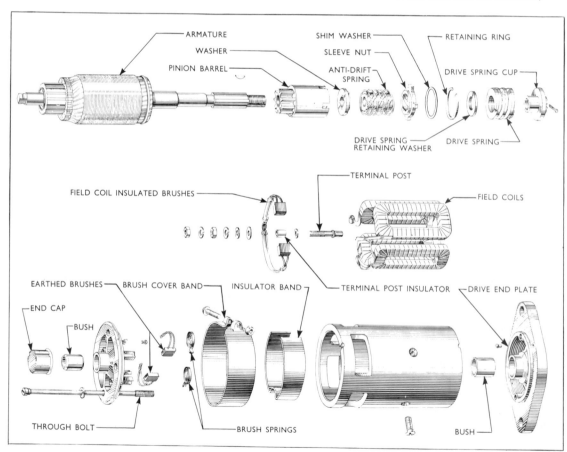

FIG 11:6 Component parts of the starter motor

The contact face of the brush is preformed so that bedding to the commutator is unnecessary when fitting new brushes.

6 Polish the commutator with very fine glasspaper. Undercut the mica insulation between the segments to a depth of $\frac{1}{32}$ inch with a hacksaw blade ground down to the thickness of the mica (see **FIG 11 : 4**) or the width of the spaces between the commutator segments.

Finally, polish the commutator with fine glasspaper and remove all copper dust. Check the armature for shortcircuits to the shaft or core.

7 Examine the front bearing for wear and if it is found in need of replacement, see **FIG 11 : 2** and press the armature shaft out of the drive end bracket.

Drill out the four rivets which secure the bearing retainer plate to the end bracket and remove the plate.

Press the bearing out of the end bracket and remove the bearing washer, felt washer and retainer from the housing.

Clean the bearing housing and lubricate the new ballbearing with high melting point grease.

Place the retainer, felt washer and bearing washer in the housing.

Locate the bearing and press it home, using a driver sufficient diameter to take the thrust on the outer race of the bearing.

Fit the bearing retainer plate. Insert four new rivets from the inside of the end bracket and open the rivet ends by means of a punch to secure the plate rigidly in position.

Ensure that the flat metal clip and retainer are located in the groove on the armature shaft and press the drive end bracket onto the shaft so that the retainer plate abuts the clip.

8 Examine the porous bronze type bush in the commutator end plate (see **FIG 11 : 2**) and if in need of replacement remove the plug from the commutator end bracket, then remove the lubricating felt and the felt retainer plate (early models have a wick assembly). Press the bush from the end bracket by means of a suitable driver.

Before fitting a new bush it should be allowed to stand in engine oil for 24 hours. Drive the bush home until its end is flush with the bottom of the chamfer on the end plate. The bush now requires reaming (Tool No. A/CET.10128). Clean the end bracket assembly carefully, replace the felt and felt retainer and tap the plug into position. On early models with a wick lubricator, pack the lubricator with petroleum jelly.

Testing the field coils for continuity:

9 To check field coils suspected of being faulty, first unsweat the field coil tappings from the field terminal post (see **FIG 11 : 2**).

A plastic insulator is fitted between the terminal tags and the terminal post should be removed before before unsoldering the tappings.

10 With the aid of the vehicle battery, connect either a voltmeter or a bulb between the two coil tappings, as shown in **FIG 11 : 5**. If the bulb lights or the voltmeter shows a reading then the field coils are unbroken.

It is recommended that renewal of the field coils be left to a service station.

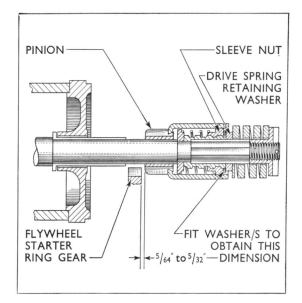

FIG 11 : 7   Checking starter drive out of mesh clearance

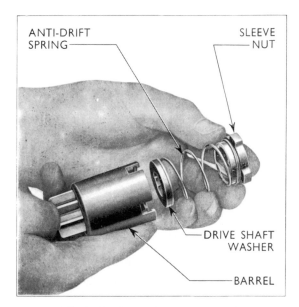

FIG 11 : 8   Assembling the starter drive

The armature:

11 Apart from giving attention to the commutator as already described, armature windings can only be tested at a service station or by substitution. Never attempt to straighten a bent armature shaft.

Should either the field coils or the armature become unserviceable then it will probably be advantageous to substitute the complete generator for an exchange unit.

11 : 5 Reassembly and replacement of the generator

This is largely a reversal of dismantling procedure but the following information will be of assistance when read in conjunction with **FIG 11 : 2**.

1 Place the armature and drive end bracket assembly in the generator yoke from the front end, so that the dowel on the bracket locates in the slot in the yoke end face. Replace the spacer washer on the commutator end of the armature shaft. Ensure that the insulator strip is fitted between the field coil connections and the generator yoke. Place the insulator on the field coil terminals and, on early assemblies, check that the cover band is located around the generator yoke.

2 **On later models** secure the brush leads to the brush holder terminals with screws and lockwashers. Enter the brushes into their holders and turn the springs until they rest against the sides of the brushes, thus holding them clear of the commutator. Position the commutator plate on the armature shaft so that there is a small space between it and the generator yoke which will allow access to the brushes.

3 Press the brushes into contact with the commutator and ensure that the springs are then resting on the top of the brushes. Refit the commutator end plate to the generator yoke so that the head of the dowel engages in the slot of the yoke end face.

4 **On early models** position the commutator end plate on the armature shaft so that the head of the dowel engages in the slot of the yoke end face.

Now position the brushes in the holders, ensure that the springs rest on top of the brushes, 'wind up' the springs if necessary so that they exert pressure on the brush holders, then slide the cover band over the brush apertures and tighten the clamp screw.

5 Replace the two through-bolts from the commutator bracket end, screwing them into the drive end bracket. Make sure that the righthand bolt (looking from the commutator end) passes between the insulator strip and the generator yoke, thus clearing the field coil bridge connection. Refit the generator terminal insulator, noting that the 'D' terminal has a square shank and the field terminal 'F' has a round shank. Loosely fit the terminal nuts and spring washers. Locate the spacer on the front of the armature shaft and fit the key in the shaft keyway. Align the keyway in the pulley with the key on the shaft and gently tap the pulley into position, using a hide mallet. Refit the generator pulley nut and lockwasher and tighten securely.

6 Slacken the bolt securing the generator adjusting racket to the cylinder block. Place the generator on its support brackets with the end brackets in front of the support bracket legs and locate it with the three securing bolts. Refit the fan belt and adjust the tension as described in **Chapter 4, Section 4 : 2**.

7 Reconnect the leads to the terminals on the generator end bracket. Yellow-red tracer to 'F' terminal. Yellow-black and red tracer to 'D' terminal.

11 : 6 The starter motor, description and testing in the vehicle

The starter motor is mounted on the front of the flywheel housing on the righthand side of the engine.

The motor has four polepieces and four sets of field coils. Four commutator brushes are fitted, two of which are earthed, the other two being insulated and connected to the ends of the field coils. Component parts are shown in **FIG 11 : 6**.

A square is machined on the end of the armature shaft, beneath the small metal cap, to assist in freeing the pinion if it jams in the flywheel ring gear.

Another method of freeing a jammed starter is to engage a gear and with the ignition switched off, rock the car backwards and forwards when the pinion should free itself from the flywheel teeth.

If the starter armature does not rotate when the ignition switch is operated, first depress the centre spindle on the switch located on the engine rear bulkhead. If the starter now operates, the cable should be checked at the connector behind the bulkhead.

If the starter does not operate, check the condition of the battery connections as described in section 2 of this Chapter.

If the battery is in good condition and fully charged, check the starter switch. If the starter still does not operate, the motor should be removed for examination.

11 : 7 Removing, testing and servicing the starter

(a) Removal:

Disconnect the battery and the cable at the terminal on the starter motor end plate. Unscrew the two starter motor securing bolts evenly and pull the starter motor forward from the flywheel housing.

(b) The starter drive:

1 Later-type starter drive assemblies have a dished retaining ring fitted, which supersedes the shim washer and retaining ring fitted to earlier models.

If the starter drive pinion is tight on the drive sleeve, wash in paraffin but do not oil the pinion or sleeve.

If the starter motor jams due to fracture of the shim washer, the shim washer and retaining ring should be removed and replaced by the dished retaining ring (see **FIG 11 : 7**).

Adjusting washers are available from dealers where cases of starter motor jamming occur.

One or two washers, as necessary, may be fitted between the sleeve nut and drive spring retaining washer, to reduce the out of mesh clearance between the pinion and ring gear.

2 The out of mesh clearance should be checked by reference to **FIG 11 : 7**.

Measure the distance between the rear face of the flywheel starter ring gear and the starter motor mounting face on the cylinder block. Push the starter motor drive shaft towards the starter motor body. (to eliminate drive shaft end float) and measure the distance between the front face of the pinion and the starter motor mounting face.

The difference between these two measurements is the out of mesh clearance (see **FIG 11 : 7**).

If the clearance exceeds $\frac{5}{32}$ inch fit one or two adjusting washers to obtain the specified clearance, which must not be less than $\frac{5}{64}$ inch.

3 Remove the splitpin securing the drive spring cup, and carefully unscrew the cup (see **FIG 11 : 6**).

Detach the drive spring and retaining washer and

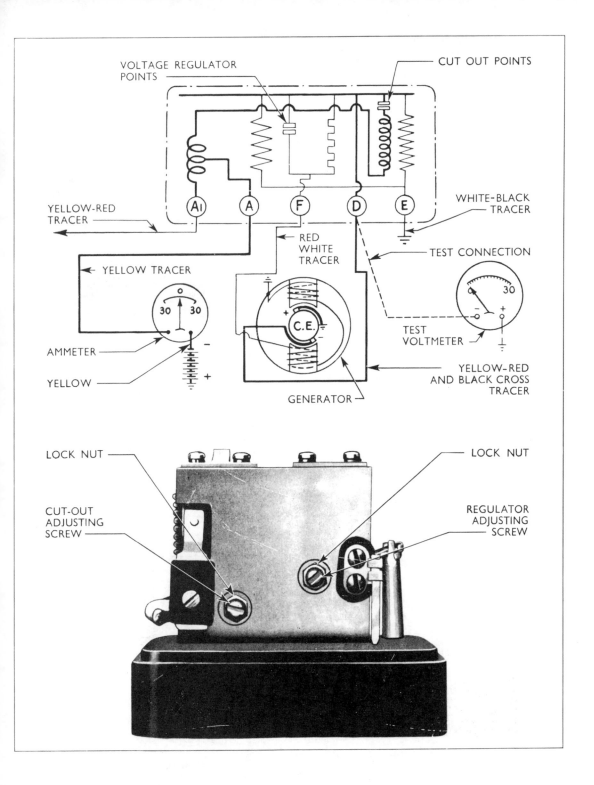

VOLTAGE REGULATOR
POINTS

CUT OUT POINTS

YELLOW-RED
TRACER

A1   A   F   D   E

WHITE-BLACK
TRACER

RED
WHITE
TRACER

YELLOW TRACER

TEST CONNECTION

C.E.

30   30

TEST
VOLTMETER

30

AMMETER

YELLOW

GENERATOR

YELLOW-RED
AND BLACK CROSS
TRACER

LOCK NUT

LOCK NUT

CUT-OUT
ADJUSTING
SCREW

REGULATOR
ADJUSTING
SCREW

FIG 11:9   The voltage regulator and wiring diagram (early models)

pull the drive pinion barrel assembly from the armature shaft. To dismantle the barrel assembly, screw the sleeve (lefthand thread) out of the sleeve nut. Extract the retaining ring securing the sleeve nut in the barrel and detach the thin shim washer, sleeve nut, anti-drift spring and drive shaft washer.

On later models the shim washer and retaining ring are not fitted. These parts are replaced by a single dished retaining ring.

(c) The starter brushes

1 Loosen the screw and slide the brush cover band away from the brush apertures. Lift the brush springs, using a piece of wire shaped into a hook and check the movement of the brushes in the holders. If the brushes are sticking, clean them with a petrol-moistened cloth and, if necessary, ease the sides of the brushes by polishing on a smooth file. If the brushes are worn so that they do not bear on the commutator or the brush lead is exposed on the wearing face, new brushes must be fitted.

If the commutator is blackened or dirty, clean by holding a petrol-moistened cloth against it while the armature is rotated.

If this is ineffective, carefully polish with a strip of fine glasspaper, **not emery cloth,** while the armature is rotated.

Do not undercut the mica insulation between the segments as is the normal practice with generators.

Check that the commutator segments are not earthing to the armature shaft and core by checking with a battery and bulb.

2 To further dismantle the starter, unscrew the starter cable terminal nuts and detach the spring, flat and fibre washers. Unscrew the two through-bolts and carefully pull the commutator end plate from the starter motor, together with the earth brushes. Remove the

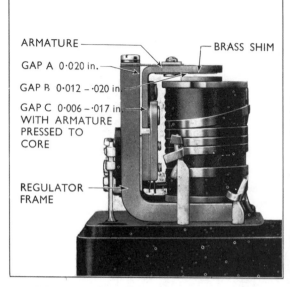

FIG 11:10   The voltage regulator (early models)

armature. The brush leads are soldered into tags on the earthed brush holders on the end plate and to the ends of the field coils. Carefully unsweat the brush leads from their connections and detach the brushes.

(d) Testing the field coils and armature

1 Check for continuity between the two ends of the field coils, using a line tester, having a suitable bulb in circuit.

If the lamp does not light, there is an open circuit in one of the field coils. If the lamp lights, it does not

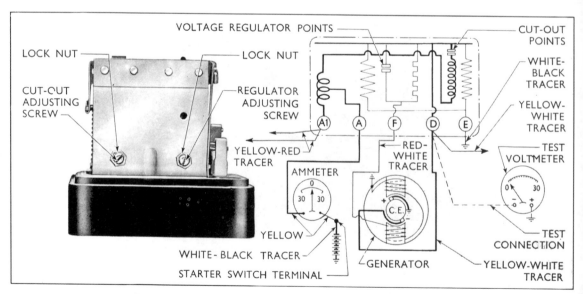

FIG 11:11   The voltage regulator and wiring diagram (later models)

necessarily mean that the field coils are in order, as it is possible that one of the coils may be earthing to the polepieces or starter yoke.

2 The armature can be inspected after it has been removed from the starter motor yoke. Visual examination will usually reveal any cause of failure, such as conductors lifting away from the commutator due to the starter pinion being jammed in engagement with the flywheel teeth while the engine is running.

Any operations on either the field coils or armature should be left to a service station having the appropriate equipment.

(e) Reassembly and replacement:

1 Resolder the brush leads to the field coils and earthed brush holders. Before fitting the end plate, check the brush springs and renew if necessary. Take care to close the ends of the brush spring posts after fitting new springs. Check the insulated brush holders to ensure that they are not earthing. Use a battery and bulb for this test. Check that the fibre washers are fitted on the field coil terminal post and a fibre bush is located in the terminal post hole in the commutator end plate.

2 Check that the insulator band is located between the yoke and the end of the field coils, and pass the insulated brushes through the apertures in the yoke. Replace the commutator end plate on the starter motor yoke, passing the earthed brushes through the other apertures in the yoke and engage the dowel pin in the end plate with the notch in the yoke end. Replace a fibre washer, flat washer, spring washer, nut, spring washer and nut on the field coil terminal post and tighten the inner nut securely.

3 Replace the armature and drive end plate, if removed, engaging the dowel pin on the plate in the notch at the drive end of the yoke.
   Replace the two through-bolts and tighten securely. Lift the brush springs and insert the brushes into their holders, ensuring that they slide freely. (The field coil brushes locate in the insulated brush holders.)
   Slide the brush cover band over the brush apertures and tighten the screw.

4 See **FIG 11:8** and reassemble the starter drive by locating the drive shaft washer, anti-drift spring and sleeve nut in the barrel and secure with the shim washer and retaining ring. On later vehicles, secure the barrel assembly with the dished retaining ring.
   Replace the sleeve in the sleeve nut. Refit the barrel assembly on the armature shaft, with the pinion teeth towards the armature.
   Locate the retaining washer and drive spring on the shaft and screw on the drive spring cup. Tighten the cup down against the shoulder of the shaft and refit the splitpin.

5 The assembled starter may now be fitted to the engine by passing the drive end of the starter motor into the flywheel housing aperture and locating the motor on the mounting flange. Replace the two bolts and spring washers and tighten securely but evenly. Reconnect the cables to the starter motor terminal and the battery.

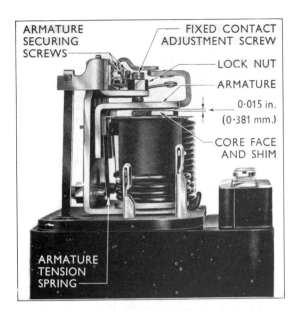

FIG 11:12   The voltage regulator (later models)

FIG 11:13   The cut-out (early models)

11:8 The control box

Combined in the control box are the cut-out and the voltage regulator. The unit normally requires very little attention but if it does not function correctly, check the following before giving attention to the control box.

Ensure that the fan belt is not slipping. Check the condition and state of charge of the battery. Watch for corroded terminals which can cause a low output even if the regulator setting is correct.

Check the earth connections both from the battery and the regulator to the vehicle body. Test the generator as described in **Section 11 : 3.**

Two types of regulator have been fitted, the following details applying to the earlier design. After approximately Engine No. 100E.323014 (October 1956) a modified design was introduced, details of this are included later in this Section. Both types are directly interchangeable.

To remove:

Disconnect the various leads to the regulator and remove the two screws and lockwashers retaining it to the righthand side of the engine compartment.

(a) Testing and adjusting the regulator (early models):

1 Insulate the cut-out points with a thin strip of mica or withdraw the cables from the terminals marked 'A' and 'A1' (see **FIG 11 : 9**) and join them together.

Connect the negative lead of an accurate voltmeter (0-30 volts) to terminal 'D' on the regulator and the positive lead to a good earth. Adjustment must be made with the regulator cold, so immediately on starting the engine the atmospheric temperature should be noted by means of a thermometer.

2 Start the engine and gradually increase the speed until the voltmeter needle 'flicks' and then steadies. This should occur at a voltmeter reading between the limits given below for the approximate temperature of the regulator unit.

Atmospheric temperature	Regulator setting
50°F (10°C)	15.9 to 16.5 volts
68°F (20°C)	15.6 to 16.2 volts
80°F (27°C)	15.3 to 15.9 volts
104°F (40°C)	15.0 to 15.6 volts

3 If the reading is not between these limits, the regulator needs adjusting. Increase the speed gradually to maximum rev/min when the voltmeter needle should not rise more than half a volt above the readings shown above.

If the voltmeter reading continues to rise as the engine speed is increased, possibly swinging the needle right over, it is indicative that either the regulator points are not opening or there is a poor or no earth between the regulator and the body.

4 If the points are not opening, the regulator should be renewed, as it is probable that they are 'welded' or shorted, or there is an open circuit in the shunt coil.

If the voltage at which the reading becomes steady occurs outside these limits, the engine should be maintained at the same speed and the regulator adjusted. Release the locknut (see **FIG 11 : 9**) holding the regulator adjusting screw and turn the screw in a clockwise direction to increase the voltage or in an anticlockwise direction to decrease the voltage, keeping as near to the minimum figure as possible. Make sure that the locknut is tightened securely after the adjustment is completed.

Reconnect the wires to terminals 'A' and 'A1' or remove the insulation from the cut-out points, whichever method was used.

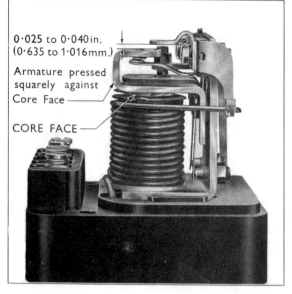

FIG 11 : 14 The cut-out (later models) armature stop arm

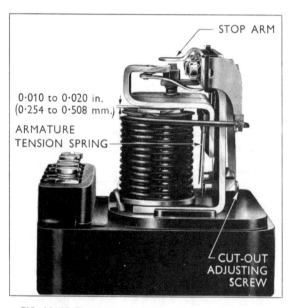

FIG 11 : 15 The cut-out (later models) fixed contact

(b) Ampere output test (all models):

Connect a test ammeter in series with the lead 'A' and terminal 'A'. Speed up the engine and observe the charging rate. This will vary according to the state of charge of the battery. Check the vehicle ammeter for accuracy.

(c) Cleaning and resetting the regulator points (early models):

If the contact points are found to be badly worn, replace the regulator.

1 To render the regulator contacts accessible for cleaning, slacken the screws securing the plate carrying the fixed contact (see **FIG 11 :10**). It will be necessary to loosen off the upper screw so that the contact can be swung outwards and downwards.

2 Remove the moving contact (two screws) then thoroughly clean the contact points with a carborundum stone operated in a circular movement. Carefully wipe away all traces or dirt or other foreign matter.

3 Finally wipe both points with methylated spirit to remove any traces of film present. Return the fixed contact to its upright position and tighten the two screws securely. Replace the moving contact. Ensure that the contact securing screws are each fitted with a spring washer.

4 Insert a .020 inch feeler gauge between the armature and the frame (gap 'A', **FIG 11 :10**) and a .016 inch feeler gauge between the armature and the core of the bobbin (gap 'B', **FIG 11 :10**). Adjust as necessary, remove the feeler gauges, press down the armature on to the core and check the gap 'C' of the contact points.

This should be .006 to .017 inch and may be adjusted either by increasing or decreasing the .005 inch thick shims located between the contacts and the packing plate. Do not allow the shims to 'short' to the back frame.

5 After ensuring that the gap is correct, the screws securing the moving contact should be tightened securely.

(d) Testing and adjusting the regulator (later models):

1 The procedure in the previous section (a), paragraphs 1, 2 and 3 only should be adhered to but reference should be made to **FIGS 11 :11** and **11 :12**, used in conjunction with the following voltmeter limits.

Atmospheric temperature	Regulator setting
50°F (10°C)	15.7 to 16.1 volts
68°F (20°C)	15.6 to 16.0 volts
86°F (30°C)	15.5 to 15.9 volts
104°F (40°C)	15.4 to 15.8 volts

If the voltage at which the reading becomes steady occurs outside these limits the regulator must be adjusted by the following method.

Shut off the engine and remove the cover. Slacken the locknut of the regulator adjusting screw (see **FIG 11 :11**) and turn the screw in a clockwise direction to raise the setting or in an anticlockwise direction to lower the setting. Turn the screw only a fraction of a turn at a time and then tighten the locknut. Again run up the engine and repeat as above until the correct setting is obtained.

2 Adjustment of regulator open circuit voltage should be completed within 30 seconds, otherwise heating of the shunt winding will cause false settings to be made. Remake the original connections.

A generator run at high speed on open circuit will build up a high voltage, always increase engine speed slowly when adjusting the regulator otherwise you may make a false setting. Reconnect wires to terminals 'A' and 'A1' or withdraw the insulation from the cut-out whichever method was used.

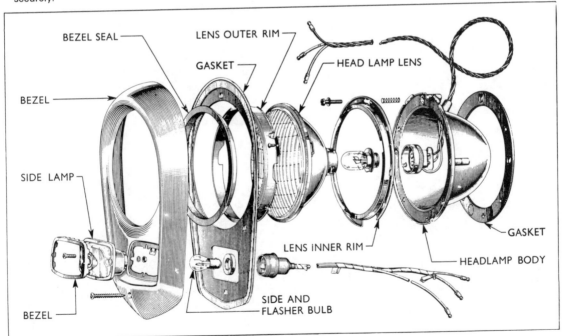

FIG 11 :16 Exploded view of the head and side lights

(e) Cleaning and resetting the regulator points (later models):

1 Remove for cleaning by first slackening the locknut (see **FIG 11 :12**) which secures the fixed contact and screw to its bracket and removing them.

Now remove the two armature screws and locknuts and detach the metal strip.

2 Move the fixed contact mounting over slightly, enabling the moving contact bracket to be lifted out. Take care not to lose the insulating strips positioned on either side of the fixed contact mounting bracket. Clean the contact points with carborundum stone operated in a circular movement. Carefully wipe away all traces of dirt and wipe both points with methylated spirit.

Replace the points in the reverse sequence to that described above and reset the gaps.

3 The armature or moving contacts should not normally be removed, as the gaps between the core and the frame are accurately set and are of great importance to the satisfactory operation of the regulator. If, for any reason, however, the armature has been removed, or its setting altered, it should be reset as follows:

Disconnect the battery. Slacken the fixed contact screw locknut and unscrew the contact screw until it is clear of the armature moving contact (refer to **FIG 11 :12**). Slacken the regulator adjusting screw locknut and unscrew the adjusting screw until it is completely clear of the armature tension spring. Slacken the two armature assembly securing screws. Using a .015 inch feeler blade, wide enough to cover the complete core face, insert the blade between the

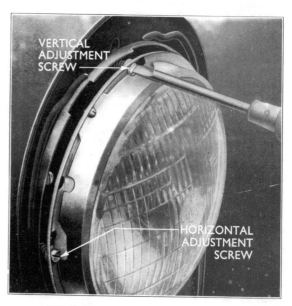

FIG 11 :17   Adjusting the headlight beams

armature and core shim, taking care not to damage or burr the edge of the shim.

4 Press the armature squarely down against the blade and, holding it firmly, retighten the two armature assembly securing screws. With the blade and armature

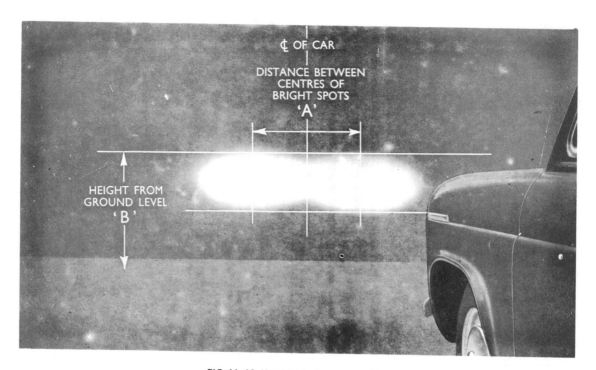

FIG 11 :18   Headlight alignment guide
Key to Fig 11 :18   **A** 46 inches   **B** 29½ inches

still in this position, screw the adjustable contact down until it just touches the armature contact. Retighten the locking nut. Reset the regulator adjusting screw and reconnect the battery.

11:9 The cut-out

(a) Early models:

Examine the cut-out points and, if necessary, clean with a carborundum stone. Ensure that the points are meeting correctly (see **FIG 11:13**).

1 Connect the voltmeter between the 'D' terminal and a good earth see **FIG 11:9**).
2 Speed up the engine slowly and note the voltage immediately before the points close.

This voltage should be between 12.7 and 13.3 volts. The voltage may be adjusted by turning the cut-out adjusting screw in an anticlockwise direction to decrease the voltage and vice versa. Turn the adjusting screw a little at a time, tighten the locknut and retest.

This voltage should be obtained when gap 'A' is .014 inch, gap 'B' is .011 to .015 inch when the cut-out points are just closed, gap 'C' is .002 to .006 inch, and gap 'D' is .030 to .034 inch measured with the armature held down firmly against the core. Note that gap 'C' should be obtained with a .025 inch feeler gauge between the armature and core (see **FIG 11:13**).

(b) Later models:

1 Examine the cut-out points and, if necessary, clean with a carborundum stone. Ensure that the points are meeting correctly (see **FIGS 11:14** and **11:15**).
2 To test and adjust the cut-out connect the voltmeter between the 'D' terminal and a good earth, or the 'E' terminal.

Speed up the engine slowly and note the voltage immediately before the points close.

This voltage should be 12.7 to 13.3 volts. The voltage may be adjusted by slackening the locknut and turning the cut-out adjusting screw (see **FIG 11:11**) in an anticlockwise direction to decrease the voltage and vice versa. Turn the adjusting screw a little at a time, tighten the locknut and retest.

3 If it is suspected that the above setting is incorrect and the cut-out points setting has been disturbed, then slacken the adjusting screw locknut and unscrew the cut-out adjusting screw until it is clear of the armature tension spring. Slacken the two armature securing screws. Press the armature down squarely against the copper-coated core face and, holding it there, re-tighten the armature securing screws. Still holding the armature down against the core, bend the armature stop arm so that a gap of .025 to .040 inch exists between it and the armature tongue (see **FIG 11:14**). Insert the end of a .010 to .020 inch feeler blade between the outer end of the armature and core face, and set the fixed contact, by bending the arm, so that the points are just touching (see **FIG 11:15**).

Reset the cut-out adjusting screws as previously described.

11:10 The headlamps

Pre-focus bulbs are used in semi-sealed units (see **FIG 11:16**).

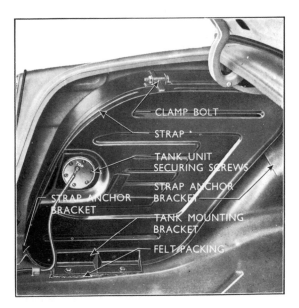

FIG 11:19 Petrol tank unit location in Anglia and Prefect

1 To remove, unscrew and remove the nut and lock-washer the headlamp bezel at its upper mounting location. This nut and washer is reached from inside the engine compartment.

Unscrew the cross-headed screw and spring nut which secure the bezel at its lower point. The spring nut can be reached from under the wheel arch, a circular aperture being provided for this purpose.

Later models have a spring plate fitted to seal this aperture.

Earlier vehicles had the headlamp bezel secured at three points. The upper mounting being similar to that described above for later models, and the lower mounting consisting of two screws located just below the headlamp lens aperture, and passing through into the front wing. The lower mounting screws were each secured by a spring nut.

2 Now ease the bezel out of its upper mounting and remove the sidelamp bulb and holder by turning the holder slightly anticlockwise. Then detach the bezel gasket. Turn the headlamp lens and reflector assembly slightly anticlockwise when it can be lifted away, complete with the lens gasket, from its mounting location. Turn the headlamp bulb socket slightly anticlockwise and detach the socket.

The headlamp bulb will still remain in the lens and reflector assembly. Lift the bulb carefully from the lens and reflector assembly. Remove the four screws securing the headlamp body to the front wing, and detach the body and gasket.

The inner and outer lens rims are secured at the front and rear of the headlamp lens assembly by three self-and rear of the headlamp lens assembly by three self-tapping screws, and these rims can be separated.

Reassembly and replacement is a reversal of the dis-mantling procedure. If due to damage or rust it is necessary to fit a new headlamp bezel then reference should be made to **Section 11:15** which describes the necessary modification due to a change in fitting methods.

Headlamp alignment:

It is strongly recommended that headlamp beam setting should be carried out at a service station having the necessary equipment but a reasonable result may be obtained by following the procedure given here.

1 Ensure the vehicle is unladen, and standing on level ground 25 feet from a wall. Unless you have facilities in a darkened building then this is obviously a night job.

2 Remove the headlamp bezel and rubber gasket and screw either the horizontal or vertical adjusting screws in or out (see **FIG 11:17**) until the projecting beams of light correspond to the position shown in **FIG 11:18**. **For this operation the headlamps will of course be in the undipped position.**

11:11 The flasher unit

1 Flasher type direction indicators are fitted and a flasher unit is mounted at the rear of the parcels tray, on the engine rear bulkhead.

The flasher unit has three contacts, which press into the adaptor.

A 5-amp fuse is fitted in a plastic holder in the black-blue tracer wire. The yellow wire passes from the adaptor to the direction indicator switch, and a red-white tracer wire to the indicator warning lights (see wiring diagrams in **Technical Data**).

From engine No. 100E.176761, a 42-watt flasher unit assembly is fitted and replaces the 36-watt unit previously used. The components are clearly marked to show the wattage.

Use 12V 21/6W sidelamp and front flasher bulb and rear flasher bulbs when this later-type flasher unit is fitted.

2 Should the flashers fail to operate, first check for broken filaments in the bulbs, then using the wiring diagram in **Technical Data**, check all leads and connections for continuity, also the fuse.

3 Switch on the ignition and using a voltmeter between the flasher unit position 'B', terminal and earth check for battery voltage. Now connect the flasher unit terminals 'B' and 'L' together, and if the flasher lamps light then the flasher unit needs renewing.

Take great care to mark the cables for connecting to the terminals on the new flasher unit, as if incorrectly done severe damage can be caused when the direction indicator switch is operated.

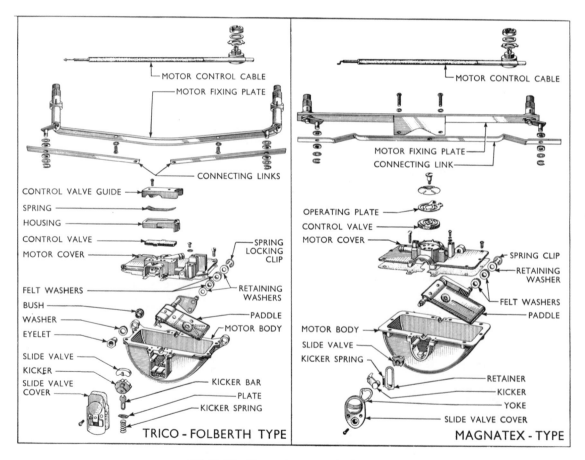

FIG 11:20 Alternative types of wiper motor

11:12 The horns

Dual-tone horns are fitted on all de luxe vehicles and estate cars, and a single-tone horn is fitted on standard passenger vehicles and 5 and 7 cwt vans.

The dual horns are fitted one each side of the engine compartment, on the body panel adjacent to each front suspension unit. The single-tone horn is fitted on the righthand panel, and later vehicles have the necessary holes drilled in the lefthand panel to enable twin horns to be fitted if required.

The horn relay is fitted adjacent to the righthand horn mounting when the dual horns are fitted. This is necessary because of the high current flow which would otherwise arc across the horn switch on the steering wheel.

The feed wire for the horn on **later** models is now taken from the switch terminal of the ignition coil and not the 'A1' terminal of the regulator as previously, and the horn will therefore only operate with the ignition switched on.

The dual horns must be adjusted individually, disconnecting one horn to adjust the other.

1 Remove the screws securing the horn cover. Tone adjustment is effected by increasing or decreasing the gap.

2 **Single-tone.** Adjust by means of the large countersunk head screw on the back of the horn. Do not touch the adjusting screw and locknut in the centre of the horn as this controls the setting of the magnet.

Turning the screw clockwise increases the pitch of the note. The horn should be tuned to give a clear and steady note without mechanical vibration.

If there is mechanical vibration, check the horn bracket mounting bolt for tightness. If vibration persists, check the diaphragm for cracks around the outer edge.

3 **Dual-tone.** Adjust these, one at a time by disconnecting the other horn during the operation. Remove the screws which retain the horn cover. Loosen the locknut and turn the adjusting screw either in or out until the desired note is obtained, retighten the locknut. Repeat on the other horn.

11:13 The fuel gauge and tank unit

If the fuel gauge is not reading correctly, the following test should be applied:

1 If the gauge permanently reads 'EMPTY' when the ignition is switched on there is a shortcircuit to earth in the fuel gauge, tank unit or wiring.

2 If the gauge permanently reads 'FULL' with the ignition switched on, there is an open circuit in the gauge, wiring or tank unit. To locate the fault, disconnect the fuel gauge wire at the snap connector behind the panel.

3 With the ignition switched on the gauge should read 'FULL' when the wire is disconnected, and 'EMPTY' when it is shortcircuited to earth.

4 If both these conditions are fulfilled, the gauge and the wiring are satisfactory. Reconnect the wire at the snap connector and remove the inspection cover in the luggage compartment over the fuel tank unit. Disconnect the tank unit lead. With the ignition switched 'On' the gauge should read 'EMPTY' when the wire is shortcircuited to earth, and 'FULL' when disconnected. If both these conditions are fulfilled, the gauge and wiring are satisfactory and the fault lies in the tank unit, which should be checked.

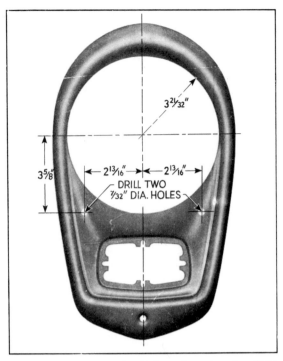

FIG 11:21 Diagram for fitting a later type headlight bezel

5 The tank unit is mounted in the side of the tank on Anglia and Prefect cars, and in the top of the tank on 5 and 7 cwt vans, and Escort and Squire estate cars. In each case an inspection plate or cover is fitted to enable the gauge tank unit to be removed or inspected.

The unit consists of a float mounted on a hinged arm and is provided with a wiper contact for the rheostat, so that as the float rises or falls according to the fuel level, a greater or lesser number of turns in the rheostat are put into the circuit by the wiper contact.

The voltage applied at the fuel gauge therefore varies according to the fuel level in the tank and indicates the quantity of fuel contained in the tank.

6 On Anglia and Prefect cars, remove the gauge tank unit inspection cover from its locating clip on the side of the fuel tank. On 5 and 7 cwt vans and Escort and Squire estate cars an inspection plate is fitted over the tank location and is secured to the floor of the vehicle by three screws. Disconnect the fuel gauge lead from the terminal post of the gauge tank unit. Remove the six securing screws and washers and withdraw the tank unit, taking great care to avoid bending the float arm.

7 Replacement of the new unit is a reversal of removal procedure **but it is important that the unit is fitted in the correct position,** and on Anglia and Prefect cars the word 'TOP' will be found stamped on the face of the unit, and when correctly fitted the word 'TOP' must incline towards the front of the car, as shown in **FIG 11:19.**

On Escort and Squire estate cars the terminal post must point towards the petrol tank filler neck, when the tank unit is correctly positioned.

When fitting the tank unit on 5 and 7 cwt vans, the terminal post must point towards the lefthand rear of the van.

11:14 The wiper motor

Although the wiper motors fitted to the vehicles covered by this manual are of the vacuum-operated type information has been given here in the interests of ease of reference.

The standard Anglia and Prefect cars have dual wipers operated by two individual wiper motors, one motor being the operating unit, and the other an auxiliary unit.

On standard 5 cwt and 7 cwt vans a single wiper motor is normally fitted.

De luxe vehicles have a single large wiper motor to operate both wipers. The motor is of either the Magnatex or Trico-Folberth type (see **FIG 11 : 20**).

Early models are fitted with a direct push-pull control but a kit is available for conversion to a rotary-type cable operated switch if required.

Removal and dismantling

(a) Standard cars and vans :

1 Detach the wiper blades and lever the arms off their splined shafts. Unscrew the nut on each wiper arm shaft and detach the spacers and rubber grommet. Pull the wiper motors down and detach the vacuum hose from its connection adjacent to the control valve.

Slacken the screw securing the wiper control cable to the motor, and detach the operating cable. On very early vehicles the control is of the push-pull type and can be removed complete with the motor. Disconnect the two motor connecting tubes. Detach the motor connecting link, after removing the spring clip, retaining washer and felt washer at each drive lever. location. This will separate the operating and auxiliary motors.

2 Remove the screw securing the wiper arm driver to the paddle spindle, then ease the driver from its location. Unscrew the two screws securing the wiper motor fixing plate to the motor body when this plate can be detach. Remove the six cross-head screws securing the motor cover to the body and detach the cover complete with its gasket. Unscrew the shouldered screw from the top of the motor cover, and dismantle the control valve assembly which comprises the cover operating plate and control valve.

Remove the slide valve cover, which is secured by two screws, then detach the kicker spring where it is secured to the lower part of the slide valve retainer, when the spring together with the yoke can be lifted out.

Pull the kicker from the paddle spindle then lift out the retainer and slide valve.

The paddle assembly can then be removed from the motor body.

The auxiliary motor fitted to Anglia and Prefect cars is dismantled in a similar manner to that described above, with the exception of the control valve and slide valve mechanisms which are not incorporated in this auxiliary unit.

(b) De luxe vehicles (see FIG 11 : 20) :

1 Detach the wiper blades and carefully lever the arms off their splined shafts.

Unscrew the nut on each wiper arm shaft, detach the spacer and rubber grommet. Pull the wiper motor down and detach the wiper hose. Slacken the screw securing the control conduit to the motor and detach the operating cable.

2 **Magnetex type.** Remove the three spring clips, retaining washers and felt washers from the connecting link, when the link can be detached from the motor fixing plate and the drive lever.

Detach the motor fixing plate by removing the two screws securing it to the front face of the motor cover.

3 **Trico-Folberth type.** Disconnect the two connecting links. These links are each connected at one end to the swivel link on the motor fixing plate and at the other end on one spigot of the drive lever. Detach the spring clip and remove the felt and retaining washers.

Detach the motor fixing plate which is secured by two screws and lockwashers to bosses at each side of the motor body. The mounting bosses have a bush, washer and eyelet through which the screw passes, and these need not be dismantled.

Remove the control valve assembly which is secured to the upper face of the motor cover by two screws. This assembly comprises the control valve guide, spring, housing and valve.

Unscrew the two screws securing the slide valve cover and remove the cover complete with its gasket.

Detach the lower end of the kicker bar from the spigot in the slide valve housing which will release the kicker spring, plate and kicker bar. Lift the kicker and slide valve from their location.

Remove the motor cover, which is secured with eight screws, when the cover and the paddle assembly can be withdrawn.

Reassembly and replacement of all types is a reversal of the appropriate dismantling procedure.

11:15 Modifications

Headlamp bezel. If it is required to replace a headlamp bezel on early model vehicles then the following operations will have to be carried out as the original design part is no longer available as a replacement.

1 Drill two $\frac{7}{32}$ inch holes $2\frac{13}{16}$ inch either side of the centre line of the bezel, and on a line running horizontally $3\frac{5}{8}$ inch below the centres of the headlamp aperture. This line will be found to coincide approximately with the bottom edge of the aperture (see **FIG 11 : 21**). If it is intended to use the original screws it will be necessary to countersink the holes.

2 Fill up the original hole for the locating screw at the base of the bezel with body filler. When fitting the bezel, locate the stud in the hole, previously used for the self-tapping screw at the top, and retain in position by means of a flat washer, spring washer and nut.

Retain the lower part of the bezel by means of two flat-headed self-tapping screws, or the original screws if the holes have been countersunk.

(a) Battery discharged

1 Terminals loose or dirty
2 Lighting circuit shorted
3 Generator not charging
4 Regulator or cut-out units not working properly
5 Battery defective internally

(b) Insufficient charging current

1 Loose or corroded battery terminals
2 Generator driving belt slipping

(c) Battery will not hold a charge

1 Low electrolyte level
2 Battery plates sulphated
3 Cracked battery casing or sealing
4 Plate separators ineffective

(d) Battery overcharged

1 Voltage regulator needs adjusting

(e) Generator output low or nil

1 Belt broken or slipping
2 Regulator unit out of adjustment
3 Worn bearings, loose polepieces
4 Commutator worn, burned or shorted
5 Armature shaft bent or worn
6 Insulator proud between commutator segments
7 Sticking brushes, weak or broken springs
8 Field coil wires shorted, broken or burned

(f) Starter motor lacks power or will not operate

1 Battery discharged
2 Starter pinion jammed in mesh with flywheel gear
3 Starter switch faulty
4 Brushes worn or sticking, leads detached or shorting
5 Commutator dirty or worn

6 Starter shaft bent
7 Engine abnormally stiff

(g) Starter motor runs but does not turn engine

1 Pinion sticking on screwed sleeve
2 Broken teeth on pinion or flywheel gears

(h) Noisy starter pinion when engine running

1 Restraining spring weak or broken

(j) Starter motor inoperative

1 Check 1 and 4 in (f)
2 Armature or field coils faulty

(k) Starter motor rough or noisy

1 Mounting bolts loose
2 Damaged pinion or flywheel gear teeth
3 Main pinion spring broken

(l) Lamps inoperative or erratic

1 Battery low, bulbs burned out
2 Faulty earthing of lamps or battery
3 Lighting switch faulty, loose or broken wiring connections

(m) Unsatisfactory windscreen wiper operation

1 Carburetter or distributor in need of adjustment
2 Engine in poor condition generally
3 Punctured hoses
4 Air leaks at motor valves or flanges

(n) Fuel gauge does not register

1 No battery supply to gauge
2 Gauge casing not earthed
3 Cable between gauge and tank unit earthed

(o) Fuel gauge registers 'FULL'

1 Cable between gauge and tank unit broken or disconnected

CHAPTER 12

THE BODYWORK

12:1 The door trim

The trim panels on Anglia and Prefect cars are secured to the door with spring clips attached to the underside of the trim panel. On later vehicles these clips engage in nylon inserts fitted in the door.

Estate cars and vans have the door trim panel secured with cup washers and self-tapping screws.

Removal:

1 Depress the spring-loaded cap behind the door lock remote control and window regulator handles, push out the locking pin with a piece of wire and detach each handle. Remove the spring and escutcheon plate.
2 Detach the door pull handle by removing the securing screws. Carefully pull the edges of the trim panel away from the door to release the spring clips, and detach the trim panel.

On estate cars and vans unscrew the self-locking screws and cup washers.

Replacement:

1 Position the trim panel on the door and carefully press the clips into the holes around the edge of the door.

On estate cars and vans, secure the trim with the self-tapping screws.
2 Fit an escutcheon plate, spring and cap on both the remote control arm shaft and the window regulator shaft. Locate each handle on its shaft, depress the cap and insert the locking pin. Locate the door pull in position on the trim panel, and refit the securing screws.

12:2 The door locks

Late model vehicles have remote control type door locks as illustrated in **FIG 12:1**. Very early production vehicles had a door lock operated by a handle which engaged directly with the lock assembly.

On all vehicles the exterior handle has a square shank which engages in the lock assembly, and the handle is secured to the exterior of the door with a single setscrew.

Removal (later vehicles):

1 Detach the exterior locking handle, after unscrewing the setscrew securing it to the door, and withdrawing the squared shank from the lock assembly. Remove the interior handles and door trim as described in the previous section. Disconnect the remote control arm after removing the spring clip securing the arm to the lock assembly.

2 Remove the three screws and lockwashers securing the remote control arm and bracket to the door, and lift away.

Remove the door inspection panel, after unscrewing the four self-tapping screws. Unscrew the two screws and lockwashers which secure the lock assembly to the door frame, then detach the lock assembly through the inspection aperture.

Removal (early vehicles):

With this type of door lock remove the door trim panel and detach the exterior handle.

Depress the interior handle, to expose the two countersunk screws securing the escutcheon at the door frame. Unscrew these two screws and detach the interior handle, disengaging the forked link from the lock assembly. Remove the two screws securing the lock assembly to the door frame, and detach the lock assembly through the inspection aperture.

Should any part of the door lock gear be worn or broken it is recommended that a complete component is fitted, do not waste time trying to repair these assemblies. When refitting, oil and grease the working parts before installing in the door cavity and ensure that the anti-vibration felt is in position between the door and the remote control arm.

Replacement is a reversal of dismantling procedure.

A striker plate is fitted to the door pillar, and when correctly closed the door lock will engage on the inner face of this striker. Dovetails are fitted on the door face, and also on the door pillar, to provide adequate support at the rear end of the door. The dovetails include a spring-loaded wedge.

The striker plate and both dovetails are each secured with two lockwashers and setscrews. Serrations are provided on the rear face of the striker so that adjustment may be made to ensure that the door lock engages correctly.

12:3 The ventilators (swivel quarter lights)

Late model vehicles are fitted with an opening-type vent window in each front door. A non-opening type quarter window was fitted at this location on very early vehicles.

Removal:

Detach the front door trim panel, as described in **Section 12:1.** Remove the screw, flat washer and rubber grommet from the lower depression in the door, which secures the vent window frame in the door. Remove the self-tapping screw securing the upper window channel in the top front corner of the door window and pull the fabric channel to one side. Unscrew and remove the two screws passing through the top front of the vent window frame, into the door frame. Wind the window right down, pull the top of the vent window back and detach it from the door, as shown in **FIG 12:2**.

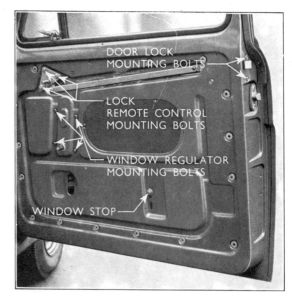

FIG 12:1 Door control gear (late model vehicles)

FIG 12:2 Removing a front door ventilator

The ventilator relies upon the compression spring fitted to the bottom pivot for friction to hold it open in any predetermined position and by adjustment of the self-locking nut the desired amount of friction may be obtained.

Replacement is a reversal of removal procedure but do not forget the window must be fully wound down.

12:4 Window winders and glass

A handle-operated type of window winder is fitted to all later vehicles.

Very early Prefect cars had push-down type rear door windows (see **FIG 12:3**), the operating linkage incorporating a large coil spring. Three slots are provided on the lower arm of the regulator to which the lower end of the spring is fitted, to allow for adjustment of the spring tension, as necessary, to ensure that the window is properly counterbalanced.

To fit the winder type control see **Section 12:9.**

Removal:

Remove the door trim panel as described in **Section 12:1.**

Detach the inspection cover which is secured to the door with four self-tapping screws.

Lower the window until the winder arm and the window guide are exposed. Unscrew the four screws and flat washers securing the winder assembly to the door, then remove the assembly through the inspection aperture, disengaging the spring-loaded boss on the winder arm, from the window glass guide channel.

The early type rear door window gear fitted to Prefect cars can be removed in a similar manner to that described above; in this case the linkage is secured to the door with two spring washers and screws (see **FIG 12:3**).

Replacement:

Pass the winder assembly through the aperture in the door, engaging the spring-loaded boss on the regulator arm in the slotted guide channel at the base of the window.

Secure the winder in position, using four bolts and spring washers (two bolts and spring washers for the push-down type gear fitted to early Prefect cars).

Check the operation of the winder and if satisfactory refit the inspection cover securing it with four self-tapping screws.

Refit the door trim and interior handles as previously described.

Window glass:

In the event of replacement being necessary, the following procedure should be carried out but in the case of front door windows, the ventilator will first have to be removed as described in **Section 12:3.**

Squire estate cars have a fixed and sliding window in each side panel. These windows are retained in position by a moulding, secured with self-tapping screws.

Removal:

1 Remove the door trim panel as previously described.
   In order to extract this glass, it is necessary to remove either the inner or outer window moulding. To prevent scratching the paintwork, apply a smear of grease at one side of the moulding clip and push the clip away from the joint. The moulding can now be removed.
2 Remove the inspection cover which is secured to the door by four self-tapping screws, and expose the window winder arm. Ease the window guide from the spring-loaded boss on the winder arm. The rear door window may now be lifted up and out of the door frame. On front door windows, twist the glass through

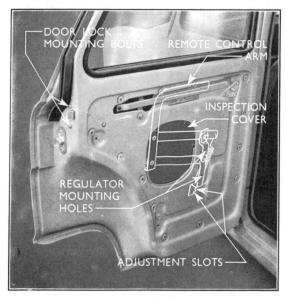

FIG 12:3 Push down type early Prefect rear window gear

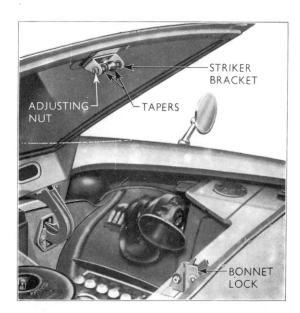

FIG 12:4 The bonnet lock component parts

90 deg. until the bottom channel is to the front of the vehicle, then lift the window up, passing the channel through the vent window aperture, previously removed.

Replacement:

Replace the windows in the reverse order, ensuring that the winder arm correctly engages in the window guide, and when reassembled check to ensure that the windows will move up and down satisfactorily.

12:5 The bonnet lock and hinges

Provision for adjustment is made on the bonnet hinges, and also on the bonnet lock striker (see **FIG 12:4**).

If the bonnet appears to close correctly, but the lock does not engage around the striker, the striker can be adjusted by screwing the threaded spindle in or out, to align the two tapers on the striker around the bonnet lock. The striker mounting bolt holes are elongated to allow for slight fore and aft adjustment.

If when closed, the bonnet does not lie equally between the two mudguards and the cowl top panel, the adjustment can be made on the elongated holes provided in each bonnet hinge (see **FIG 12:5**).

12:6 Seat belts

Seat belt anchorages are not fitted to the vehicles covered by this manual and it is strongly recommended that seat belt kits are purchased from Ford authorized dealers which will have the appropriate fitting instructions and strengthening plates supplied for the model in question. Do not be tempted to fit a standard belt by just drilling holes in the floor pans and door pillar. In an impact or emergency stop the anchorages just will not hold up to the strain. **If in any doubt, leave the fitting to a service station.**

12:7 The heater

This is mounted below the parcels tray, in the centre of the vehicle, as shown in **FIG 12:6**.

The heater comprises a blower unit, a heater box containing a radiator and suitable flap valves, and

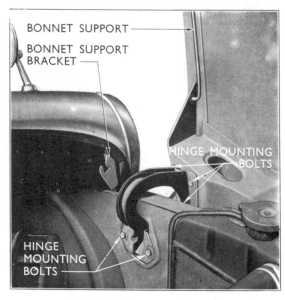

FIG 12:5   The bonnet hinges

connecting piping to the demister nozzles at each end of the windscreen.

The blower is driven by an electric motor mounted in the base of the heater box. The radiator in the heater box

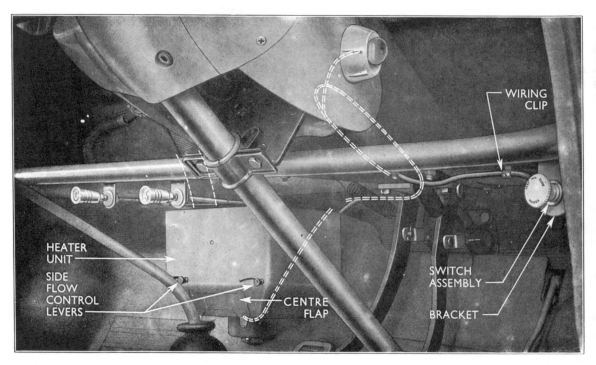

FIG 12:6   The heater installation

is supplied with hot water from the engine cooling system.

Two pipes, one at each end of the heater radiator, are connected to the engine cooling system by two hoses, as shown in **FIG 12:7**.

A rheostat switch mounted on the parcels tray edge, adjacent to the driver's door, controls the heater blower motor. When the control knob is turned fully anticlockwise the motor is switched 'Off'. With the control turned slightly clockwise, the motor speed is at maximum. Further clockwise rotation of the control reduces the motor speed. Three flaps on the heater box control the air flow to the vehicle interior, and can be adjusted. A short hose from the demister outlet at the top rear of the heater box is connected to each demister nozzle hose by means of a two-way union. To obtain maximum air flow for defrosting, all flaps on the heater should be closed. A tap on the cylinder head can be turned to the 'Off' position (groove on tap at right angles to pipe), to prevent water circulation during the summer months.

(a) Removal and dismantling:

1 Ensure that the heater valve on the cylinder head is 'Open' and drain the engine cooling system (see **FIG 12:7**). Retain the coolant if it contains antifreeze. Disconnect the blower motor feed wire at its snap connector. Loosen the spring clip on each heater water hose and disconnect each water hose from its heater pipe. Detach the short hose from the heater demister outlet, at its location on the two-way connector. This demister hose is a push fit on the connector.

2 Unscrew the three nuts and washers securing the heater to the engine rear bulkhead, and lift away the

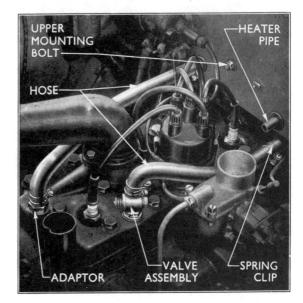

FIG 12:7 The heater connections to the cooling system

assembly from inside the vehicle. Removal of the heater box will release the blower motor earth wire which is fitted around the heater lefthand lower mounting stud. Ease the short hose from the demister

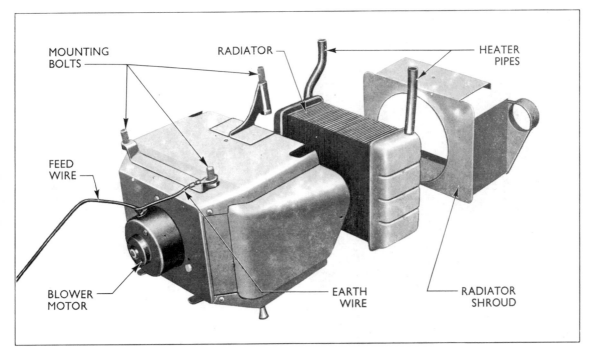

FIG 12:8 Exploded view of the heater assembly

outlet of the heater. Remove the four self-tapping screws securing the radiator shroud to the heater casing. Lift out the radiator and shroud; if necessary the shroud can be removed by easing it over the radiator fins (see **FIG 12 : 8**).

3 Unscrew the three nuts, washers, grommets and bolts which secure the blower motor to the heater base, and remove the blower assembly. The blower fan can be removed, if required, after extracting the fan securing splitpin. The side flaps can be removed, if necessary; remove the screw at each end of each flap, and unscrew the flap control knobs. The centre flap is secured in position by two rivets.

If dismantling was required because of a blocked heater radiator, it may be possible to clear it by attaching a cold water hose to each heater pipe in turn. Do not attempt to repair a leak as it is rarely successful, exchange the unit.

Reassembly and replacement are a reversal of the removal and dismantling procedure. **Refill slowly with coolant to prevent air locks.**

Reference should be made to **Section 12 : 9** for the method of fitting a heater to vehicles not equipped with one as original equipment.

12 : 8 The facia panel

Information is given here on the method of facia panel removal in order to gain access to instruments and panel lights. Three types of panel are described.

(a) Standard vehicles built prior to September 1957:

Remove two countersunk screws which secure the instrument panel and lower housing or shroud (see **FIGS 12 : 10** or **12 : 11** as appropriate).

The individual instruments can be removed without first removing the entire instrument panel. On Prefect cars it is necessary to remove the entire instrument cluster before any removal of instruments can be effected.

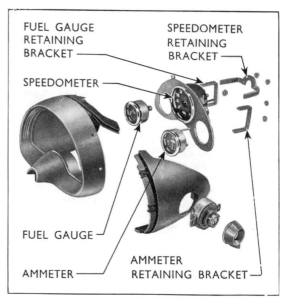

FIG 12 : 10   The facia panel (standard Anglia and Vans prior to September 1957)

When replacing bulbs on the instrument cluster on standard vehicles, it is only necessary to remove either the lefthand or righthand cluster cheek (see **FIGS 12 : 10** and **12 : 11**) when the bulb socket can be withdrawn.

(b) De luxe vehicles built prior to September 1957:

The mounting points for this type of facia panel are shown in **FIG 12 : 12**.

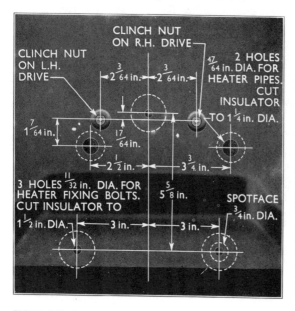

FIG 12 : 9 Engine bulkhead diagram for heater installation

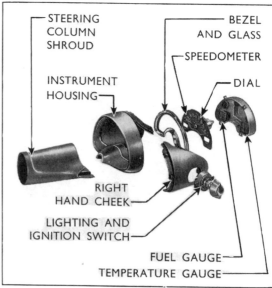

FIG 12 : 11   The facia panel (standard Prefect vehicles prior to September 1957)

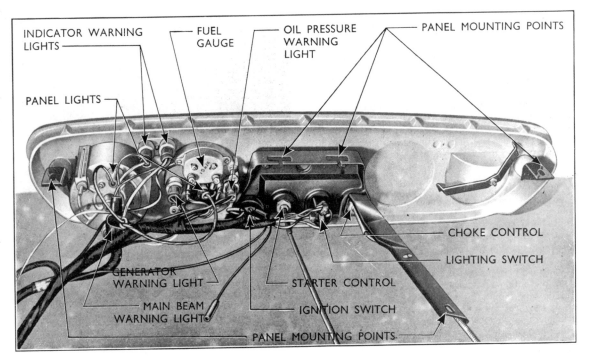

FIG 12:12　The facia panel (de luxe vehicles prior to September 1957)

Individual instruments may be removed without withdrawing the entire facia panel.

Bulbs may be replaced by simply reaching under this type of facia panel and withdrawing the bulb socket.

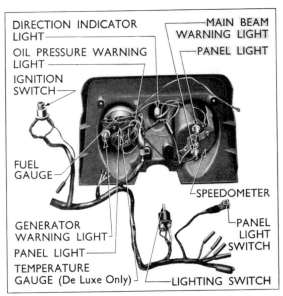

FIG 12:13　Rear view of facia panel (all vehicles after September 1957)

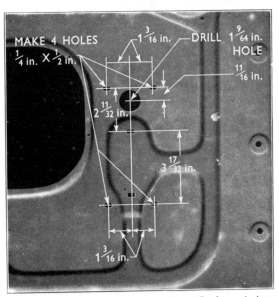

FIG 12:14　Drilling diagram for fitting Prefect window winding gear

(c) All vehicles built after September 1957, incorporate a facia panel, the rear view of which is shown in **FIG 12:13**. The panel of later vehicles is secured by means of two crosshead screws at the top and by a single crosshead bolt centrally locate at the bottom of the panel. On all de luxe vehicles a temperature gauge is fitted in the instrument panel.

The flasher indicator warning light is mounted on the instrument panel between the speedometer unit and the fuel gauge unit.

Use care when removing the flasher indicator warning light. Do not pull the warning light clear of the panel with any undue force, as the bulb holder may then become detached from the sleeve assembly and fall back through the aperture in the instrument panel. Should this occur, it would entail removing the facia panel to retrieve the bulb holder.

To change the warning light bulb, it is necessary to prise the chrome lens retainer and sleeve assembly gently out of its housing in the instrument panel. When the sleeve assembly is just clear of the panel, the bulb holder can be detached from the sleeve and the bulb changed. As a safety precaution it is advisable to pass a loop of covered wire or string around the sleeve, sliding the loop downwards and over the bulb holder as the sleeve is being withdrawn. In this way, the holder can be securely held after being detached from the sleeve.

12:9 Modifications

(a) Fitting winder type rear window mechanism to early model Prefect cars:

1 Remove the door trim and interior handles as previously described. Detach the old type push-down window gear and lock remote control as described in **Section 12:4**.
2 Remove the window glass as also described in **Section 12:4**. Drill out the window catch to door lock remote control arm rivet.
3 Drill holes in accordance with diagram **FIG 12:14**.
   Cut out the material between the original two slotted holes used to provide clearance for the spring on the new winder (see **FIG 12:15**). Obtain four machined collars, $\frac{7}{8}$ inch outside diameter and $\frac{1}{4}$ inch inside diameter, two being $\frac{9}{32}$ inch thick for fitting behind the upper slots and the other two being $\frac{11}{32}$ inch thick for fitting behind the lower two slots, when mounting the winder. Slacken off the large screwdriver-slotted hinge bolt on the window winder and insert it in the door.
4 Remove the channel from the window glass and fit a new channel, Part Nos. 100E.7326228.B (righthand) and 100E.7326229.B (lefthand). Insert the window glass and channel assembly in the door, and slip the spring-loaded boss of the regulator onto the glass channel. Slip two lockwashers, Part No. 34927.S7/8 over the two pan-headed screws, Part No. 38189.S7/8, and pass these through the upper two slotted holes.

(b) Installing a heater in a vehicle not so equipped:

Vehicles manufactured after engine No. 100E.7755 and not fitted with a heater as original equipment already have the engine rear bulkhead and package tray drilled with the necessary holes for installation.

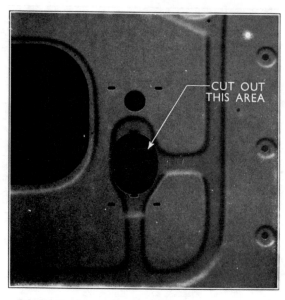

FIG 12:15 Area to cut to give clearance for window winder spring

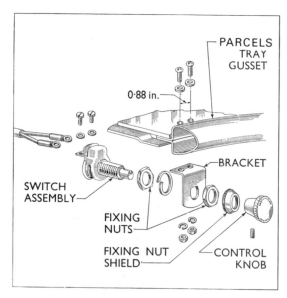

FIG 12:16 Drilling diagram for fitting heater control switch

Earlier models should be modified in accordance with the diagram **FIG 12:9**.

Installation:

1 Drain the radiator and disconnect the battery. Drill holes and cut the facia panel insulator, as shown in **FIG 12:9**.
2 Drill two holes in the parcels tray of $\frac{15}{64}$ inch diameter

and $\frac{7}{8}$ inch between centres for the heater control switch, as shown in **FIG 12:16**. Now drill a $\frac{1}{4}$ inch hole for the cable clip.

3 Cut a $2\frac{1}{4}$ inch diameter hole in the parcels tray for the demister hose. The centre of the hole should be $5\frac{1}{8}$ inch to the left of the existing rivet hole on the centre line of the parcels tray, and $3\frac{1}{4}$ inch from the front edge of the tray.

4 Mark out and drill a $\frac{9}{64}$ inch diameter hole for the two-way connector, in accordance with the dimensions shown in **FIG 12:17**. Fit a rubber grommet in each heater pipe hole in the facia panel.

5 Locate the heater unit in the prepared bulkhead holes in the vehicle, ensuring that the heater earth terminal spade lug has been placed over the lower lefthand fixing bolt and that the lead to the switch passes up between the heater and facia panel. Secure the heater unit to the bulkhead, using a washer, spring washer and nut to each of the three fixing bolts. Secure the switch bracket to the parcels tray by means of the two screws and washers. Assemble the switch to the bracket and connect the two switch leads to the switch terminals, as shown in **FIG 12:16**.

6 Remove the three screws on the righthand side of the instrument cluster housing on standard vehicles and detach the housing cheek, exposing the ignition switch terminal. Connect the third (short) heater lead to the centre terminal of the ignition switch assembly, replace the instrument cluster housing cheek and secure with the three screws. On de luxe vehicles make a similar connection to the ignition switch, in the instrument panel. Secure the control switch lead to the underside of the parcels tray gusset by means of a clip, as shown in **FIG 12:6**.

7 To each demister nozzle assembly attach a length of hose. The longer branch hose is connected to the right-hand nozzle, the shorter to the left. Attach a spring nut over each nozzle bracket tab, and secure each nozzle beneath the appropriate vent in the facia panel with self-tapping screws. Pass the large diameter length of hose through the hole in the parcels tray, locating the lower end of the hose over the demister port in the heater unit.

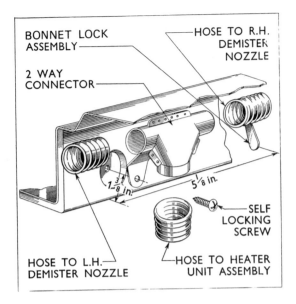

FIG 12:17 Drilling diagram for fitting demister tubes

Screw the two-way demister connector into the panel adjacent to the bonnet lock assembly and connect the hoses (see **FIG 12:17**).

Remove the brass plug at the front centre of the cylinder head and fit the adaptor and washer (see **FIG 12:7**).

8 Fit the longer water hose between the adaptor and to the righthand heater pipe.

Remove the brass plug at the front lefthand side of the cylinder head and fit the valve with washer. Fit the shorter water hose between the valve and the lefthand heater pipe.

9 Refill the cooling system slowly and check for leaks, reconnect the battery.

APPENDIX

TECHNICAL DATA

Engine   Cooling system   Fuel system   Ignition system
Clutch   Transmission   Steering   Suspension   Brakes
Electrical equipment Capacities Dimensions Torque wrench settings

WIRING DIAGRAMS

HINTS ON MAINTENANCE AND OVERHAUL

GLOSSARY OF TERMS

INDEX

TECHNICAL DATA

Dimensions are in inches unless otherwise stated

ENGINE

Type	4 cylinder, in-line, side valve
Bore	2.5
Stroke	3.64
Cubic capacity	1172 cc
Brake horsepower (max.)	36 at 4500 rev/min
Torque (max.)	53 lb ft at 2500 rev/min
Compression ratio	7.0:1
Firing order	1, 2, 4, 3
Block bore for cylinder liners	2.624 to 2.625
Oversize liners available	.001 and .005
Pistons:	
Type	Auto-thermic, full skirt
Material	Aluminium alloy with steel inserts
Number of piston rings	2 compression, 1 oil control
Width of ring groove:	
Top	.078 to .079
Centre	.095 to .096
Oil control	.156 to .157
Oversizes available	.001, .0025, .005, .010, .020, .030
Piston fitting:	
By grading:	
Selected fit to give .0011 to .0016 clearance at top of skirt, at the thrust axis	
By pull scale:	
Feeler thickness	.0015
Pull to remove feeler	8 to 11 lb
Piston pin bore	.6877 to .6880
Piston removal	From top of block
Gudgeon pin:	
Type	Fully floating, retained by circlips
Clearance in piston	Up to .0002
Piston rings:	
Compression rings:	
Upper	Chrome plated taper or parallel faced
Lower	Parallel faced stepped O.D.
Oil control ring	One-piece slotted channel
Width:	
Top	.0760 to .0765
Centre	.0930 to .0935
Lower	.1545 to .1550
Ring to groove clearance:	
Top—mfg.	.0015 to .0030
wear limit	.0045
Centre—mfg.	.0015 to .0030
wear limit	.0045
Lower—mfg.	.0010 to .0025
wear limit	.0040
Gaps (in position):	
Top—mfg.	.007 to .012
wear limit	.015
Centre—mfg.	.008 to .014
wear limit	.017
Lower—mfg.	.007 to .012
wear limit	.015

Ring to wall pressure:
Top	...	...	...	...	...	4 to 8.12 lb
Centre	...	...	...	...	...	6.28 to 7.70 lb
Lower	...	...	...	...	...	4 to 7 lb

Connecting rods:

Type	...	...	...	...	'I' beam design with integral big-end studs
Bearing clearance—mfg.	...	...	...	...	.0005 to .0020
wear limit	...	...	...		.0045
Bearing width	...	...	...	...	.835 to .857
Small-end bearing	...	...	...	...	Bronze bush
End float of connecting rod on crankpin	...	...		...	.004 to .010

Undersizes available:

Small-end bearing	...	...	...	...	.004
Big-end bearing	...	...	...	...	.010, .015, .020, .030, .040

Crankshaft:

Type	...	...	...	...	4-throw fully counterbalanced
Main bearing	...	...	...	...	Replaceable steel-backed babbitt liners
Number of main bearings	...	...	...		3
Main bearing journal diameter	...	...	...		2.0010 to 2.0015
Undersize bearings	...	...	...		.010, .020, .030
Bearing liner wall thickness—mfg.	...	...			.072 to .07225
wear limit	...				.0705
Block bore bearing liners	...	...	...		2.1460 to 2.1465
Bearing clearance—mfg.	...	...	...		zero to .0015
wear limit	...				.005
End float crankshaft—mfg.	...	...	...		.002 to .001
wear limit	...				.015
Position of end float washers	...	...			Rear main bearing
End float washer thickness—mfg.	...	...			.091 to .093
wear limit	...				.0895
Oversizes available	...	...	...		.0025, .005, .0075, .010

Camshaft:

Type	...	...	...	...	One-piece, chain driven
Bearings	...	...	...	...	Steel-backed babbitt liners
Number of bearings	...	...	...		3
Journal diameter—mfg.	...	...	...		1.560 to 1.5605
wear limit	...	...			1.559

Bearing length:

Front	...	...	...	...	...	1.42
Centre	...	...	...	...	...	1.52
Rear	...	...	...	...	...	1.15
Bearing liner I.D.—mfg.	...	...	...	...		1.5615 to 1.5620
wear limit	...	...	...			1.563
Bearing clearance—mfg.	...	...	...	...		.001 to .002
wear limit	...	...	...			.004
Camshaft thrust washer thickness	...	...	...			.123 to .127
Camshaft drive	...	...	...	...		Duplex chain
Camshaft sprocket	...	...	...	...		Located by offset dowels and 3 bolts
Crankshaft sprocket	...	...	...	...		Located by keyway
Cam lift (max.)	...	...	...	...		.295
Cam heel to toe dimension—mfg.	...	...	...			1.263 to 1.267
wear limit	...	...				1.235

Valves:

Head diameter:

Inlet	...	...	...	...	...	1.15 to 1.16
Exhaust	...	...	...	...	...	1.05 to 1.06

Angle of seat (cylinder head)	...	...	...	45 deg.
Angle of seat (valve)	...	...	...	$45\frac{1}{4}$ deg.
Diameter of valve stem:				
Inlet				.3095 to .3105
Exhaust				.3086 to .3096
Valve guide bore:				
Inlet—mfg.				.3113 to .3125
wear limit				.3130
Exhaust—mfg....				.3113 to .3125
wear limit				.3135
Stem to valve clearance:				
Inlet—mfg.				.0008 to .0030
wear limit				.0045
Exhaust—mfg....				.0017 to .0039
wear limit				.0069
Valve lift				.28
Valve seating contact width				.044

Valve springs:
   Number of springs per valve 1
   Free length 1.98
Test pressure:
   Valve closed ... ... 20 to $26\frac{1}{2}$ lb
   Valve open ... ... 53 to 59 lb
Length under test pressure:
   Valve closed 1.80
   Valve open 1.52
Valve clearance (cold) ... ... .0115 to .0135
Tappets:
   Type ... ... Adjustable, self-locking
   Tappet stem diameter—mfg. ... ... .4906 to .4911
      wear limit ... ... .4891
   Block bore for tappet ... ... .4915 to .4925
   Clearance of tappet in block—mfg. ... ... .0004 to .0019
      wear limit .0035
Valve timing (measured at .015 clearance):
   Inlet opens ... ... 3° 30′ BTDC
   Inlet closes ... ... 56° 30′ ABDC
   Exhaust opens ... ... 47° 30′ BBDC
   Exhaust closes ... ... 12° 30′ ATDC
Engine lubrication:
   Lubrication system ... ... Pressure fed
   Pressure fed bearings ... ... Main, connecting rod and camshaft
   Time chain lubrication ... ... Controlled flow from front camshaft bearing
   Crankcase ventilation ... ... Directed flow incorporating breather cap, and ventilation tube on valve chamber cover

Oil pump:
   Type ... ... Gear, driven from camshaft
   Oil pump shaft diameter—mfg. ... ... .497 to .498
      wear limit ... ... .496
   Shaft bearing I.D.—mfg.... ... ... .4995 to .5015
      wear limit ... ... .5025
   Shaft to bearing clearance—mfg. ... ... .0015 to .0045
      wear limit ... ... .0065
   Driven gear I.D.—mfg. ... ... .4370 to .4380
      wear limit ... ... .4390

Driven gear shaft diameter—mfg.	...	.4345 to .4350
wear limit ...	...	.4340
Driven gear to shaft clearance—mfg. ...	...	.002 to .0035
wear limit ...	...	.005
Pressure relief valve	...	Incorporated in oil pump

Relief valve spring:
Test length at pressure of 26 to 32 ozs. ...	...	1.38
Relief valve pressure	...	30 lb/sq in

Grade of oil:
Moderate Summer and Winter	...	SAE 20 or 20W

Severe Winter:
Down to —10°F	...	SAE 10W
Below —10°F	...	SAE 5W

Sump capacity:
Prior to April 1955	...	$4\frac{1}{2}$ pints
After April 1955	...	$3\frac{1}{2}$ pints

Oil filter:
Type	...	Bypass, replaceable element

Capacity:
Prior to April 1955	...	$\frac{3}{4}$ pint
After April 1955	...	1 pint
Oil level indicator	...	Dipstick

Oil pressure warning light:
Operating pressure	...	5 to 7 lb/sq in

COOLING SYSTEM

Cooling system capacity	...	12 pints
Radiator capacity (approx.)	...	$5\frac{1}{2}$ pints
Car heater capacity (approx.)	...	1 pint

Radiator:
Number of tubes	...	114
Number of rows of tubes	...	3
Frontal area of core	...	207.9 sq in

Thermostat:
Starts to open	...	170°F to 179°F (76.7°C to 82.2°C)
Fully open	...	190°F (87.8°C)
Identification	...	80°C, 176°F marked on valve
Radiator cap	...	Valve opens at 4 lb per sq in

Fan:
Diameter (2-blade)	...	11
Diameter (4-blade)	...	13
Belt tension	...	$\frac{1}{2}$ inch free movement

FUEL SYSTEM

Carburetter	Downdraught-type		

Jet sizes:	Prior to December 1955	After December 1955	After January 1956 (5 cwt van only)
Main jet	110	110	95
Idling jet	50	50	50
Starter jet	130	120	120
Idling air bleed	1.20 mm	1.20 mm	1.20 mm
Starter air jet	5 mm	—	—
Main air correction jet ...	160	160	185
Choke diameter	21 mm	21 mm	18 mm
Fuel level below top face of float chamber bowl	15 mm ± 2 mm		

Fuel pump:
Type	...	Diaphragm, operated by eccentric on camshaft

Fuel tank:
  Capacity:
    Passenger and estate cars   ...   .   7 Imperial gallons
    Vans   ...   . $5\frac{1}{2}$ Imperial gallons
  Location:
    Passenger cars...   ...   .   Lefthand rear wing panel
    Estate cars   ...   .   Below floor at rear
    Vans   ...   .   Below floor behind driver's seat

IGNITION SYSTEM

Distributor:
  Type   ...   .   Single contact breaker point
  Drive   ...   .   Spiral gears from camshaft
  Ignition advance ...   .   Centrifugal control
  Initial advance   ...   .   5 deg. before TDC
  Automatic—advance   ...   .   14 deg.
            starts   ...   .   1000 rev/min (crankshaft)
            ends...   ...   .   3800 rev/min (crankshaft)
  Ignition advance characteristics:

Rev/min (engine)						*Automatic advance (deg. crankshaft)*
1000 ...	...	...	...	...	...	0
2200 ...	...	...	...	...	...	6
3800 ...	...	...	...	...	...	14
Per cent dwell ...	...	...	...	...	63 to 70	
Contact breaker point gap	...	...	...	.014 to .016		
Condenser capacity	...	...	...	...	.18 to .23 microfarad	

Distributor shaft:
  Diameter ...   .   .4895 to .4900
  End float 005
  Maximum side play in bush   ...   .   .005 inch
  Bush internal diameter   ...   .   .4906 to .4916
Coil:
  Resistance at 68°F:
    Primary   ...   .   4 to 4.4 ohms
    Secondary   ...   .   7000 to 8000 ohms
Sparking plugs:
  Type   ...   .   Champion L10
  Size   ...   .   14 mm
  Points gap 025

THE CLUTCH

Type   ...   .   Dry, single plate
Clutch disc linings:
  Outside diameter 7.38
  Inside diameter 4.50
  Thickness...   ...   .   .132 to .142
  Total friction area...   ...   .   53.62 sq in
  Number of springs in clutch hub   4
Pressure plate coil springs:
  Colour (early)   ...   .   Black or Aluminium
  Colour (late)   ...   .   Blue or Gold

THE GEARBOX

Grade of lubrication...				SAE 80 EP
Oil capacity ...				1.68 Imperial pints (approx.)

Overall ratios:

	Prior to August 1955	August 1955 to May 1957	May 1957 onwards
First	15.07:1	16.23:1	17.24:1
Intermediate	8.25:1	8.89:1	8.89:1
Top	4.429:1	4.429:1	4.429:1
Reverse	19.71:1	21.22:1	21.22:1

Main drive gear:

	Prior to August 1955	August 1955 to May 1957	May 1957 onwards
Number of teeth ...	14	13	13

Countershaft gear:

Number of teeth (prior to May 1957)	...	30, 23, 17, 13
Number of teeth (May 1957 onwards)	...	30, 23, 16, 13
End float ...	...	.004 to .016
Wear limit ...	...	.025

Thrust washers:

Material—front and rear ...	Brass or phosphor bronze
Thickness...	.0615 to .0635
Wear limit ...	.0565

Countershaft:

Diameter ...	.6247 to .6252
Wear limit ...	.624

Intermediate gear:

End float ...	.008 to .016
Wear limit ...	.020
I.D. ...	1.1645 to 1.1650
Wear limit ...	1.168
Thrust washer thickness (rear) ...	.154 to .155
Wear limit ...	.150

Reverse idler gear:

Gear I.D. ...	.618 to .619
Wear limit ...	.620
Shaft O.D. ...	.6247 to .6252
End float ...	.004 to .015
Wear limit ...	.025

Selector shaft spring:

Free length ...	1.03 to 1.09

REAR AXLE

Type ...	¾ floating, spiral bevel crown-wheel and pinion
Ratio ...	4.429:1
Oil capacity ...	1½ Imperial pints
Grade of lubricant ...	SAE 90—Extreme pressure gear oil
Track ...	3 ft 11½ in

FRONT SUSPENSION

Type—Independent, coil spring combined with vertical hydraulic dampers

Coil spring:

Anglia and Prefect (1953 onward)
5 cwt van (August 1954 to September 1955)

Free length ...	14.22
Number of coils ...	10.33

Escort and Squire 5 and 7 cwt van
(September 1955 onwards)

Free length ...	14.28
Number of coils ...	10.33

REAR SUSPENSION

Rear springs:
    Type   ... ... Longitudinal, semi-elliptic
Anglia and Prefect cars (1953 onwards):
    Number of leaves... 7
    Width of leaves ... ... 1.50 to 1.53
    Length (eye to eye):
       Loaded   ... ... 41.94 to 42.06
Thames 5 cwt van (August 1954 to September 1955):
    Number of leaves... 7
    Width of leaves ... ... 1.50 to 1.53
    Length (eye to eye):
       Loaded   ... ... 41.94 to 42.06
Thames 5 cwt van (September 1955 onwards):
    Number of leaves... 7
    Width of leaves ... ... 1.75 to 1.78
    Length (eye to eye):
       Loaded   ... ... 43.94 to 44.06
Escort and Squire estate cars and Thames 7 cwt van:
    Number of leaves... 8
    Width of leaves ... ... 1.75 to 1.78
    Length (eye to eye):
       Loaded   ... ... 43.94 to 44.06

DAMPERS

Front:
    Type—Hydraulic integral with suspension legs
Rear:
    Type—Hydraulic telescopic, except Escort, Squire and 7 cwt van. Double acting vertical
    Fluid   ... ... Ford damper fluid

STEERING GEAR

Type   ... ... Worm and ball peg
Ratio 11.5:1
Grade of oil ... ... SAE 90 EP
                                            SAE 140 EP. White or Yellow
                                               paint spot on box
The following figures are applicable when the vehicle to be tested is unladen:
Castor   ... ... 1° to 3°
Camber   ... ... 0° 30' to 2° 15'
Kingpin inclination   ... ... 3° 30' to 5°
Toe-out on 20 deg. turns... ... ... 3° to 5°
Toe-in   ... ... $\frac{1}{16}$ to $\frac{1}{8}$
Track   48
Turning circle   ... ... 34 ft 6 in

BRAKING SYSTEM

Type   ... ... Drum front and rear
Fluid   ... ... Ford brake fluid
Diameter of brake drum: *7 inch dia.*   *8 inch dia.*
    Front   ... ... 7 to 7.005   8 to 8.005
    Rear   ... ... 7 to 7.005 to 8 to 8.005
Brake lining:
    Material ... ... Woven   Woven
    Length 6.72   7.68
    Width   ... ... $1\frac{1}{4}$ $1\frac{1}{4}$
    Thickness... ... ... $\frac{5}{32}$ to $\frac{11}{64}$ $\frac{5}{32}$ to $\frac{11}{64}$
    Total lining area ... ... 67.2 sq in   76.8 sq in

Brake shoe return springs:
Front brakes:

Colour ...	Red	Black
Overall free length	$2\frac{25}{32}$	$3\frac{1}{16}$

Rear brakes (top):

Colour ...	Red	Yellow
Overall free length	$4\frac{27}{64}$	$4\frac{25}{64}$

Rear brakes (bottom):

Colour ...	Black	Green or Black
Overall free length	$4\frac{27}{64}$	$4\frac{25}{64}$

ELECTRICAL EQUIPMENT

Battery:

Type	Lead/Acid
Voltage ...	12-volt
Plates per cell ...	7
Specific gravity (charged) at 70°F	1.270 to 1.285
Minimum S.G. (discharged)	1.110
Terminal earthed ...	Positive
Capacity at 20-hour rate ...	40 amp/hrs
Electrolyte capacity	5.3 pints

Generator:

Type	12-volt, 2-brush
Speed (ratio to engine) ...	1.33:1
Brush length	.61 to .64
Maximum output...	234 watts

Voltage control regulator:

Atmospheric temperature:	Regulating voltage	
	Prior to October 1956	*After October 1956*
50°F (10°C)	15.9 to 16.5	15.7 to 16.1
68°F (20°C)	15.6 to 16.2	15.6 to 16.0
86°F (30°C)	15.3 to 15.9	15.5 to 15.9
104°F (40°C)	15.0 to 15.6	15.4 to 15.8
Cut-in speed (engine)		837 rev/min
Maximum reverse current		5 amps at 12 volts
Cut-in voltage		12.7 to 13.3 volts
Cut-out voltage		8.5 to 10 volts

Starter motor:

Type	12-volt, 4-pole
Number of brushes ...	4 (2 earthed)

TORQUE WRENCH SETTINGS

Engine:

Cylinder head bolts ...	65 to 70 lb ft
Main bearing cap bolts ...	55 to 60 lb ft
Connecting rod nuts ...	20 to 25 lb ft
Connecting rod locknut ...	2.5 to 3 lb ft
Flywheel to crankshaft flange	21 to 23 lb ft
Oil filter centre bolt ...	8 to 10 lb ft
Clutch cover to flywheel ...	12 to 15 lb ft
Oil sump bolts	15 to 18 lb ft

Rear axle:

Universal joint flange	15 to 18 lb ft
Crownwheel to differential case	15 to 18 lb ft
Pinion bearing locknut ...	70 to 80 lb ft
Pinion oil seal retainer	20 to 25 lb ft
Axle housings	20 to 25 lb ft
Steering wheel nut ...	20 to 25 lb ft

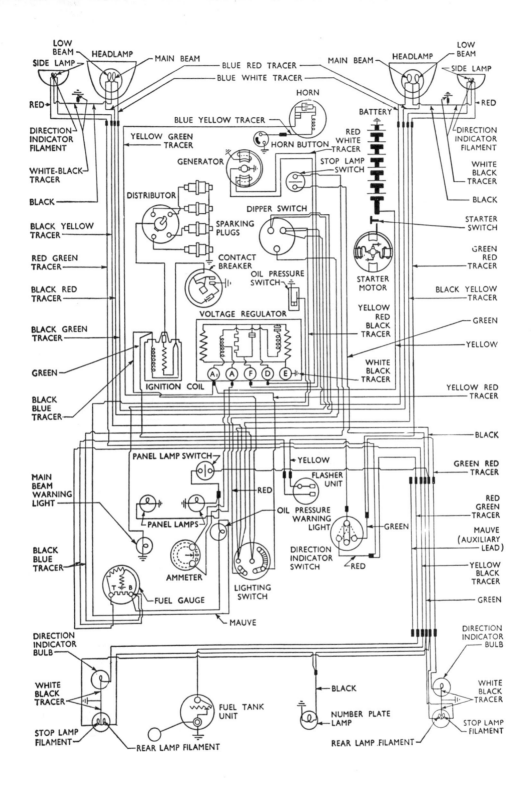

LOW BEAM
SIDE LAMP
HEADLAMP
MAIN BEAM
BLUE RED TRACER
BLUE WHITE TRACER
MAIN BEAM
HEADLAMP
LOW BEAM
SIDE LAMP

RED
DIRECTION INDICATOR FILAMENT
WHITE-BLACK TRACER
BLACK
BLACK YELLOW TRACER
RED GREEN TRACER
BLACK RED TRACER
BLACK GREEN TRACER
GREEN
BLACK BLUE TRACER

HORN
BLUE YELLOW TRACER
HORN BUTTON
YELLOW GREEN TRACER
GENERATOR
DISTRIBUTOR
SPARKING PLUGS
DIPPER SWITCH
CONTACT BREAKER
OIL PRESSURE SWITCH
VOLTAGE REGULATOR
IGNITION COIL

BATTERY
RED WHITE TRACER
STOP LAMP SWITCH

STARTER MOTOR

A₁ A F D E

RED
DIRECTION INDICATOR FILAMENT
WHITE BLACK TRACER
BLACK
STARTER SWITCH
GREEN RED TRACER
BLACK YELLOW TRACER
GREEN
YELLOW
YELLOW RED BLACK TRACER
WHITE BLACK TRACER
YELLOW RED TRACER

PANEL LAMP SWITCH
MAIN BEAM WARNING LIGHT
PANEL LAMPS
RED
YELLOW
FLASHER UNIT
OIL PRESSURE WARNING LIGHT
GREEN
RED
DIRECTION INDICATOR SWITCH

BLACK
GREEN RED TRACER
RED GREEN TRACER
MAUVE (AUXILIARY LEAD)
YELLOW BLACK TRACER
GREEN

BLACK BLUE TRACER
AMMETER
FUEL GAUGE
LIGHTING SWITCH
MAUVE

DIRECTION INDICATOR BULB
WHITE BLACK TRACER
STOP LAMP FILAMENT
REAR LAMP FILAMENT
FUEL TANK UNIT
BLACK
NUMBER PLATE LAMP
REAR LAMP FILAMENT
DIRECTION INDICATOR BULB
WHITE BLACK TRACER
STOP LAMP FILAMENT

FIG 13:1   Anglia, 1953 to February 1955

100E

135

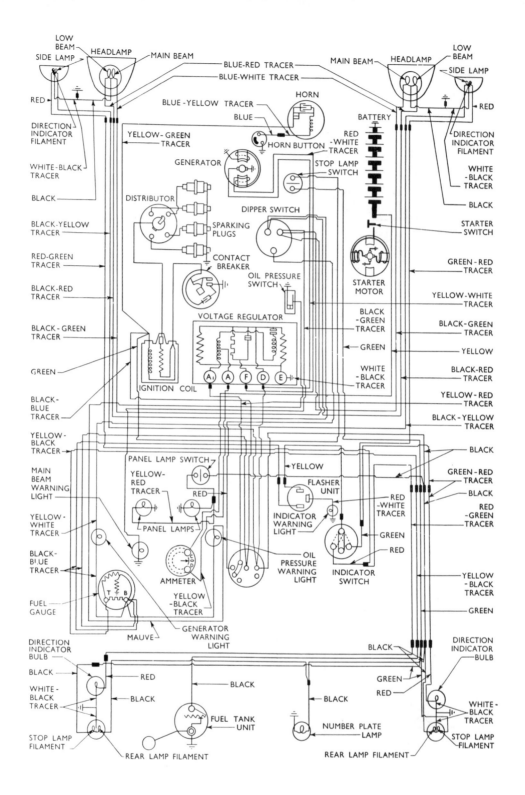

FIG 13:2 Anglia, February 1955 to October 1957 (excluding de luxe)

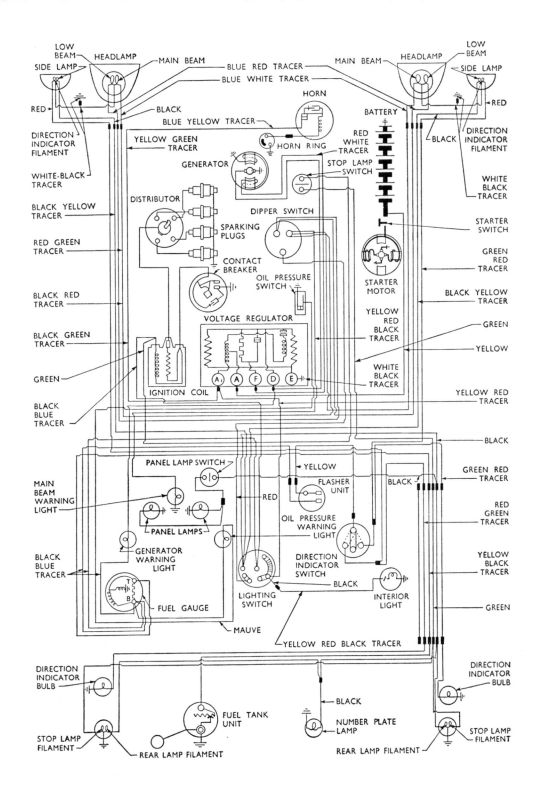

FIG 13:3   Prefect, 1953 to February 1955

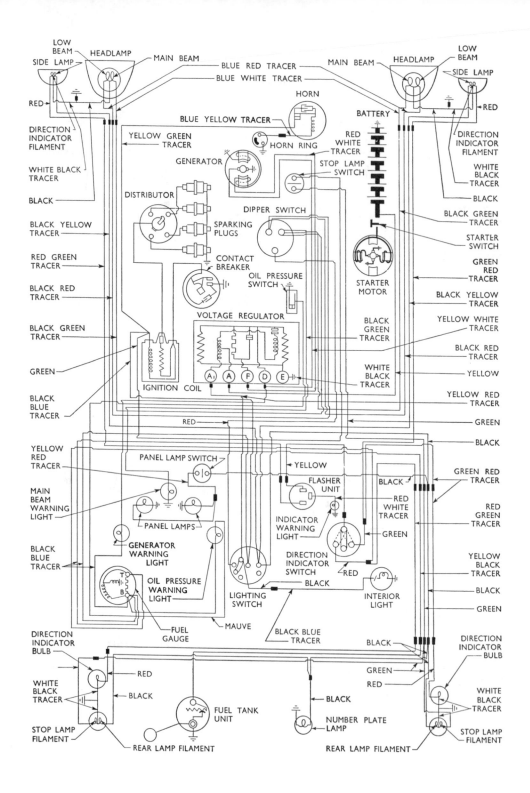

FIG 13:4 Prefect, February 1955 to October 1957 (excluding de luxe)

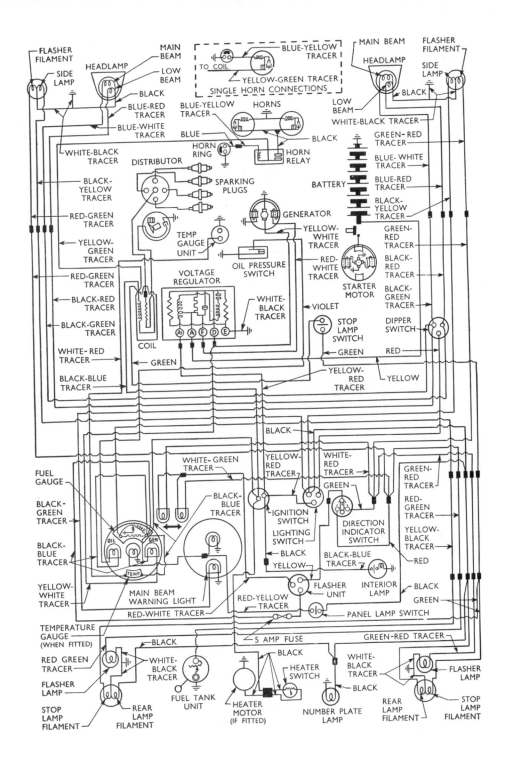

FIG 13:5 Anglia and Prefect, all models 1957 onwards and Anglia and Prefect de luxe (prior to October 1957), Escort and Squire

100E

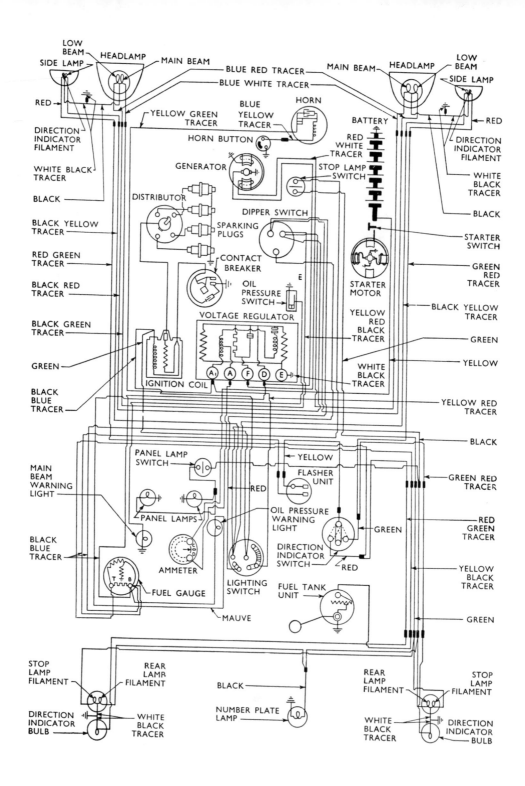

FIG 13:6   5 cwt van, 1954 to February 1955

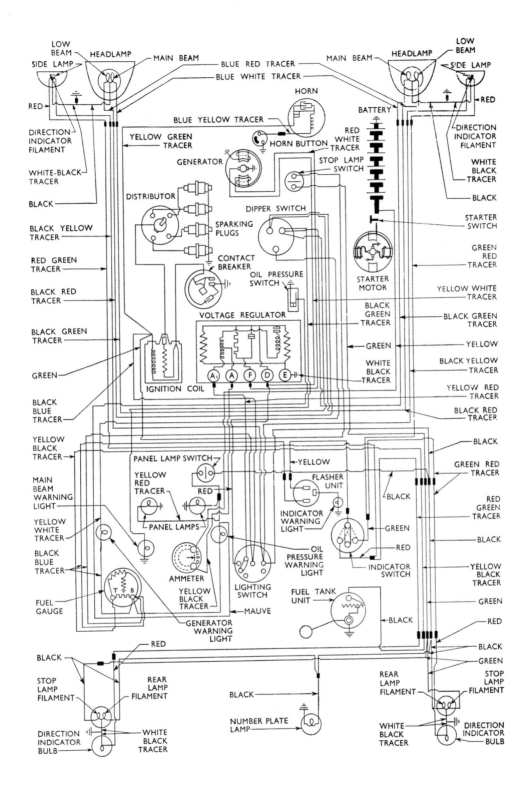

FIG 13:7 5 cwt van, February 1955 to October 1957. 7 cwt van prior to October 1957 and Export

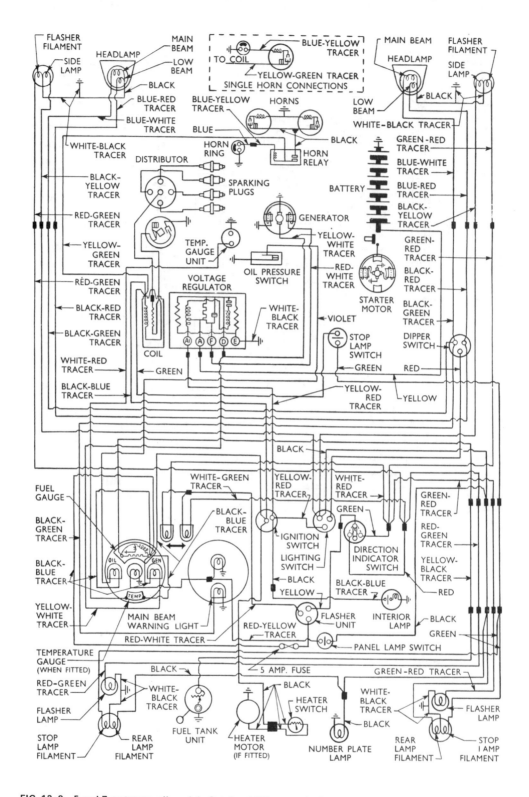

FIG 13:8   5 and 7 cwt vans, all models October 1957 onwards. 7 cwt van de luxe prior to October 1957

HINTS ON MAINTENANCE AND OVERHAUL

There are few enterprises more rewarding than the restoration of a car to its original peak of efficiency and smooth performance. The following notes are intended to help the owner to reach that state of perfection. Providing that he possesses the basic manual skills he should have no difficulty in performing most of the operations detailed in this manual. It must be stressed, however, that highly-skilled work which entails the use of expensive special tools and gauging equipment should be entrusted to the experts who have such equipment. Also, these notes must not be regarded as in any way superseding or modifying the specific information contained in this book.

Problems

The chief problems which may face an operator are:
1 External dirt
2 Difficulty in undoing tight fixings
3 Dismantling unfamiliar mechanisms
4 Deciding in what respect parts are defective
5 Confusion about the correct order for reassembly
6 Adjusting running clearances
7 Final tuning

Practical suggestions to solve the problems

1 Use newspaper instead of rag for preliminary cleaning. Having removed most of the dirt, continue with a brush and paraffin. Progressive cleaning is best done with two containers of paraffin, using the second one for those parts which are almost clean.

Finish off with clean petrol. This will dry, eliminating the use of rag which may leave clogging fibres behind. Do not dismantle anything until the outside has been cleaned, particularly round joints which will be separated. This ensures that gritty dirt cannot fall inside. Be careful not to wash dirt into holes. Plug them first, but do not use matchsticks, as these may break off short. If dirt can enter, blank off all orifices in parts which will be dismantled for some time, but be sure that the material used cannot be pushed into a place where it would be difficult to remove. This applies, for example, to the plugging of water passages in the top face of a cylinder block.

2 It is not advisable to hammer on the end of a screw thread, but if it must be done, first screw on a nut so that it is flush with the end. This applies particularly to the removal of cotters. Nuts and bolts seem to 'grow' together, especially in exhaust systems. If penetrating oil does not work, try plenty of heat, but be careful of starting a fire. Asbestos sheet or cloth is useful to isolate heat.

Tight bushes or pieces of tail pipe rusted into a silencer can be removed by splitting them with an open-ended hacksaw. Tight screws can be started by hammering on the end of an all-metal screwdriver. Many tight fixings will yield to the judicious use of a hammer, but it must be a soft-faced hammer if damage to surfaces is to be avoided. This treatment is very useful when trying to part tapered fixings such as those of a steering ball joint pin in a steering arm. Distortion of the arm is prevented by holding a heavy metal block or 'dolly' on the opposite side of the boss.

3 It often happens that an owner is baffled when trying to dismantle an unfamiliar piece of equipment. So many modern devices are pressed together or assembled by spinning-over flanges, that they must be sawn apart. The intention is that the whole assembly must be renewed. However, parts which appear to be in one piece to the naked eye, may reveal close-fitting joint lines when inspected with a magnifying glass, and this may provide the necessary clue to dismantling.

Be very careful when dismantling mechanisms which may come apart suddenly. Work on a sheet of paper which will catch everything as it falls, and drape a piece of cloth over the device if springs are likely to fly in all directions. Mark everything which might be reassembled in the wrong position, scratching a line across joint faces before parting them, and using scratch symbols where necessary. A sequence of tiny dots from a centre punch are also useful to identify the position of apparently identical parts, but be quite sure that any marks will not weaken the part or damage working surfaces. **Springs and torsion bars, for instance, must never be scratched or marked.** Store parts which look alike in the correct order for reassembly. Never rely upon memory to assist in the assembly of complicated mechanisms, especially when they will be dismantled for a long time. Make notes, draw diagrams, and put labels on detached wires.

4 Rust stains may indicate unlubricated wear. This can sometimes be seen around the outside edge of a bearing cup in a universal joint.

Look for bright rubbing marks on parts which normally should not make heavy contact. These might prove that something is bent or running out of truth. For example, there might be bright marks on one side of a piston, at the top near the ring grooves, and others at the bottom of the skirt on the other side. This could well be the clue to a bent connecting rod.

Test parts for wear, especially ball- and roller-bearings, by first washing them free from lubricants. Accurate checks are best made with expensive tools like micrometers, but much can be done by getting the right 'feel' with a pair of calipers or a vernier gauge, especially if the latter has jaws for both inside and outside measurements. Sometimes it is possible to make quite accurate dimensional checks by using something of known diameter, like a twist drill shank, to set the calipers or vernier gauge.

The clearance between parts can often be measured by bolting them together with a tiny piece of lead wire or cored solder in between. This will be flattened to the dimension of the clearance. Such a method is very handy when trying to shim a housing which locates a bearing endwise, as it does in some hubs and gearboxes. Alternatively, use a proprietary material like 'Plastigage'.

Sometimes joint faces leak persistently, even after gasket renewal. The fault will then be traceable to distortion, to dirt or to burrs. The last-named can be found by rubbing a smooth flat file over the faces, spanning opposite surfaces if possible, so that the file is kept flat. This will remove burrs without damaging the joint faces. Studs which are screwed into soft metal frequently raise burrs at the point of entry. A quick cure for this is to chamfer the edge of the hole in the part which fits over the stud.

Always check a replacement part with the original one before it is fitted.

5 If parts are not marked, and the order for reassembly is not known, a little detective work will help. Look for marks which are due to wear to see if they can be mated. Joint faces may not be identical due to manufacturing errors, and parts which overlap may be stained, giving a clue to the correct position. Most fixings leave identifying marks especially if they were painted over on assembly. It is then easier to decide whether a nut for instance, has a plain, a spring, or a shakeproof washer under it. All running surfaces become 'bedded' together after long spells of work and tiny imperfections on one part will be found to have left corresponding marks on the other. This is particularly true of shafts and bearings and even a score on a cylinder wall will show on the piston.

6 Checking end float or rocker clearances by feeler gauge may not always give accurate results because of wear. For instance, the rocker tip which bears on a valve stem may be deeply pitted, in which case the feeler will simply be bridging a depression. Thrust washers may also wear depressions in opposing faces to make accurate measurement difficult. End float is then easier to check by using a dial gauge.

It is common practice to adjust end play in bearing assemblies, like front hubs with taper rollers, by doing up the axle nut until the hub becomes stiff to turn and then backing it off a little. **Do not use this method with ball bearing hubs as the assembly is often preloaded by tightening the axle nut to its fullest extent.** If the splitpin hole will not line up, file the base of the nut a little.

Steering assemblies aften wear in the straight-ahead position. If any part is adjusted, make sure that it remains free when moved from lock to lock. Do not be surprised if an assembly which is know to be carefully adjusted outside the car, becomes stiff when it is bolted in place. This will be due to distortion of the case by the pull of the mounting bolts, particularly if the mounting points are misaligned or the bolts unevenly tightened. This problem may be remedied by careful attention to the alignment of mounting points, and correct fitting.

7 When a spanner is stamped with a size and A/F it means that the dimension is the width between the jaws and has no connection with ANF, which is the designation for the American National Fine thread. Coarse threads like Whitworth are rarely used on cars today except for studs which screw into soft aluminium or cast iron. For this reason it might be found that the top end of a cylinder head stud has a fine thread and the lower end a coarse thread to screw into the cylinder block. If the car has mainly UNF threads, it is likely that any coarse threads will be UNC, which are not the same as Whitworth. Small sizes have the same number of threads in Whitworth and UNC, but in the $\frac{1}{2}$ inch size for example, there are twelve threads to the inch in the former and thirteen in the latter.

8 **It is useless to tune an engine which has not reached its normal running temperature.** In the same way, the tune of an engine which is stiff after a rebore will be different when the engine is again running free. Remember too, that rocker clearances on pushrod operated valve gear will change when the cylinder head nuts are tightened after an initial period of running with a new head gasket.

Trouble may not always be due to what seems the obvious cause. Ignition, carburation and mechanical condition are interdependent and spitting back through the carburetter, which might be attributed to a weak mixture, can be caused by a sticking inlet valve.

For one final hint on tuning, never adjust more than one thing at a time or it will be impossible to tell which adjustment produced the desired result.

GLOSSARY OF TERMS

AF — Across flats of nut or bolt head. Width between spanner jaws.

Allen key — Wrench of hexagonal bar used to turn socket-head screws.

Ambient temperature — Surrounding temperature.

ANF — American National Fine screw thread.

Annulus — Ring-like space.

Armature — Of generator or starter motor—part which revolves in a magnetic field. Of a solenoid—plunger which is pulled into a hollow magnet.

Asymmetrical — Not quite symmetrical.

AVC — Automatic voltage control.

Axial — Something belonging to, or revolving round, an axis.

BA — British Association screw thread. Frequently used for small screws associated with electrical equipment.

Backlash — Play between parts, e.g. between teeth of meshing gears.

Balance lever — A cross-lever which divides a central push or pull equally between two rods or cables attached to the outer ends.

Ball peg — Engages in steering box worm to transmit motion.

Banjo axle — Hollow rear axle casing with large diameter housing to accommodate the drive gears.

Bendix pinion — Self-engaging drive on starter motor shaft.

Bevel pinion — Small gear with sloping teeth on side face. Meshes with another gear at an angle to it (usually a right angle).

bhp — Brake horse power.

bmep — Brake mean effective pressure. Average pressure on piston during working stroke.

BSF — British Standard Fine screw thread. Now almost superseded by UNF on cars.

BSP — British Standard Pipe screw thread. A fine thread for pipe work. Can be parallel or tapered. Size indicates bore of thick-walled pipe, not top of thread diameter.

BSW — British Standard Whitworth screw thread. A coarse thread no longer used on cars.

Bulkhead — Usually the rear vertical panel of the engine compartment.

Bypass — Oil filter—one which cleans a small volume of oil from the pump and returns it to the sump.

Camber — Angle at which a wheel is tilted from the vertical.

Capacitor — Modern term for electrical condenser. Chiefly used in ignition distributor.

Castellated nut — Top face slotted across to take a locking splitpin.

Castor — Angle at which the kingpin or swivel pin is tilted when viewed from the side.

Clevis — A U-shaped fork much used in brake cable connections.

Clockwise — Like onward rotation of clock hands when viewing face of object.

Collet — Collar, often split and located in a groove in a shaft, e.g. on a valve stem.

Commutator — Rotating segmented current distributor between armature windings and brushes in a generator or motor.

Condenser — See 'Capacitor'.

Core plug — Thin metal discs blanking off manufacturing holes in castings. See 'Welch plug'.

Crownwheel — Large gear with ring of teeth at shallow angle on one face. Typically meshes with bevel pinion in rear axle.

'C' spanner — Like a 'C' with an extended handle. The top hook engages in slots round the periphery of a part.

CVC — Constant voltage control.

Damper — Latest term for shock-absorber. Used in suspension systems to damp out spring oscillations.

Depression — The lowering of atmospheric pressure, e.g. in the inlet manifold and carburetter.

Dowel — Close-fitting peg, tube or bolt which accurately locates holes in mating parts.

Drag link — Rod connecting steering gearbox arm to nearest road wheel.

Drop arm — Forged rod splined to steering box.

Dry liner — Thin tube pressed into bored-out engine cylinder.

Dry sump — Does not store main oil supply, which is pumped into a separate tank.

Dynamo — Original term for 'Generator'.

Electrode — Terminal point in electrical circuit, e.g. sparking plug points.

Electrolyte	In car batteries, a solution of sulphuric acid and distilled water.
Element	Air, oil or fuel internal filtration component.
End float	Or end thrust. Free endwise movement of a part, e.g. shafts and parts mounted on shafts.
EP	Extreme pressure lubricants for arduous duties, e.g. between the teeth of rear axle gears.
Eye	Circular attachment point
Fade	Of brakes. Reduced efficiency due to heat.
Field coils	Stationary windings to produce magnetism in generators or motors.
Fillets	Narrow finishing strips usually applied to interior bodywork.
First motion shaft	Input shaft from clutch into gearbox.
Fullflow	An oil filter which cleans all the oil all the time unless the element is clogged, when a relief valve opens.
Gear pump	For oil. Pumps it round between the outer teeth of two meshing gears and a close-fitting casing.
Generator	Latest term for 'Dynamo'. Produces electricity from rotating energy.
Grommet	A ring of protective or sealing material.
Halfshaft	One of a pair transmitting power from the differential gearing to the rear wheel hubs.
h.c.	High-compression ratio in an engine combustion chamber.
Helical	Spiral, as in a valve spring. Helical gear—a thin section of teeth in a spiral form.
Hot spot	Warms mixture from carburetter on its way to engine. Usually provided by clamping inlet and exhaust manifolds together.
HT	High-tension electricity. Produced by coil for sparking plugs.
Hydrometer	Used to test Specific Gravity of battery electrolyte. Withdraws sample to lift graduated float.
Hypoid bevel	Small bevel pinion meshing below centre line of crownwheel in rear axle. Gives lower propeller shaft line.
Idler	Passes on movement, e.g. a gear between input and output gears. Transmits track rod movement to side rods in steering gear.
i.f.s.	Independent front suspension.
Impeller	Of a water pump. Centrifugal fan rotating to stimulate flow.
Insulator	Electrical or anti-vibration mounting.

Journals	Those parts of a shaft which are in contact with the bearings.
Kerosene	Paraffin.
Key	Square section retainer fits in machined grooves in shaft and hub.
Kingpin	Main vertical pin. Typically carries front stub axle and road wheel.
Laminations	Leaves, as in a suspension spring.
Layshaft	Often called the second motion shaft. A cluster of gears driven by the input or first motion shaft in a gearbox.
lb ft	Value of torque or twisting effort. Pull of ten pounds at a radius of one foot equals 10 lb ft.
lb/sq in	Pounds per square inch.
l.c.	Low-compression ratio in engine combustion chamber.
Little-end	The small end of a connecting rod. Takes the gudgeon pin.
l.s.	The leading shoe in a brake. Tries to wedge into drum, so increasing the braking effect.
LT	Low-tension electricity, usually battery rating in cars.
Mandrel	Axle or cylindrical rod used for centring purposes.
Manifold	A pipe with several branches.
Needle rollers	Bearing rollers which are many times longer than their diameter.
Oil bath	A reservoir which lubricates working parts by immersion. In air filters, a separate oil supply for wetting a wire-mesh element.
Oil wetted	In air filters, the wetting of a wire mesh element by dipping in oil and allowing to drain.
Overlap	Period during which the inlet and exhaust valves are open simultaneously.
Panhard rod	One which is connected between a fixed point and an axle to restrict sideways movement.
Pawl	Pivoted lever catching in teeth of a ratchet wheel to prevent reverse rotation.
Peen	To rivet or spread the end of a pin.
Peg spanner	One with two spaced pegs which engage in holes in a part which must be rotated.
Pendant pedals	Pedal levers which are pivoted at the top.
Phillips screwdriver	Fluted blade with a cross point to engage the crossed slots in a special screw head.
Pinion	Usually the smaller of two gears, originally a spur gear.

Piston-type damper	Damping pistons work in cylinders in a housing fixed to chassis. Pistons reciprocated by linkage to suspension system.
Preloading	Built-in end pressure on ball or roller bearings. Pressure is not due to working loads.
Radial	Like rays or spokes in a wheel.
Radius rod	Pivoted arm restraining a moving part to make it travel in an arc.
Ratchet	Toothed wheel or rack which can move in one direction only, return being prevented by a pawl.
Recessed-head screw	Crossed slots in head need special (Phillips) screwdriver.
Rheostat	A wire-wound electric control.
Ring gear	Ring of gear teeth attached to flywheel. Starter pinion engages with it.
Runout	Amount by which a rotating part is out of truth.
SAE	Society of Automotive Engineers.
Semi-floating axle	Outer end of rear axle halfshaft is carried on bearing inside axle casing. Wheel hub secured to end of shaft.
Servo	Additional power applied to a control, often by vacuum, e.g. vacuum-servo for powerful brake operation.
Setscrew	Hexagon-headed screw with shank threaded for entire length.
Shackle	Coupling link. Two parallel pins connected by side plates to control the moving end of a leaf spring.
Shell bearing	Thin steel tube lined with anti-friction metal. Used in halves for main bearings and big-end bearings.
Silentbloc	Rubber bushed bonded to inner and outer metal sleeves. Permits small rotational movements.
Snail cam	Semi-circular in section.
Socket-head screw	Deep screw head with central hexagonal socket. Turned by hexagonal Allen key.
Solenoid	Coil of wire which becomes a magnet when electric current passes. Will draw in a soft iron plunger.
Spur gear	One with straight teeth.
Starter dog	Pulley wheel connector for starting handle.

Stator tube	Stationary tube inside moving steering column to carry horn and indicator wiring.
Stub axle	Short projecting axle at one end only.
Tachometer	Instrument which shows rotating speed, usually in revolutions per minute.
TDC	Top-dead-centre when piston is at top of its travel. BTDC and ATDC indicate before and after top-dead-centre.
Thermostat	Automatic device for regulating temperature.
Third-motion shaft	Output shaft of gearbox carrying gears which mesh with those on the layshaft.
Three-quarter floating axle	Inner end of axle shaft splined to differential side gear, outer end flanged and bolted to hub. Hub runs on bearing mounted on outside of axle casing.
Thrust bearing or washer	Reduces friction caused by end thrust of shafts or rotating parts.
Torque	Twisting effort, se 'lb ft'.
Track rod	Bar across vehicle which connects both steering arms together.
t.s.	Trailing shoe in brake. Has tendency to be pushed away from drum.
U.J.	Universal joint in propeller shaft or drive shaft.
UNF	Unified National Fine screw thread.
Vacuum-servo	Gives extra power, particularly for brake operation by using the partial vacuum in the inlet manifold.
Venturi	A smooth specially-shaped throat in a tube which increases the speed of air or fluid passing through it.
Venturi	A smooth specially-shaped throat in a tube which increases the speed of air or fluid passing through it.
Vernier	A small graduated scale used to obtain fractional readings of a coarser scale.
Welch plug	A domed thin-metal disc which is partially flattened to make it lock in a machined recess. Much used as a core plug in castings like cylinder blocks.
Wet liner	Renewable cylinder barrel with sealing rings at each end. Is surrounded by engine coolant.
Wet sump	The usual form, consisting of a pan beneath the crankcase which holds all the lubricating oil.
Worm	Endless gear found in steering boxes, axles and hose clips.

INDEX

THE AUTOBOOK SERIES OF WORKSHOP MANUALS

Make						Author	Title			Price
AUSTIN										
A30 1951–1956	..	..	..	..	..	Ball	Austin A30/A35/A40 Autobook	..	..	40/–
A35 1956–1962	..	..	..	..	..	Ball	Austin A30/A35/A40 Autobook	..	..	40/–
A40 Cambridge 1954–1957	..	..	..		..	Ball	BMC Autobook Three	..	..	40/–
A50 Cambridge 1954–1957	..	..	..		..	Ball	BMC Autobook Three	..	..	40/–
A55 Cambridge Mk I 1957–1958		..	..		..	Ball	BMC Autobook Three	..	..	40/–
A55 Cambridge Mk II 1958–1961		..	..		..	Smith	BMC Autobook One	..	..	40/–
A60 Cambridge 1961 on	..	..	..		..	Smith	BMC Autobook One	..	..	40/–
A40 Farina 1957–1967	..	..	..		..	Ball	Austin A30/A35/A40 Autobook	..	..	40/–
A99 1959–1961	..	..	..	..	..	Ball	BMC Autobook Four	..	..	40/–
A110 1961–1968	..	..	..	..	..	Ball	BMC Autobook Four	..	..	40/–
Mini, Cooper, Cooper S 1959 on		..	..		..	Ball	Mini Autobook	..	..	40/–
1100 1963 on	..	..	..	..	..	Ball	1100/1300 Autobook	..	..	40/–
1300 1967 on	..	..	..	..	..	Ball	1100/1300 Autobook	..	..	40/–
AUSTIN HEALEY										
Sprite 1958 on	..	..	..	..	..	Ball	Sprite/Midget Autobook	..	..	40/–
BEDFORD										
CA Mk I and II 1961 on	..	..	..		..	Ball	Victor I/II/FB Autobook	..	..	40/–
Beagle HA 1964–1966	..	..	..		..	Ball	Viva Autobook One	..	..	40/–
COMMER										
Imp Vans 1963 on	..	..	..	..	..	Smith	Imp Autobook One	..	..	40/–
DE DION BOUTON										
One-cylinder 1899–1907	..	..	..		..	Mecredy	De Dion Autobook One	..	..	40/–
Two-cylinder 1903–1907	..	..	..		..	Mecredy	De Dion Autobook One	..	..	40/–
Four-cylinder 1905–1907	..	..	..		..	Mecredy	De Dion Autobook One	..	..	40/–
FORD										
Anglia 100E 1953–1959	..	..	..		..	Ball	Ford Anglia, Prefect 100E 1953–62 Autobook			40/–
Anglia 105E 1959–1967	..	..	..		..	Smith	Anglia Prefect Autobook One	..	..	40/–
Anglia Super 123E 1962–1967	..	..	..		..	Smith	Anglia Prefect Autobook One	..	..	40/–
Prefect 100E 1953–1959		..	..		..	Ball	Ford Anglia, Prefect 100E 1953–62 Autobook			40/–
Prefect 107E 1959–1961		..	..		..	Smith	Anglia Prefect Autobook One	..	..	40/–
Popular 100E 1959–1962		..	..		..	Ball	Ford Anglia, Prefect 100E 1953–62 Autobook			40/–
Consul (inc. Lowline) I, II 1950–1962		..	..		..	Page	Ford Autobook Three	..	..	40/–
Zephyr I, II 1950–1962	..	..	..		..	Page	Ford Autobook Three	..	..	40/–
Zephyr 4 Mk III 1962–1967	..	..	..		..	Ball	Zephyr/Zodiac Autobook Two	..	..	40/–
Zephyr 6 Mk III 1962–1967	..	..	..		..	Ball	Zephyr/Zodiac Autobook Two	..	..	40/–
Zodiac I, II 1950–1962	..	..	..		..	Page	Ford Autobook Three	..	..	40/–
Zodiac Mk III 1962–1967	..	..	..		..	Ball	Zephyr/Zodiac Autobook Two	..	..	40/–
Classic 109E 1961–1962	..	..	..		..	Smith	Classic/Capri Autobook One	..	..	40/–
Classic 116E 1962–1963	..	..	..		..	Smith	Classic/Capri Autobook One	..	..	40/–
Capri 109E 1962	..	..	..		..	Smith	Classic/Capri Autobook One	..	..	40/–
Capri 116E 1962–1964	..	..	..		..	Smith	Classic/Capri Autobook One	..	..	40/–
Corsair V4 3004E 1965 on	..	..	..		..	Smith	Ford Corsair V4 Autobook	..	..	40/–
Corsair V4 GT 1965–1966	..	..	..		..	Smith	Ford Corsair V4 Autobook	..	..	40/–
Corsair 2000/2000E 1966 on	..	..	..		..	Smith	Ford Corsair V4 Autobook	..	..	40/–
Escort 1100 1967 on	..	..	..		..	Ball	Escort Autobook	..	..	40/–
Escort 1300 1967 on	..	..	..		..	Ball	Escort Autobook	..	..	40/–
Cortina GT 118E 1963–1966	..	..	..		..	Smith	Cortina Autobook One	..	..	40/–
Cortina 1300 1967 on	..	..	..		..	Smith	Cortina Autobook Two	..	..	40/–
Cortina 1500 1967 on	..	..	..		..	Smith	Cortina Autobook Two	..	..	40/–
Cortina 1600 (including Lotus) 1967 on		..	..		..	Smith	Cortina Autobook Two	..	..	40/–
Cortina 113E 1962–1966	..	..	..		..	Smith	Cortina Autobook One	..	..	40/–
Cortina Super 118E 1963–1966	..	..	..		..	Smith	Cortina Autobook One	..	..	40/–
Cortina-Lotus 125E 1963–1966	..	..	..		..	Smith	Cortina Autobook One	..	..	40/–

Make	Author	Title	Price
HILLMAN			
Imp 1963 on	Smith	Imp Autobook One	40/–
MG			
TA 1936–1939	Ball	MG Autobook One	40/–
TB 1939	Ball	MG Autobook One	40/–
TC 1945–1949	Ball	MG Autobook One	40/–
TD 1950–1953	Ball	MG Autobook One	40/–
TF 1953–1954	Ball	MG Autobook One	40/–
TF 1500 1954–1955	Ball	MG Autobook One	40/–
Magnette ZA, ZB 1955–1959	Ball	BMC Autobook Three	40/–
Magnette III, IV 1959–1968	Smith	BMC Autobook One	40/–
MGA 1500, 1600 1955–1962	Ball	MG Autobook Two	40/–
MGA Twin Cam 1958–1960	Ball	MG Autobook Two	40/–
MGB 1962 on	Ball	MG Autobook Two	40/–
Midget 1961 on	Ball	Sprite/Midget Autobook	40/–
1100 1962 on	Ball	1100/1300 Autobook	40/–
1300 1967 on	Ball	1100/1300 Autobook	40/–
MORGAN			
Four-wheelers 1936 on	Clarke	Morgan Autobook One	40/–
MORRIS			
Minor Series II 1952–1956	Ball	Morris Minor Autobook	40/–
Minor 1000 1957 on	Ball	Morris Minor Autobook	40/–
Oxford II, III 1956–1959	Ball	BMC Autobook Three	40/–
Oxford V, VI 1959 on	Smith	BMC Autobook One	40/–
Mini, Cooper, Cooper S 1959 on	Ball	Mini Autobook	40/–
1100 1962 on	Ball	1100/1300 Autobook	40/–
1300 1967 on	Ball	1100/1300 Autobook	40/–
RILEY			
1.5 1957–1965	Ball	BMC Autobook Three	40/–
4/68 1959 on	Smith	BMC Autobook One	40/–
4/72 1961 on	Smith	BMC Autobook One	40/–
Elf 1961–1966	Ball	Mini Autobook	40/–
1100 1965 on	Ball	1100/1300 Autobook	40/–
1300 1967 on	Ball	1100/1300 Autobook	40/–
ROVER			
60 1953–1959	Ball	Rover Autobook One	40/–
75 1954–1959	Ball	Rover Autobook One	40/–
80 1959–1962	Ball	Rover Autobook One	40/–
90 1954–1959	Ball	Rover Autobook One	40/–
95 1962–1964	Ball	Rover Autobook One	40/–
100 1959–1962	Ball	Rover Autobook One	40/–
105R 1957–1958	Ball	Rover Autobook One	40/–
105S 1957–1959	Ball	Rover Autobook One	40/–
110 1962–1964	Ball	Rover Autobook One	40/–
SINGER			
Chamois 1964 on	Smith	Imp Autobook One	40/–
Chamois Sport 1964 on	Smith	Imp Autobook One	40/–
SKODA			
440, 445, 450 1957 on	Skoda	Skoda Autobook One	40/–
SUNBEAM			
Imp Sport 1963 on	Smith	Imp Autobook One	40/–
Stilletto 1967 on	Smith	Imp Autobook One	40/–

Make					Author	Title			Price
TRIUMPH									
Herald 948 1959–1964 ..	..	..	..	Smith	Triumph Herald Autobook	..	..	40/–
Herald 1200 1961–1967 ..	..	..	..	Smith	Triumph Herald Autobook	..	..	40/–
Herald 12/50 1963–1967	..	..	..	Smith	Triumph Herald Autobook	..	..	40/–
Herald 13/60 1967 on ..	..	..	..	Smith	Triumph Herald Autobook	..	..	40/–
Spitfire 1962 on ..	..	..	..	Smith	Triumph Spitfire/Vitesse Autobook	..	..	40/–
Vitesse 1600 and 2 litre 1962 on..	..	..	..	Smith	Triumph Spitfire/Vitesse Autobook	..	..	40/–
GT Six 2 litre 1966 on ..	..	..	..	Smith	Triumph Spitfire/Vitesse Autobook	..	..	40/–
VANDEN PLAS									
3 litre 1959–1964	..	..	..	Ball	BMC Autobook Four	..	..	40/–
1100 1963 on ..	..	..	..	Ball	1100/1300 Autobook	..	..	40/–
1300 1967 on ..	..	..	..	Ball	1100/1300 Autobook	..	..	40/–
VAUXHALL									
Victor I 1957–1959	..	..	..	Ball	Victor I/II/FB Autobook	..	..	40/–
Victor II 1959–1961	..	..	..	Ball	Victor I/II/FB Autobook	..	..	40/–
Victor FB 1961–1964	..	..	..	Ball	Victor I/II/FB Autobook	..	..	40/–
VX 4/90 1961–1964	..	..	..	Ball	Victor I/II/FB Autobook	..	..	40/–
Victor 101 series FC 1961–1967 ..	..	..	Page	Vauxhall Autobook One	..	..	40/–
VX 4/90 series FC/H 1964–1967	..	..	Page	Vauxhall Autobook One	..	..	40/–
Viva HA (including 90) 1964–1966	..	Ball	Viva Autobook One	..	..	40/–
Viva HB (including 90 and SL90) 1966 on	..	Ball	Viva Autobook Two	..	..	40/–
VOLKSWAGEN									
1200 Beetle 1954–1966 ..	..	..	..	Ball	Volkswagen Autobook One	..	..	40/–
1200 Karmann Ghia 1955–1965 ..	..	..	Ball	Volkswagen Autobook One	..	..	40/–
1200 Transporter 1954–1964	..	..	..	Ball	Volkswagen Autobook One	..	..	40/–
1300 Beetle 1965–1967 ..	..	..	..	Ball	Volkswagen Autobook One	..	..	40/–
1300 Karmann Ghia 1965–1966 ..	..	..	Ball	Volkswagen Autobook One	..	..	40/–
1500 Beetle 1966–1967 ..	..	..	..	Ball	Volkswagen Autobook One	..	..	40/–
1500 Karmann Ghia 1966–1967 ..	..	..	Ball	Volkswagen Autobook One	..	..	40/–
1500 Transporter 1963–1967	..	..	..	Ball	Volkswagen Autobook One	..	..	40/–
WOLSELEY									
1500 1959–1965..	..	..	..	Ball	BMC Autobook Three	..	..	40/–
15/50 1956–1958	..	..	..	Ball	BMC Autobook Three	..	..	40/–
15/60 1958–1961	..	..	..	Smith	BMC Autobook One	..	..	40/–
16/60 1961 on ..	..	..	..	Smith	BMC Autobook One	..	..	40/–
6/99 1959–1961 ..	..	..	..	Ball	BMC Autobook Four	..	..	40/–
6/1100 1961–1968	..	..	..	Ball	BMC Autobook Four	..	..	40/–
Hornet 1961–1966	..	..	..	Ball	Mini Autobook	..	..	40/–
1100 1965 on ..	..	..	..	Ball	1100/1300 Autobook	..	..	40/–
1300 1967 on ..	..	..	..	Ball	1100/1300 Autobook	..	..	40/–